LIGHT & TRUTH

Volume Five

The Journey Home

A Historical Novel

Based on a True Story

Library of Congress Control Number: 2006930075
ISBN: 0-9747376-4-X

First printing: July 2006

Printed at Falls Printing (a subsidiary of Harris Publishing, Inc.), Idaho Falls, Idaho, USA.

Dedicated to the wives of Mormon Battalion soldiers; especially to my great-great-great grandmother, Hannah Maria Eagles Harris, and her sister-in-law, Elizabeth Harris Browett—my aunt.

"Our government called upon us to raise a battalion of 500 men to go to Mexico to fight the battles of our country. This draft was ten times greater, according to the population of the Mormon camp, than was made upon any other portion of our nation…Whether our government expected we would comply with the request or not, is not for me to say. But I think I am safe in saying that plan was laid by certain parties for our destruction if we did not comply."

Wilford Woodruff, 1880

Foreword

The story told in *Light & Truth* began six years earlier when I began assembling the history of Robert Harris, Jr., who was converted to the Church by Elder Wilford Woodruff in 1840. Little did I know when I began the history that it would lead to a series of five novels about his life.

I had originally planned to limit the series to four volumes but the fourth, detailing his life in the Mormon Battalion, grew and grew until it was more than a thousand pages. At that point I divided the book into two parts—volumes four and five.

This fifth volume tells the story of the release of Robert Harris, his brother-in-law, Daniel Browett, and the other Mormon soldiers after their one year of service in the Battalion, and their struggles to find their families. They were released in California in July 1847, just before the arrival of Brigham Young's Pioneer Company into the Salt Lake Valley.

When the returning Battalion members reached the Sierras they met Samuel Brannan and other members of the Church with a message from Brigham Young: half the men were advised to return to California and work for a year. The other half, men with large families, were instructed to proceed to the Salt Lake Valley. At this point, Robert and Daniel split up. Robert continued his trip; Daniel went to work for Captain Sutter.

This volume tells the details of Robert's trip to reach the Salt Lake Valley. Daniel and other members of the Battalion were at Sutter's Mill in January 1848 when James Marshall discovered gold. This gold strike had a profound impact upon the life of Daniel, as you will read.

Again, I would like to thank the many people that have made this series possible, especially the late Dr. Ben Bloxham, who provided key research to the first volume. Most recently, I would like to thank members of the Mormon Battalion organization for their support and proofreading, namely: Richard Bullock, Val John Halford, Cap Cresap, and Sherman Fleek. And I would like to thank members of my family who posed for the pictures on the front cover. My sons Jason and Mike portrayed Robert and Daniel. Jason's wife, Michelle, portrayed Hannah and my daughter, Stephanie, portrayed Elizabeth.

Principal Characters

All characters are real except those indicated with an asterisk. Bold face indicates main characters. Ages are as Volume Four opens in January 1847.

THE ROBERT HARRIS FAMILY

Robert, 35

Hannah, 32

Joseph, 10

Lizzy, 8

William, 7

Thomas, 5

Enoch, 3

Sarrah Ann, 2

THE BROWETT FAMILY

Daniel, 36

Elizabeth, 33

Moroni,

Martha, 61, Daniel's mother.

Rebecca, 27, Daniel's sister.

THOMAS BLOXHAM FAMILY

Thomas, 34

Dianah, 35

Lucy, 13

Tommy, 12

Johnny, 9

Isaac, 4

HENRY EAGLES FAMILY

*Henry, 37

*Katherine, 32

*Annie, 5

OTHERS

John Benbow, 46

Jane Benbow, 54

John Cox, 37

John Hyrum Green, 47

Susannah Green, 43

Joseph Hill, 42

Orson Hyde, 44

Thomas Kington, 53

Edward Phillips, 33

Levi Roberts, 33

Richard Slater, 32

Robert Pixton, 32

Ezra Allen, 31

Henderson Cox, 17

Wilford Woodruff, 39

Brigham Young, 45

PART ONE

California

1

January 14, 1847

Alamo Mocha Well, Mexico

COLONEL PHILIP ST. GEORGE COOKE gave the command. "Get ready to move out boys. We've spent more than enough time here. General Kearny needs us in California."

General Stephen W. Kearny and his forces had been decimated by General Pico and his Californio lancers at the battle of San Pasqual. Seventeen of Kearny's soldiers had been killed. Kearny was licking his wounds somewhere on the California coast, waiting for the Mormon Battalion to reinforce him. Pico could be anywhere, looking for more Americans to rout.

Dozens of skinny mules and bony cattle, along with more than three hundred tired, starving Mormon soldiers had surrounded three slowly seeping wells in the desert, trying to quench their thirst. "Sell the worst of the mules to the highest bidders," Cooke said to his officers. Cooke's eyes were looking northwest. "There'll be new army mules waiting for us somewhere up ahead."

Sergeant Daniel Browett of Company E scanned the almost lifeless mule he was watering. If Pico and his horse-mounted lancers attacked the Battalion, the mule would be worthless as a mount. It would be worse than trying to escape on foot. A chill coursed up and down Daniel's spine as he thought of the possibility.

"You want to bid on this mule?" Daniel asked his brother-in-law, Robert Harris. Robert's dark brown hair had grown long and so had his beard.

"No," Robert answered as he slowly filled his canteen with the murky, bad-tasting desert water. "That mule might die before we find General Kearny. Besides, I'm about out of money."

Daniel and Robert had been paid a portion of their money while in Santa Fe, but like many of the soldiers, they had sent most of it back to their wives and to the Church in Council Bluffs.

"Or before Pico finds us," Daniel said, feeling the chill again. He doubted there was even one soldier in good shape to fight. The men were on half rations. Sugar and coffee had run out a week ago. There was no flour or bread. Each time a mule died, Robert cut it up into strips, divided it among the men, and the men chewed it as they marched. The only other thing they had to eat was beef, but the beeves were as skinny as the mules. And there was no salt.

"That mule is hardly worth eating," Robert said, assessing its bony frame.

"No wonder it can't pull a wagon anymore."

The Battalion had arrived at Alamo Mocha Well eight hours earlier only to find four dead wolves in the two wells, and both wells had dried to a trickle. The soldiers had cleaned them out and dug a new one, but the water seeped in so slowly that it had taken all day to water the mules, cattle, and the men, adding to Colonel Cooke's impatience.

"How far to the next water?" Robert asked. Daniel had just attended an officer's meeting.

"The guides say thirty miles to a place called Pozo Hondo," Daniel said dejectedly as he stared at his canteen and at Robert's. Both canteens would be empty in half that distance in this hot, cloudy weather. This part of the desert was frustrating; hot in the day, freezing at night.

"Will we be in California by then?" Robert asked.

"That's what they say," Daniel replied as he gave the mule to one of the teamsters to be harnessed.

At Pozo Hondo, a new guide was supposed to meet Colonel Cooke and the Battalion with a few new mules from somewhere within California, probably Warner's Ranch. The Battalion had left Santa Fe in mid-October with twenty-five wagons, each pulled by a team of eight mules. Now there were only seven wagons and the mules that pulled them looked as though they were at death's door.

Colonel Cooke called the order and the Battalion began its weary march, keeping a tight formation in case of an attack. Daniel prayed for the men.

Every day a few fainted from lack of water and food. Dr. Sanderson wouldn't let the sick ride and he forced them to take calomel and arsenic. Most men, including himself, had bare skin showing through their worn out clothing. Others were shirtless, covered only with a Mexican blanket. Daniel's shoes had long worn out and so had Robert's. Both used rawhide strips over their feet. As butcher, Robert always had access to mule and beef hides.

The Battalion had traveled no more than two or three miles when Daniel's heart came to his throat. He shielded his eyes from the bright, hazy sun. "I think I see Pico and his men up there," he said.

Robert shaded his eyes too. "Where?"

"There," Daniel said, pointing northwest.

"It's just more mesquite bushes and rocks and cactus," Robert said without a hint of concern.

Except for the soft sounds of feet sinking into the sand and the steady clanking of the wagons, the desert was silent. Buzzards flew overhead.

Daniel felt foolish. He'd seen the same mirage for several days, over and over.

"It's a poor time to have to fight," Robert said. "I hope your mirages don't turn out to be the real thing."

"There's no time good when you might have to kill another man," Daniel lamented.

The thought of facing Pico and his lancers haunted Daniel all night and into the next morning when a rainbow formed in the mountains behind the Battalion. It was the first he'd ever seen in dry weather. There had been no rain.

"What do you suppose that rainbow means?" Daniel asked as the relentless march toward Pozo Hondo continued. Dust hung in the air from the men and animals ahead of Company E. The dust caked on Daniel's skin and clothing, and worked its way into his lungs.

Robert shrugged his shoulders. "Maybe it means there's hope." He opened his canteen and took one precious sip of the unpleasant well water.

"Hope in what? More suffering?" Daniel asked. He kept his canteen closed, deciding to save the water for later.

"Hope that we'll find better water," Robert suggested. "Hope that we'll find plenty of food when we get out of this desert. Hope that we'll have time to make new boots. Hope in Brigham Young's promise that we'll not have to fight the Mexicans. Hope that Pico doesn't find us. Hope that when we do find Kearny's army, the Missourians won't bother us."

Daniel let his blue eyes scan the horizon beyond the rainbow, in the direction of Council Bluffs. "I just hope I'll see my little boy again, And Elizabeth and Harriet." He felt a little ashamed at the role reversal. As a sergeant in E company, he was supposed to be the one offering encouragement to other soldiers, especially to the five other men, all privates, in his mess—his brother-in-law, Richard Slater, Levi Roberts, Robert Pixton, and John Cox. Out here he'd passed through an endless panorama of saguaro, cholla, ocotillo, and mesquite—a sharp contrast to the lush green country along the

Missouri where Brigham Young had wintered most members of the Church of Jesus Christ of Latter-day Saints.

The comment brought a similar admission from Robert. "You're no different than me in that regard. I miss Hannah and the children."

"We must be a thousand miles away from Council Bluffs," Daniel said mournfully.

The Battalion had left Council Bluffs in July under the leadership of Colonel James Allen. Colonel Allen took sick in Fort Leavenworth and the Battalion was forced to leave without him. Upon Allen's death, a Lieutenant Andrew Jackson Smith forced his leadership upon the Battalion. But once the Battalion reached Santa Fe, a more likeable man, Colonel Cooke, took command of the Mormon soldiers.

"A thousand miles as the crow flies," Robert added.

"That means we've walked more like a thousand four hundred miles," Daniel said. "I'm plumb worn out." He reckoned his back was as sore as the shoulders of the mules. His legs and feet were sore too.

"I'd rather be here than Pueblo," Robert said suddenly. Nearly five hundred men had left Council Bluffs, but sick detachments had been sent to Pueblo, whittling the Battalion down to its current size of three hundred thirty-five men.

"That depends on whether or not Pico finds us," Daniel said. He'd first heard the news of Pico routing General Kearny while the Battalion was camped near the Maricopa Indian villages north of Tucson. Three army scouts from California had brought the news. They downplayed Kearny's defeat, but the facts were facts: Pico had suffered minor losses and still posed the menacing reality that he was still a force to contend with, him and his mighty lancers.

"Maybe Pico went north," Robert answered.

An ocean of sand surrounded Daniel, enough to swallow up the entire Mississippi River. "I hope so. I'd hate to fight here, and I'd hate to live here," he said weakly.

"It'd be worse than living in a prison," Robert replied.

"I miss the green hills of England, and the green hills of Nauvoo," Daniel said. "I even miss the green hills of Council Bluffs."

"It's not green in Council Bluffs this time of year," Robert said. "It's probably covered with snow, and freezing cold."

"It's a poor time for raising a child back there," Daniel said, thinking about Moroni.

"It's even a worse time to bring a child into the world," Robert countered.

Hannah would have her seventh child in a few weeks.

CHAPTER NOTES

The rainbow the members of the Mormon Battalion witnessed on January 15 was a meteorological phenomenon now known as rain shadow. The Cuyamaca mountain range, which rises six thousand feet from the desert floor, squeezes most of the moisture out of the air on its windward side by forcing that air up the slopes to produce rain. The air on the leeward size of the mountain, where the Battalion was marching, is forced downward and heated by compression, causing the remaining water to expand into the air.

2

Winter Quarters, Near Council Bluffs

ELIZABETH BROWETT FRAMED her tow-headed boy, Moroni, in her wide green eyes. "Can you say Daddy?"

Moroni, on semi-steady legs, acknowledged his mother's promptings with a smile but said nothing.

"He'll be able to say it in a few more weeks," said Harriet Browett, Daniel's second wife, from the interior of their sod hut along Woodruff Street.

"Where do you think your Daddy is right now?" the boy's grandmother, Martha Browett, said as she swooped the boy into her arms. "Where's Daddy? Where's Daddy?"

Elizabeth let out a delightful laugh as her son stuck out a chubby finger and pointed west, a trained response from months of the three women asking the question over and over again. "He's out there somewhere, isn't he?"

"Probably in California by now," Martha said. "Sunny California."

Harriet edged closer to the sod fireplace. Outside, the weather had dipped to below zero. Two feet of snow covered the ground. "Warm California."

"I hear it's a paradise," Martha said.

Harriet shivered again. "I don't know what's worse here on the Missouri—the terrible cold or the sickness of the summer."

Shortly after Daniel and other men who had volunteered for the Mormon Battalion had left, camps had been stricken with fever and a scorbutic disease Mormons called the black canker. In the autumn drought, the streams that discharged into the Missouri River were little better than open sewers. All during the fall they flowed sluggishly through their channels of slime and sedge, causing the encampments to be called Misery Bottoms. For several weeks it had been impossible to dig graves quickly enough for the burial of the dead. The few people not plagued with total sickness staggered from tent to tent carrying food and water to the stricken. Wasted forms of women were in every tent, brushing away the flies from their sick children, or from the putrefying corpses of the dead.

Thanks to George Bundy, Job Smith, and other men left to care for the wives of the Battalion, in late summer and fall the axe and saw had been at work night and day to build survival huts at Winter Quarters. Some houses were made of mud and sod a foot thick, others of logs, still others of turf and willows. Elizabeth's house had a dirt floor and a roof of straw and dirt. So did Hannah's.

"At least we're reasonably warm and protected for the winter," Elizabeth said cheerfully. She glanced at the ceiling. "But when the snow melts and the spring rains come, I don't think the roof will keep out much water."

The roof had been covered with willows, followed by a long coat of prairie grass, over which the men had placed six inches of dirt.

"If the roof leaks, it means the spring thaw is here," Harriet said as she rubbed her hands over the fire. "It's something to look forward to."

"At least the fireplace is drawing better today," Martha said. Yesterday, because there was no breeze, the fireplace did not draw very well and filled the sod house with smoke much of the time.

Elizabeth put on her wool coat and opened the door, letting a burst of frigid air enter the hut.

"Where're you going?" Martha asked.

"I told Hannah I'd go to the bishop's storehouse with her."

The homes of Winter Quarters were spread out in neat rows on the west wide of the Missouri. Streets bore the names of Church leaders: Joseph, Hyrum, Samuel, and Woodruff, where Hannah lived. Hannah's home had no glass windows; the only opening was covered by a blanket. Elizabeth knocked on the thin wooden door. Hannah's soft voice answered immediately.

"Come in."

Elizabeth pulled the door open and stepped inside. "It's just me. How's everyone doing?"

"Good as can be expected," Hannah answered.

Elizabeth glanced at Hannah's six children, ranging from ten-year-old Joseph to Sarah Ann, a year and a half. The only furnishings in the sod home were barrels, chests, a trunk, and one wooden chair. "Still need to go to Whitney's bishop storehouse?"

"Yes," Hannah answered. "Let me get my coat."

Newel Whitney had opened the store only a month ago, made possible only after Mormon Battalion families had turned over a large amount of cash to Church leaders. Early in August, Battalion soldiers such as Daniel and Robert had been paid forty-two dollars each in clothing money—a combined total of twenty thousand dollars. Of that amount, nearly six thousand dollars was sent back to Council Bluffs via Parley Pratt, who interrupted his journey to England to return the money to camp. Although it took considerable arm twisting by Church leaders, wives of the soldiers—including Elizabeth and Hannah—had turned over seventy-five percent of the money to Bishop Whitney. President Brigham Young had considered the money "a peculiar manifestation of divine providence," just at the right time for provisions and goods for the winter supply of the camp.

Another two thousand four-hundred dollars, collected from the soldiers in Santa Fe by John D. Lee and Howard Egan, arrived at Winter Quarters in November.

While Whitney made a trip in November to St. Joseph, Missouri, with freight wagons, construction of the store began and it opened three weeks later—even before the sixty-ton shipment of goods and supplies arrived. Now it carried a full line of foodstuffs, textiles, household and hardware goods, various herbal medicines, and some books. However, there was a heavy demand: displaced Mormons from not only Winter Quarters and settlements on the other side of the river shopped here, but so did Church members from as far away as Mt. Pisgah and Garden Grove.

"Joseph, watch the children for a few minutes," Hannah said. "We won't be gone long."

Just as Hannah was doing, Elizabeth made a shopping list in her mind as they walked to the store. Lazy smoke curled from nearly every chimney. Hard-frozen snow crunched beneath their feet.

"Good afternoon, Sister Browett and Sister Harris," Newel Whitney said as the two women entered the store.

"You remembered our names," Elizabeth said with a smile.

"I've made it a point to do that," Newel said. "If it weren't for you Battalion wives, we wouldn't have this store, let alone what's in it."

Elizabeth felt a tinge of pride. "Are the supplies going to last through the winter?"

"If we ration them carefully," he answered. "What can I get you?"

"We both need buckwheat, beans, and turnips," Elizabeth said.

"And corn meal and flour," Hannah added.

Whitney began measuring out the two women's specific orders. "I'm out of flour and corn meal, but should have some more tomorrow. The main mill's frozen up and the others can't keep up."

"I'll come back," Hannah said with an air of determination.

The frozen mill would be the overshot water driven mill that had been built at the north end of Winter Quarters, west of Brigham Young's home. There were three other small horse-drawn mills. In addition to the welfare store run by Whitney, there were two other small commercial stores, and three blacksmith shops. Schools were held in several homes. Winter Quarters also had a city council and a police force.

Whitney shook his head. "Here it is January and people are still pouring into Winter Quarters. It puts pressure on us to keep everyone supplied."

"I know," said Elizabeth. "But you're doing a great job."

When Elizabeth first reached the staging area at the Missouri River last July, there were a reported fifteen thousand Saints scattered along both sides of the river in what was known as the Grand Encampment. Many of them were now in Winter Quarters, where the population was approaching four thousand with another two thousand five hundred on the other side of the river.

"How is Sister Phelps?" Whitney asked.

"Still not good," Elizabeth answered. "I saw her yesterday. Her fever's gone away, but she's still weak."

Margaret was the wife of Alva Phelps, a private in Company E of the Battalion whose death had been reported by Lee and Egan. She lived in hovel a on the side of a hill, a house that resembled a potato cellar. Like hundreds of others, she had suffered from the ague since late summer. Around two hundred people had already died in Winter Quarters; the number was expected to double by spring.

"Do you have any dried meat?" Hannah asked. "I need some milk too." Her cow, Victoria, had gone dry. But the cow was expected to calve soon.

Whitney scratched his head. "Meat's about gone. But I can spare a few ounces. I'll write you an order for some milk."

Mormon men killed as much wild game as possible, but only a small amount of the meat ended up at the welfare store. Cattle were kept in pens south of the city. Huge stacks of hay were there too.

"Did you hear about the Sioux?" Whitney asked.

Elizabeth's heart skipped a few beats. "No. Is it bad news?"

"They killed a least thirty head of cattle north of here, at Asahel Lathrop's encampment."

Elizabeth trembled and looked away.

"Change the subject," Hannah said to Whitney. "Elizabeth hates that kind of talk. She has bad dreams about Indians. She keeps seeing a tomahawk flying toward her husband's head."

"Sorry," Whitney said. "It's a good thing Brother Brigham promised the Battalion men they wouldn't have to see battle during the war. Maybe it applies to Indians too."

"We hope so," Hannah said.

3

❦

Warner's Ranch, California

ROBERT POINTED TO AN OLD Indian, one of Jonathan Warner's ranch hands. "Ask him."

"I don't want to talk to any Indian, not even an old one," Daniel said. Two other soldiers, Ezra Allen and Henderson Cox, accompanied Robert and Daniel.

"He won't hurt you, he's a tame one," Robert said with a laugh. "He's even dressed like a white man."

Practically all Daniel had heard since his arrival at Warner's Ranch was talk about General Kearny and his battle against Pico at San Pasqual. There were conflicting reports of the battle; some said Pico won because of the number of casualties he inflicted on Kearny. Others said Kearny won because he was still in California and Pico had disappeared. Daniel wondered if any of Warner's men knew where Pico might be. Had he gone north? Or had he gone south, and if so, was he lurking in the hills nearby?

"It can wait—the old Indian probably doesn't speak much English," Daniel said. To him, the Indian was dressed more like a Californio than the white men he'd last seen in Illinois, Iowa, or Missouri.

For the first time since Santa Fe, Daniel was impressed with the country. Warner's Ranch lay in a beautiful valley and there were hot springs where the Battalion soldiers could bathe. Thousands of cattle grazed on fresh, deep, green grass. There was plenty of fresh beef, and Daniel had a full stomach for the first time since the battle of the bulls at the San Pedro.

The old Indian was one of the *vaqueros*, ranch hands who could throw lassoes from horseback, catching cattle by the head and hind feet. Now, however, he sat quietly among the barns and corrals of the ranch.

"How far to the ocean from here," Robert asked, opening up a conversation. "To San Diego?"

The old Indian didn't look up. "For good Indian rider, two, three days. For white soldier, many days."

"Did you see General Kearny?" Robert asked. Kearny had descended onto Warner's Ranch six weeks earlier, on December second. The general and his troops had been mistaken for marauding Indians. Ranch hands, including these Cupeno Indians, initially bore arms against Kearny's troops, not fully understanding the commotion of their arrival.

This time the Indian grunted and nodded his head. "I see him. I see soldiers. Scare me, first time."

Daniel chuckled only slightly but the other men laughed heartily.

"What happened to Kearny?" Robert asked.

"He fight bad. White soldiers die."

Ezra Allen posed the key question. "Where's Pico?"

The old Indian remained expressionless. "Not know."

"Do you think he's coming this way?" young Henderson Cox asked.

"Not know."

"Will he fight Kearny again?" Robert asked.

"Not know."

"Do you think we could beat Pico?" Ezra asked, referring to the Battalion.

This time the old Indian looked up. Under his *sombrero*, he had a dark, weathered, wrinkled face. "Horses you no have. Mules skinny. Men skinny. If Pico come, you smart, you run."

Daniel shuddered. The old Indian was right. The Battalion might outnumber Pico's men, but the Mormon soldiers were in no shape to fight right now.

"How long have you worked for Mr. Warner?" Robert asked, changing the subject.

The Indian shrugged his shoulders. "Long time."

"You must like him," Robert said with a smile.

"Warner good to Indian."

Robert became bolder. "You think it's a good idea for American soldiers to be here in California?"

Daniel immediately cast a concerned glance at his brother-in-law. It was a bad question to ask.

The old Indian's dark eyes bored into Robert. "The Spaniard men—white men—they here many years before. No good. I no like people who treat Indian bad."

Daniel shuddered again but his curiosity was piqued. He asked his first question. "But I thought the Spaniards did a good thing when they established missions here, all up and down California."

"Senor," the ranch hand said with a negative shake of the head, "you no understand. Bad missions. Bad Spaniards. Bad Mexicans."

The Spaniards had established missions and pueblos in a line north from San Diego all the way to San Francisco. "Why do you say bad, senor?" Daniel asked.

The old Indian's dark eyes beamed. "Senor, Spaniard try to change Indian. Padre try to change Indian. Say our ways backward. Say we heathens."

Daniel drew a deep breath. He fought to keep his voice empty of the sentimental pity he felt for Indians in California, and everywhere for that matter. Although he felt pity for them, he feared Indians—perhaps a product of his bad dreams about them. "I've heard that about the Spaniards," Daniel admitted to the man.

The old Indian turned bitter, if not eloquent. "Padres upset Indian way of life. Old culture fine. We no need change. Padres herd our people out of hills. Herd them to mission. Make Indian work for mission. Make us farm. Make us tend sheep. *Si*, padres feed Indian. But no pay Indian."

Daniel exchanged sad, concerned glances with Robert, Ezra, and Henderson. It was common knowledge in this part of California that the padres and Spaniards had tried to teach the Indians blacksmithing, how to weave, make soap, make bricks, and how to keep animals in pens instead of letting them run wild. Reportedly there had been twenty-seven active missions in California, each with a padre as administrator. But each padre held absolute authority over those who stayed in the mission. And the padres tried to extend their possession and powers over one extremity to the other, or from one mission to the other. But California, like New Mexico, actually developed into little more than an ox-cart economy. Wheels made from rounds cut from tree trunks could still be seen in both places.

"But converting your people to Christianity was good, was it not?" Henderson asked.

The old Indian frowned and then scoffed. "Humph. Padres sprinkle water over heads. Many thousands. But no catch. Not real converts. Skin no become white. Indian not take to white man's ways."

Daniel gasped at the Indian's charges against the padres. Daniel had understood that the missions had not only preached the word of God, but the padres had taught the people a mastery of letters to help the Indians socially.

They had also tried to illuminate the northern provinces with art and provide a hospice for wayfarers, too.

"But the Spaniards are gone; the padres too," Daniel said.

The Indian scoffed again. "Mexicans worse than Spaniards. Worse than padres."

"Why do you say that?" Daniel asked, trying to piece together the storied history of California.

"Big English word. Secularization."

"I've heard of it," Daniel replied as he studied the old Indian again. "What does it mean?"

"Mexico win independence. Spaniards go away. Mexicans say missions sell land, sell sheep, give money to Indian. Padres protest. Padres delay. My people end up with nothing. Secularization bad, much bad."

"You ended up with nothing?" Ezra asked with an incredulous look.

The old Indian talked in tormented tones. "My people leave missions. Except few. They objects of white man pity. Indian pity them too. They become beasts of burden, as white man say. My people angry, my people bitter. Hate Spaniards. Hate Mexicans. Hate Pico. Pico take mission lands."

"Pico took your lands?"

"He take land, lose land. Now Warner have this land. But Warner good man. Pico, bad man. Pico almost kill white man general. General Kearny."

Daniel fell silent.

The Indian was not finished. "Many Indian no like white man. Some steal from white man. Some kill white man."

Daniel winced at the words. He did not want to meet his end at the hands of angry, bitter Indians, let alone a Californio defending Mexican interests here in Alto California. He asked another question. "What happened to the padres?"

"All gone," the Indian said. "Gone; cowards. They no help my people much. Hurt more than help."

Daniel gained the sense that the padres had not been as romantic, personable, and peaceful as legend had made them out to be.

The old Indian turned and walked away.

"I hope the California Indians don't take all this out on us," Ezra said.

"Me, too," Daniel said with a concerned shake of the head.

To Robert, Warner's Ranch was a paradise, a contrast to the desert country he'd seen since Fort Leavenworth, especially the Cimmaron, the Sonoran country, and places like Alamo Mocho and Pozo Hondo. True to Cooke's prediction, the guide Tesson had showed up at Pozo Hondo with thirty-three fresh mules and twelve cattle. It took practically all one day for Indian drovers to lasso the new mules and choke them down until they were weak enough to hitch to the wagons. But under harness, and hitched to the older mules, they helped get the wagons and the Battalion to Warner's Ranch, past Carrizo Creek. Here, Robert had bathed in the hot springs, watched Indians cook their food by placing baskets in the hottest part of the springs, tasted a hog that some of the men had purchased from Warner, and had his fill of fresh beef.

"How would you like to end up like Warner and own land as far as you can see?" Ezra Allen asked Robert the next day.

Jonathan Trumbull Warner, now thirty-nine, arrived in Calfornia in 1830 from Connecticut. For a while he worked in Los Angeles but later became a Mexican citizen, changing his name to Juan Jose Warner. That qualified him for a land grant. Warner petitioned for land abandoned by Pico, all 47,000 acres. Governor Micheltorena approved his petition two years ago, making Warner's Ranch one of the largest in all California. It stretched out fifteen leagues, or forty miles square.

"Hannah and my children would get lost here," Robert said as he surveyed the land that had once been Cupeno Indian ancestral tribal grounds. Now, many of the Cupenos worked for Warner, like the old Indian they had talked to earlier.

"But you'd be a rich man," Ezra said. "Maybe a man like you or me could apply for a land grant around her somewhere. California is a big place."

Warner not only had a new house on a hill, built behind the original adobe house where Warner had lived until recently. There were also barns, corrals, and a store.

"You can sow winter wheat here anytime from September to March," Ezra continued. "They say Warner gets thirty to fifty bushels to the acre."

Robert shook his head. "But how long would a man be able to hold land like this? Pico couldn't hold it. Who knows what'll happen to Warner?"

"But the United States is going to take possession of all this country," Henderson Cox said.

"That is, if General Kearny really has California under control and keeps it that way," Ezra Allen added.

"We'll see," Daniel replied. "It'll be a few months before everything settles down. And no one knows if the United States will recognize these old land grants."

"You can have California," Robert said. "I'm looking forward to the Great Basin, wherever that is, or wherever Brother Brigham takes the Church."

In the evening, when everyone had bathed in the hot springs and had their fill of Warner beef, and after a couple hours of fiddling, singing, and dancing, Colonel Cooke made an announcement to his Mormon soldiers. "Men, we're going to make straight for Los Angeles instead of San Diego. There are reports that despite Kearny's losses, he has the southern part of California under control, albeit mighty tenuous. We need to reinforce him, and that's where he's gone. On the way we need to watch for rebels that might be trying to escape to Sonora. We'll cut off their retreat, if that is so."

The next day, as the Battalion marched north on a steep road surrounded by mountains, Daniel was in a poor mood. He'd dreamed about Indians again, California Indians this time. He woke with a sweat when he saw a tomahawk coming at his nose. "I wish we we're going to San Diego instead of Los Angeles," he said.

"You and everyone else," Robert said.

Los Angeles was at least an additional week's travel time north of San Diego. Every man in the Battalion was equally disappointed. Not only that, but a storm had soaked everything—blankets, clothing, guns, and supplies. "It's the winter rain, a bad time in California," Levi Hancock had said when he had assessed the damages. He was the only general authority of the Church in the Battalion. He also blamed the storm on the disobedience of some of the men and immediately called them to repentance.

Daniel kept a sharp lookout for Pico and his lancers, just in case. But Pico was no where to be seen. Neither were any Californios, trying to escape to Sonora. "Maybe it would help if we prayed," he said to Robert.

"I've been praying every day, almost every step," Robert said. "We're tired and weak, but we're alive."

"I mean pray that we won't have to go to Los Angeles," Daniel said.

"I have been, haven't you?" Robert replied.

Daniel felt embarrassed. He began to pray for San Diego and fell into silence for a while.

Later in the day, the praying paid off. A messenger arrived from General Kearny with instructions to proceed to San Diego. Daniel let out a cheer.

"We should make it to the San Luis Rey Mission in two days," Colonel Cooke said during a quick meeting. "From there, San Diego is only another three days."

Daniel cheered again. So did all the other soldiers.

4

January 30, 1847
San Diego, California

AS DANIEL HELPED CLEAN OUT ROOMS in the San Diego Mission, he regretted that he and Robert had prayed for this to be the Battalion's destination. The mission was in a sad state of affairs. The rooms had deteriorated into nothing more than flea-infested swine boxes, hardly worth it to have a roof over his head. The old Indian was right; secularization had ruined the mission.

"There're enough fleas here to rub us all out," Daniel complained to Robert, "I think every square inch of my body has been bit red by the danged things."

The Battalion had arrived in San Diego yesterday in intermittent rain to be greeted with good news. Colonel Cooke found General Kearny here, waiting for a ship to carry him to Monterey. Kearny had been wounded in the battle of San Pasqual, but had mostly recovered. Pico was still no where to be found. Kearny told Cooke that hostilities seemed to be over; he doubted that Pico would attack now that the Mormon Battalion had arrived. Kearny congratulated Cooke on pioneering a new road from Sonora to California.

The weather was still wet and soggy. Despite the poor condition of the mission, Daniel visualized a time when it had been a beautiful place. The mission was surrounded by gardens, vineyards, and olive trees. There was a plaza in front, a church on the west, and a burial ground to the east.

Robert removed his shirt and put it on again. "I'm red with bites too. Either the Indians, the dogs, the pigs, or the goats left these fleas here."

Only Indians had occupied the rooms from time-to-time since secularization and the rooms were now filthy. But Cooke had ordered the Battalion to clean the mission, so that's what Daniel was doing. At least the rooms were not musty. The humidity here was different than back in Illinois.

"I hope we get to stay here for a while," Robert concluded. He was tired of marching and he was already tired of cleaning. "And I hope California is a good place for food."

"You're still hoping for a lot," Daniel remarked.

Robert looked in the direction of San Diego bay. A ship from the Sandwich Islands had just docked. "I got lots of hopes. I hope that ship brought in some good food."

For breakfast, Robert and Daniel had eaten more California beef with local mustard greens—that's all there was to eat. At least now they had salt.

There were rumors that Colonel Cooke would commandeer most everything on the ship for the Battalion.

"They say there're even pineapples on that ship," Daniel said.

"Then I hope we get 'em, and I hope they taste as good as they say," Robert said.

At least there was some good news. The Battalion had received word that Kearny had recaptured Los Angeles. California—from San Diego to Monterey—now appeared to be under control of the American army; Pico had disappeared.

At this point, Daniel's fondest hope was to get a new pair of shoes. His feet were a bundle of blisters; the rawhide Robert had given him was better than nothing, but blisters had formed top and bottom. San Diego was just a small Mexican settlement; there was no store for the men to buy shoes or clothing.

"One good thing about San Diego," Robert said as the cleaning continued.

"What would that be?" Daniel asked.

"There are fleas but there are no Missourians," Robert said.

Daniel breathed a sigh of relief. "You're right about that."

That evening, a new order came from Colonel Cooke as a result of his visits with General Kearny. The Battalion was told to move back to Mission San Luis Rey and to hold that position in case hostilities should break out again. Robert and the soldiers had passed through San Luis Rey Wednesday, on the way to San Diego. It was a far prettier mission than the one they were in.

"There're probably fleas there too," Robert lamented when he heard the news.

"Worse than that, there'll be Missourians there," Daniel said.

"What?"

"Dragoons," Daniel replied, pointing to horse soldiers that had just arrived at the San Diego Mission.

"Where'd they come from?" Robert asked.

"They rode with Kearny."

"Then they fought at San Pasqual."

"That's right."

"Do you think they'll be friendly?"

"We're all part of the same army."

Robert thought for a moment. "Well, I hope there're friendly to us Mormons."

"There you go, hoping again."

"They'll be full of stories, how they fought the Californios."

"Some are still recovering from wounds," Daniel said.

"Dern, you mean we have to live with the Mormons?" Private Bernard Bogart

asked Sergeant Waldo Peck when he found out that a few members his dra-
goon company had been assigned to help occupy San Luis Rey. Others had
orders to remain in San Diego.

Peck's pupils seemed to recede into his forehead. "It's not good news," he
replied. "They'll outnumber us Missourians four to one, maybe more."

Bogart's face twisted as he saddled his black horse. His better judgment
screamed at him to reject the order. "Dern, I'd rather fight greasers than
Mormons," he said.

"At least the Mormons don't have horses," Peck said, looking frightened
and confused. "All I've seen is mules, and most of them are skinny and all used
up."

"But they all have muskets," Bogart hissed. "By now Colonel Cooke has
probably got them Mormons trained to be sharpshooters, and vicious killers."

"Lucky Mormons," Peck added. "They had the easy road to California."
As a newspaperman, he'd made a note of that fact in his last dispatch.

"Yeh," Bogart scowled, crossing his arms. "They didn't have to fight Pico
at San Pasqual, either."

"I'll bet they had all the flour they wanted on their trip. We've been off
our feed ever since we left Fort Leavenworth and had to live on mule meat
after San Pasqual."

"My shoes are worn out, and my pants and shirt, too. Dern Mormons
probably got new shoes and new uniforms by now."

Peck's eyes pooled with waves of abhorrence. "Dern Mormons have fleas, too. I hope we don't have ta sleep in the mission with 'em."

Bogart said, "Dern Mormons will make wives out of Indian women and Californio women, too."

"How many wives can they have?"

"As many as they'd want, I'd expect."

"They'll fill up the mission with wives. There won't be room for us. Dern, we'll have ta sleep in our tents again."

Mission San Luis Rey was the most impressive sight Daniel had seen since he left Nauvoo. From a distance it was beautiful—whitewashed Spanish-style adobe buildings, red tile roofs, and thirty-two arches resting on solid square pillars. The mission had been established in 1798, but construction had not begun until 1811—thirty-six years ago. The buildings were all connected around five or six acres of land, including the chapel, which stood in the southeast corner. The church had six bells and lots of statues. There were not only orange trees, but pepper trees and cocoa trees, too. Herds of wild cattle and wild horses fed on green ridges, and in the valley. Surrounding hills were covered with oats and wild grass, green and luxuriant as mid-summer. The San Luis River ran nearby.

"Now this is more like it," Daniel said a day after the Battalion had arrived. He had his eye on a long row of rooms that could be used as a barracks. A few years earlier the rooms had been used by the padres to warehouse their Indian laborers. The padres were gone. Most of the Indians were gone, too. A few old Indians loitered nearby, acting as though they were lost and confused. They were a filthy lot, and their conditions were filthier still. Most looked like victims of venereal disease, weak and hardly moving. On the bright side, the weather was the best Daniel had seen since they had left Council Bluffs almost seven months ago. Daniel had a seven-month beard, too, as did all the Mormon men. He had not shaved since leaving Fort Leavenworth.

"Gives you a peaceful feeling, doesn't it?" Robert responded as he looked over his new surroundings.

A Californian *carreta*—or traveling cart—freighted with women and children was outbound on a pleasure excursion of some kind. The women, sort of dark and sallow, wore colorful loose gowns. The children were handsome with sparkling eyes and ruddy complexions. Vineyards dotted the hillside.

The Battalion had made the fifty-mile trip from San Diego in three days. On the way they had passed near the place where the battle of San Pasqual had taken place, and Mule Hill, where Kearny's dragoons had survived by eating mule meat. There had been a lot of comment from the Battalion members that they were thankful Kearny and not the Battalion had encountered Pico's lancers. Mounted lancers against foot soldiers would have resulted in a much greater slaughter than Kearny's dragoons had endured. The Lord had truly watched over the Battalion boys, Daniel concluded.

"Do you think they'll let us stay here until we're released in July?" Robert said as he joined in the work of cleaning out the rooms. They may have been sparkly clean at one time, but since secularization they had deteriorated into what the men were calling "swine boxes."

"I hope so," Daniel commented. "This fits my vision of California a little better. At least it will when we get this cleaning done."

Daniel peered out of the doorway to see a line of mounted horsemen riding toward the mission. He could also see a beautiful view of the Pacific Ocean. "Here come the Missourians."

Robert stood motionless for a few seconds. "I hope they keep their distance," he said. Cooke had ordered Kearny's men to travel a half-day behind his Battalion just to keep the Mormons and Missourians apart. Some of the dragoons were mounted on well-worn horses, but most were riding mules.

Daniel and Robert joined Colonel Cooke and a few other curious Mormon soldiers in the mission's quadrangle to welcome the Missourians. The Missourians looked frightened, as if they had seen Pico's lancers again.

"Relax," Cooke said to one of their sergeants, a man who had introduced himself as Waldo Peck. "These Mormons ain't gonna bite you."

Daniel could sense the Missourian's rising concern. "We'll find a place to pitch our tents," Peck said after he saluted Cooke.

"Nonsense," Cooke said, his tone unyielding. "There're plenty of rooms we can use as barracks for not only the Mormons, but for you, too." He pointed to the south. "You will find empty rooms down that way."

Peck appeared shocked, as though the Mormons were resurrected ghosts. His beard was just as long as Daniel's, or longer. He didn't move.

Cooke's patience evaporated. "I said down that way."

Instinctively, Peck lowered his shoulders. "Yes, sir," he said. He began leading his horse in the direction of the mission rooms.

"One more thing, Sergeant," Cooke said.

Peck halted, and so did the other Missourians.

"Yes, sir. What would that be?"

"You can spend the day cleaning out your rooms. But tomorrow we begin drills. I expect every man to be clean shaven and have their hair trimmed off above the ear."

Daniel went rigid along with Peck. Cooke hadn't given those orders to the Mormons, but knew that he would within the hour, or within the minute.

"Dern, do we look as bad as them Mormons? I 'spect we do," Private Bogart said after he had unsaddled his horse, hobbled him, and took a look at the mission's rooms. The Mormons he'd seen had foot-long beards, were bare foot, and had ragged looking clothing. Many had trousers made from wagon canvas-tops.

"Wish they'd come and clean our rooms, too," Peck said in a mournful tone. Behind him, scores of Mormon soldiers were sweeping and cleaning. "If we have to stay here, we just as well use them as slaves."

"I wish they would too," Bogart complained. "I don't feel like sweeping."

"You will after you've slept here," a voice said.

Bogart wheeled to face not one, but two strangers. They were Mormons. Bogart tensed, fearing the worst. Had they overhead Peck wishing they were their slaves? "You part of Cooke's Mormons?" Bogart asked.

"Yep, Daniel Browett's the name," said a man of medium height, blond hair, and one of those foot-long beards. "And this is my brother-in-law, Robert Harris."

Bogart stood rigid. "What do you want?"

"We came to help you clean your rooms," the other man said. He was taller, about six feet, and had a muscular build. His beard was just as long, but darker, and his hair was dark brown. And he held a broom in his hand, not a musket.

Bogart looked at Peck. He was having a hard time believing Mormons would offer any act of kindness. "Is this normal for Mormons?"

Peck had a look of equal disbelief. "Dunno," he growled.

"Well, while you're thinking about it, and tending to your horses, we'll get started," said Browett, the first Mormon. "Fleas just about ate us up last night. They gored me 'til blood oozed from my skin just about everywhere. It was either goats, dogs, or chickens that stayed here last, but they left their fleas. It'll probably take more than sweeping, but sweeping's a good start."

"I told you these derned Mormons had fleas," Bogart said to Peck. "They probably gave 'em to the Injuns, and the Injuns gave 'em to the goats and dogs and chickens, and the animals left the fleas in these here rooms."

Both the Mormons laughed as they went to work. "I don't know about that," the blond Mormon said. "But you'll have flea bites and lice bites by morning. We've tried everything, even boiling our clothes, but nothing works."

The blond Mormon lit a dark-colored tallow candle, illuminating the murkiness and filth that enveloped the rooms.

"Rumors are that the Indians ate fleas, maybe that's what we'll have to do," the brown-haired Mormon added.

Some of the soldiers were stripping themselves in the sun and hunting for lice in their clothing. Others were boiling their clothes.

Peck took out his notebook. "What do you two know about the mission?"

"We've only been here a day, so not much," the blond Mormon said. "Just what an old Indian and Colonel Cooke has told us, and what our guides have learned from the few Californios who live near here."

Bogart felt his heartbeat slow up and his muscles soften. The chaotic panic in his mind slowly dissolved, too. These Mormons acted like real people, not the demons he'd heard about in Missouri.

As Daniel talked, Peck made notes. A French priest, Father Lasuen, had established San Luis Rey in 1798. Lasuen had named the mission in honor of Louis IX, who left France hundreds of years earlier to fight in the Crusades. But the mission was built under the order of Father Peyri, who was put in charge. An intricate aqueduct system provided water for the missions and gardens, as well as for pools used for bathing and laundry. Until 1837, the mission had been home to nearly three thousand Indians, living in the mission and in huts. Indian huts could still be seen surrounding the mission. Before its decline after secularization, the mission's far-flung ranchos managed 16,000 cattle, 25,000 sheep, and more than 2,000 horses. In one year, 1831, the mission harvested 39,500 bushels of grain and 2,500 barrels of wine. Once Mexico was free of Spain, and after secularization, the Californios began dividing the spoils. Governor Pio Pico and his brother, Andres—whom the dragoons had fought at San Pasqual—appropriated 90,000 acres of Mission San Luis Rey land for themselves.

"Dern, no wonder General Pico was so hoppin' mad," Bogart said, rubbing his old wounds.

"You're right," Sergeant Peck said. "He was protectin' the riches he stole from his own church."

"Did you fight at San Pasqual?" the dark-haired Mormon asked.

Bogart twitched a little and then exposed the scars on his body. "Sure did, and so did the sergeant. We almost died there. That's the only time I ever prayed fer Mormons to appear. Where were you boys, anyway?"

"Trying to catch up," Browett said. He told Bogart and Peck about his enlistment in Council Bluffs, the death of Colonel Allen in Fort Leavenworth, the Battalion's delayed departure from Leavenworth, and the long trek across the desert to Santa Fe. "Our commanders pushed us hard, but General Kearny was always too far out in front. And we never did have enough to eat. We about starved."

Bogart cast a disbelieving glance at Browett. "Come on, now. I'll betcha teamsters like Henry Eagles wuz ordered to bring ya new loads of flour ever' week."

"Henry Eagles?" the other Mormon gasped. "You knew Private Eagles?"

"Met 'im on a steamboat headin' fer Independence," Bogart stammered. "We enlisted together. Why?"

"He's my brother-in-law," Robert stammered back.

Bogart was confused and pointed to the other Mormon. "But I thought you said this man was your brother-in-law."

Robert chuckled. "He is—he married my sister. Henry Eagles is my wife's brother."

"But Henry Eagles ain't no Mormon—at least he didn't act like one."

Robert considered the remark a compliment to his religion. "No, he's not Mormon."

"Well, I ain't seen Eagles since I left Leavenworth," Bogart said. "How's he doin'?"

"He made it to Santa Fe with Colonel Price's regiment," Robert said. "Last I saw him he was complaining that he might get transferred to Colonel Doniphan's outfit."

"What would that mean?"

"Doniphan was ordered to invade northern Mexico."

5

February 22, 1847

Winter Quarters

HANNAH ONLY SMILED WHEN LIZZY expressed her disappointment. Hannah's seventh child was a boy.

"But now we have five boys in our family and only two girls," eight-year-old Lizzy commented when she first saw her new baby brother. Lizzy and all the rest of Hannah's children had waited at the Browett mud home with Martha while Elizabeth and Harriet helped deliver the baby.

Joseph reached out to touch the baby, wrapped tightly in a blanket. Fifteen inches of new snow had fallen yesterday, covering Winter Quarters in its own blanket. "What are we going to call him?"

"I told your Father that I was going to name the baby after him if it was a boy," Hannah said as she rocked the child in her arms.

"Hello, little Robert," Joseph said.

"I guess Papa will need all the boys he can get when we have our new farm out west," Lizzy said. "Welcome to the world, Robert number two."

"Number three," Hannah corrected. "Remember what you grandfather's name was—Robert Harris, Sr. Your father is Robert Harris, Jr."

"So the baby is Robert Harris—junior, junior?" Lizzy asked, puzzled.

"We'll call him Robert Harris the third," Hannah explained.

"He's a healthy child," Elizabeth said. "You should feel lucky in that regard, all of you."

A tear came to Hannah's eye. News had spread throughout Winter Quarters of the death of three women during the previous night. Even Brigham Young was ill, but he was nevertheless meeting with members of the Council of the Twelve to make additional plans for the trip to the Great Basin.

Lizzy's brown eyes bore into her new baby brother. "Mother, how old will little Robert be when Papa first sees him?"

Hannah thought for a moment. "That depends."

"Depends on what?" Lizzy asked.

"We don't know yet which company we'll be in."

"But I want to be in the first company," Lizzy said.

"I don't think that's possible," Hannah said. "The first company has to be led by strong men. Our family, especially now that we have a new baby, will have to go along with one of the later companies."

"Brigham Young has asked that all the captains get together and decide how to assign the Battalion families," Harriet said.

"Guess who was chosen as one of the captain's in Wilford Woodruff's company?" Elizabeth asked.

"Who?" Hannah asked.

"John Benbow."

"Oh, that's nice."

"He's one of the captains of ten, under Abraham Smoot," Elizabeth explained. Both the Browett and Harris families felt a special attachment to Benbow, the man who had been instrumental—along with Thomas Kington—in organizing the United Brethren congregation in England.

"Have you talked to him recently?" Hannah asked.

"Yes, just the other day," Elizabeth said. "He said there is a possibility that not all the Battalion families will be able to travel west this spring."

Hannah's heart did a tumble. "Did he say why?"

"Lots of reasons," Elizabeth said. "Too many cattle have been killed by Indians for one."

"How will they choose?"

"They've got to take us," Lizzy cried. "Papa will be expecting us."

"The baby will only be two or three months old when the first companies leave," Hannah said quickly. "It depends on how healthy he'll be by then."

Lizzy touched the baby's forehead. "You be healthy. Hear?"

6

March 18, 1847

San Luis Rey Mission

JUST WHEN DANIEL THOUGHT HIS RELATIONSHIP with Sergeant Peck and Private Bogart was progressing, Daniel and Robert broke out in an argument with them over the controversial John C. Fremont.

"Fremont ain't my kind of man," Daniel said as he wrapped his feet with rawhide in preparation for the trip to Los Angeles. The boots he'd been issued at Fort Leavenworth were long worn out and there was no chance of getting new ones until he reached Los Angeles, a four-day march north. "I'm sticking with Kearny."

"You boys ought to support Kearny, too, since you fought under him," Robert said to Peck and Bogart.

Peck had been trying to sort the whole controversy out for his newspaper article.

General Kearny had let it be known that he had been ordered by the President of the United States to assume the role of governor once California had been taken. However, Commodore Stockton had bestowed that authority on John C. Fremont back in October following the capture of San Diego and Los Angeles. Fremont now publicly stated that he wouldn't give up the governorship to Kearny and the whole thing seemed to be erupting into an ugly confrontation.

"But Fremont was here first, and if it weren't for him we'd still be battling the Californios and the Mexicans," Private Bogart said.

"You just say that because Fremont is a Missourian, and so are you," Robert said.

"I've always been proud to be a Missourian," Bogart said. "What's so wrong with Fremont?"

"Well," Robert said. "First of all, he's Senator Benton's son-in-law."

Bogart pulled a face. "You don't like Fremont because he's our senator's son-in-law?"

"Perhaps you don't know it," Robert said, "but Senator Benton is one of the worst anti-Mormons in the entire world."

Sergeant Peck stopped writing.

According to the captain, Fremont was refusing to give up the governorship.

Peck slowly said, "I've heard General Kearny has ordered Colonel Fremont to not only step down but to either muster his California volunteers into the regular army, or discharge them and surrender them to his own army."

Daniel felt helpless about all these California political events; they seemed to take a strange twist as days went by. Daniel was no newspaperman, but he understood them very well. Fremont had arrived at Sutter's Fort in December of 1845 ostensibly to conduct the third of his highly publicized explorations of the Far West. His actions and the military makeup of his command—former trappers, American emigrants, and Indian volunteers—suggested that his real purpose had been to overthrow Mexican rule. Some, mostly Kearny's men, alleged that Fremont's conduct during the Bear Flag revolt disgusted professional army officers because they had to deal with its consequences. Fremont, others had said, allowed his conquests to serve as an illusion to himself that he alone was the liberator of the former Mexican province of California, and ruler of a new nation on the West Coast.

There were still others who claimed General Kearny was spreading himself thin, trying to effectively occupy California. He lacked adequate money and credit from the United States government to do everything he wanted. Kearny hoped Mexico was worse off, being poorer still, and didn't have the means to launch a counterattack. Fremont was still in control of Los Angeles, despite the conflict. Commodore Stockton held San Diego. Commodore Shubrick held Monterey. Cooke had been holding San Luis Rey.

Daniel had an immediate reaction to Peck's statement, based on his personal bias. "I've never met General Kearny, and I've never met Colonel Fremont. But I'd support Kearny over Fremont as governor in a heartbeat."

"Why?" Bogart asked.

"Because Fremont's a Missourian," Daniel responded. "He'll carry built-in anti-Mormon sentiment."

"That's not a very fair judgment," Bogart said.

Daniel searched Bogart's craggy face. "Until you met us, you were anti-Mormon."

"I see what you mean."

Robert nodded his agreement. "Well, from what I know of Kearny, he's a good man."

Daniel felt Kearny's army service, dating back to the War of 1812, was worthy of respect. Since that war Kearny had worked his way up through the ranks without benefit of political influence or a West Point education. Many in California had claimed that Kearny held superior performance to be the norm and was not given to bestowing munificent praise on those who served under him.

Daniel had one reservation about the general, however.

"Well, Kearny hasn't said much about the accomplishments of the Mormon Battalion yet," Daniel said with a reluctant nod. "But given the fact that he's been confronted with the so-called mutiny of Fremont and a handful of resentful Californians, he's had his hands full."

The last thing Daniel ever thought a Missourian would do was to tell Daniel that he liked him.

"Dern," a half-flustered Private Bernard Bogart said to Daniel as both Mormon and Missouri soldiers began packing, "I thought I'd never say this, but I'm glad that we're going to Los Angeles with ya'll. I've decided I like you Mormons."

Daniel let out a choked laugh. The argument over Fremont had not been the only difference between him and Bogart. "You like us?"

He was having trouble believing what he'd just heard. Most of the Missourians remained hostile toward the Battalion boys, so Daniel felt that perhaps he had missed a step or two in their relationship somehow. Yes, they'd helped the Missourians clean their rooms in the mission, and true Bogart and Peck offered to take Daniel and Robert to a grog shop and buy them some whiskey. But that's when Daniel told Bogart and Peck about the Word of Wisdom. Daniel thought the two Missourians were somewhat offended when they were turned down.

Bogart drew his face into a half smile. "Hate to admit it. Don't tell the other boys."

Daniel felt his insides take a happy grip on the fact that good deeds had dissolved the hatred of at least two Missourians. "And we've decided we like some of you Missourians," Daniel answered back.

"Are all you Mormons going to Los Angeles?" Sergeant Peck asked. Peck had a full beard, shiny with beef drippings. Daniel wondered when the order to shave would reach the Missourians. Beef was plentiful in California and both the Missourians and the Mormons were getting their fill of it.

"No," Daniel said. "Company B has been assigned to stay in San Diego. But all four of the other companies have been ordered to occupy the presidio in Los Angeles. Only about thirty of our men will stay here, but they're the sick ones. Eventually they'll go to Los Angeles, too."

"Then I guess it's good news," Peck said. "General Kearny must have concluded that there is no immediate threat to San Luis Rey Mission."

Daniel hardly gave Peck a chance to finish his sentence. "But all this is going to place us smack dab into the middle of the big controversy."

"I'll bet we'll be able to all shake hands with General Kearny when we get to Los Angeles," Robert said hopefully.

"I look forward to that," Daniel said.

"You'll like General Kearny," Bogart said, obviously recalling the trip from Santa Fe and the battle at San Pasqual. "He's earned my respect."

"We still have time to get you baptized before we leave," replied Daniel as he removed the rawhide and cut another small piece away. He was no shoemaker, but he knew where the blisters might form, if any. His feet, like the other soldiers', were a mass of hardened calluses after the long walk from Council Bluffs.

Bogart held up a hand and laughed. "I didn't say I liked the Mormons that much."

"Well, I suppose we can do the baptizing after we arrive in Los Angeles,"

Daniel countered with a smile of his own.

The Mormon soldiers had struck their tents at sunrise. The route to Los Angeles would take them by the ocean.

Daniel, along with Levi Hancock, David Pettigrew, and Robert, had been trying for several days to teach the gospel to Bogart and Sergeant Peck. Helping the Missourians clean their quarters at the mission had been key in breaking down the animosity of the dragoons, especially with Bogart and Peck. Since shortly after their arrival at San Luis Rey, Cooke had been determined to make soldiers out of the Mormon Battalion men, dividing them into ten squads, and drilling them twice a day. Their daily routine had become a little monotonous to Daniel—roll call at daylight, sick call at 7:20, room cleaning, breakfast at 8:40, drilling in the morning and in the afternoon, roll call at sundown, and taps at 9 p.m. Some of the men had rebelled a little at the rigorous schedule, but most accepted it. Cooke occasionally became frustrated at the men. And Dr. Sanderson remained the same—he hated Mormons and he treated them accordingly. There had been little time to develop friendships, but Bogart and Peck's opinion of the Mormons had changed drastically.

Daniel refitted his rawhide and began imagining what Los Angeles would be like. If it were anything like San Luis Rey, it would be a good place. He had liked everything about San Luis Rey, except for food. Until the last few days, there was nothing to eat but beef, but there was plenty of it. Cattle roamed the hills everywhere, and Robert had been kept busy butchering them, almost a daily event. A week ago Daniel had been able to purchase a little wheat from some Indians. He had ground it in a hand mill and made a griddlecake, which was a treat. And just a few weeks ago Cooke had been able to obtain some flour and beans from a nearby rancho, a place called Robidoux Ranch.

Another thing that had made army life a little more enjoyable in San Luis Rey was the fact that there had been time for Church services on a regular basis. Levi Hancock had organized the men into quorums, too. Sermons on gospel principles had become a regular event. Hancock, Pettigrew, and others preached against swearing and other vices.

There had been little trouble in San Luis Rey, and no battles with the Mexicans. Andres Pico's lancers made no appearance. A company of Mexicans and Indians had been camping near the mission the past two weeks, but they were friendly. One of the Indian children was bitten by a rattlesnake and died. The child was buried with Catholic rites that including ringing the mission bell. Aside from the death of the child, the worst event had been the day when four soldiers killed a cow that belonged to an Indian, and Cooke put them in the guardhouse as a penalty. Another man had been fined for sleeping on duty.

A few times he and Robert and the other men had received permission to walk down to the Pacific Ocean. The seawater had been cold and foamy. Whalebones littered the beach. At night, a heavy mist came in from the ocean most of the time. For the most part, the weather in San Luis Rey had been chilly. This had brought an additional hardship on Daniel and the other men because they had traded most of their extra clothing for food along the way. All Daniel had was the clothes on his back and his makeshift rawhide shoes, and the wool blanket he curled up in at night.

Despite the constant drilling, the lack of an adequate diet, and spending time making friends with the Missourians, the thing that occupied Daniel's mind most of the time was thoughts about his family. He especially wondered about Moroni. Daniel imagined what Moroni would look like when he saw him again, whether the boy's features would be like his, or more like Elizabeth's. He imagined Moroni crossing the plains in a wagon, sitting by his mother in a wagon, or even toddling a bit behind a cow, one step at a time getting closer to the Mormon's new home in the Great Basin. Daniel imagined still another son, and a daughter, and even several children—despite Elizabeth's past inability to have children. And he imagined having children with Harriet, too. Having a large posterity was Daniel's fondest dream.

7

Tuesday, March 23, 1847
Los Angeles, California

RIGHT NOW, ROBERT HATED COLONEL John C. Fremont. And he was losing respect for Colonel Cooke, too. The two men were arguing about everything—from who had the right to be governor of California to where the Mormons should camp. Robert had been standing in formation in front of the government buildings with the Battalion for two long hours during the heated exchange. Robert shifted his weight on one leg and then the other, stared at the rawhide that served as his makeshift shoes, and let his eyes gaze over the presidio and the pueblo known as the City of Angels.

"They're both acting like a couple of school children," Robert whispered to Daniel. He closed his eyes, his thoughts a swirling tempest of regret that two

Americans could be at each other's throat.

"You're right," Daniel whispered back.

"It makes me feel gloomy," Robert said.

Fremont had bowed his neck. He had openly resisted Kearny's instructions that he and his men should be placed under the command of Colonel Cooke. Word was out that Fremont openly opposed the Mormon Battalion, and had publicly stated as the Battalion marched toward Los Angeles that if he could get control of his volunteers he would run the Mormons out of California. "All the people in the United States are fighting Mormons, and I have a right to fight them, too," Fremont had said.

"Maybe it's more like a school marm and a disobedient child," Robert commented on second thought. "Cooke ought to take Fremont over his lap and give him a real spanking. At least it's not hot and humid here like it was at Fort Leavenworth, or we'd be dying."

Fremont had openly declared opposition to all of Kearny's orders: that he was to muster his volunteers into the regular army, that he was to send Archibald Gillespie to Washington and have him report to the U.S. Marine Corps for duty, that he was to fall under command of Colonel Cooke, and that all property Fremont had seized was to be turned over to Cooke—including howitzers and ammunition.

"I don't think Cooke dares do that," Levi Hancock stated. "Technically, until the matter is settled, Fremont outranks Cooke."

To Robert's relief, Cooke soon emerged from the building where the argument had taken place and led the Battalion a mile away from the presidio to a beautiful green area near an Indian village.

"Sorry for the delay, boys," Cooke said apologetically. "This is where we'll make camp for a few days. "I didn't get anything settled with Colonel Fremont. He not only hates you Mormons, but he hates me, too. He's going to leave Los Angeles immediately and confront General Kearny in Monterey."

Now there's a meeting I'd like to attend, Robert thought to himself. He hoped Kearny had the backbone to put Fremont in his place.

For a while Cooke spoke to the Battalion about their duties. The Battalion was to protect Los Angeles from a counterattack and from hostile Indians who had constantly marauded the area. The American army was spread thin in California and there were no replacements on the way. Even if there were, training them would be costly and time consuming. Troops would have to sail around the horn of South America to get to California from places back East. Volunteers from New York were expected to arrive in a month or two.

"It's time you men began thinking about re-enlisting," Cooke said. "We need you here."

In 1781, to secure California for Spain, the Spaniards had created a series of *pueblos* or towns. Robert understood that Los Angeles was the second of those *pueblos*. In 1836 it had been elevated to the status of a cuidad, or city. Los Angeles was still a small oasis in a remote hinterland; few buildings had any pretensions of architectural taste, or convenience of plan or arrangement.

It had a reputation for the beauty of its setting, but also for thieves, gamblers, and drifters. Robert wanted nothing to do with those types of people; he longed for the comfortable company of Mormon neighbors again.

As Robert settled into an unappetizing meal of meat acquired from town that already had an odor of decay, he stiffened his resolve at Cooke's suggestion that he and the others re-enlist. The image of Hannah and his children were locked in his mind. Everything told him that re-enlisting was a lousy idea. "I've got exactly a hundred and twelve days left until we're released," he said to Daniel. "Then I'm starting home—wherever that is."

"Me, too," Daniel agreed. "There might be a few men who'll be attracted to the offer to serve for another year, but not me. I want to see Moroni again, and Elizabeth and Harriet."

Robert began imagining again. In his mind's eye he could see Brigham Young leading companies of Mormon pioneers from Winter Quarters to their destination somewhere in the Great Basin. He could see Hannah and his children trudging across the prairie, anxious to meet up with him. "How will we find our families?" he asked Daniel.

"We either have to backtrack in the direction of Tucson and Santa Fe and find our way from there," Daniel said, "or hope there's a way through the mountains north of Los Angeles, around the Sutter's Fort area. If we have faith, the way will be shown to us."

At daybreak, Robert and Daniel ate their morning meal with their messmates and prepared to go to town. To their surprise, a few Missouri dragoons had camped nearby. Private Bogart and Sergeant Peck were there. The dragoons had killed four outlaw Indians along the way, a retaliation for Indian depredations against ranchers in the area. "Cooke's not too happy with us," Bogart said sheepishly.

"Why?" Robert asked, sensing that Cooke might be overreacting.

"He didn't mind us killing the Injuns, but we wore out our horses. My little black horse came in so lame he can hardly walk. Cooke said if the Mexican lancers attacked us now we'd be helpless to defend the city."

"We should've had our horses shod," Peck admitted.

"Cooke says he wished he had the horseshoes he left behind somewhere in Arizona," Bogart added. "If he did, he'd introduce horseshoeing to the Californians."

"Cooke's not as worried about the Mexican lancers coming up this way as he is the renegade Indians pouncing on us," Daniel said. "As soon as our Battalion can round up some good horses, Cooke wants us to go hunt down Indians. I hope it's not me."

"Why?" Bogart asked.

Daniel shuddered. "I just hate the thoughts of an arrow or a tomahawk coming at my face. I have bad dreams about it."

"Dern," Bogart said. "That's really too bad and not realistic. The Injuns around here run away just like the Mexicans did in New Mexico. Nothing to fear."

Peck caught the sight of three riders leaving town. "Hey—ain't that

Colonel Fremont?"

"It is," Daniel acknowledged. "He's on his way to Monterey to confront General Kearny."

"We're glad to see him go," Robert said as his eyes followed the riders over the northern horizon. "He's spreading lies about the Mormons to the Californians. Soon the locals will hate us as much as most of the Missourians do."

Bogart snorted a laugh. "We'll have to correct that."

Colonel John C. Fremont rode north with a Californio, Don Jesus Pico, and a black servant, Jacob Dodson. Never in his life had Fremont felt such tense anxiety over political problems. Commodore Stockton had promised him the governorship and Fremont aimed to cling to that title at any cost.

"Why can't anyone see what I see?" he complained to Pico as he turned in the saddle, taking a look at Los Angeles from a hillside. For an instant Fremont's dark eyes focused, lingering on California's largest community and the political opportunities it presented him. He could see himself not only as governor, but perhaps someday as U.S. senator, and maybe even president.

Pico had learned to tell Fremont what Fremont wanted to hear. "No one else has your insight, not even General Kearny, and certainly not Colonel Cooke, or any of his Mormons."

Fremont nodded in agreement. Now that the Mormons were here, he could see the growing unrest of the Californians about Los Angeles. Little bands of armed Mexicans were galloping about the country. Californians seemed uneasy, and rumors flew about that a bloody uprising was at hand. It was all Kearny's fault, and, of course, the Mormons. The discontent in Los Angeles was strictly because Cooke had marched the Mormons into Los Angeles without his permission. The Californians hated and feared the Mormons. Also, Kearny had issued a proclamation when the general came into California, annulling some of the wise and mild provisions of what Fremont called the Capitulation of Cahuenga—the surrender of California that he had personally negotiated. Before long, Kearny would undo everything good that Fremont had accomplished. To counter Kearny's unauthorized show of power, Fremont had spread the rumor that if he, Fremont, were replaced as governor, a much harsher officer would likely take his place. Also, Fremont had spread the rumor that Kearny's policy opposed any payment for the cattle, horses, and goods taken, and the property destroyed, in the conquest of California.

"The people of Los Angeles will not stand for anyone to be governor of California except you, Colonel Fremont," Don Jesus Pico said as the three men spurred their horses toward Monterey, four hundred twenty miles north. Their goal was to reach Monterey in four days, settle the issue with Kearny, and dash back to Los Angeles before Cooke and the Mormons could do any further damage.

The three men had nine horses with them, or three apiece. The loose mounts were to be driven ahead and every twenty miles or so, as a fresh steed was wanted, one would be lassoed and saddled, so that a sweeping gallop could be maintained most of the way.

"I've maintained a perfect peace," Fremont called back. "Someday I'll be a senator, and, who knows? Perhaps president one day."

As Fremont and his companions sped away, Robert, Daniel, and their two Missourian friends went to town, located a few miles inland from the ocean.

"If the Californios here throw rocks at us, we'll blame it on Fremont," Robert said as he scanned the city and its people. He gave Daniel and the other two men a dogged determined look.

"Just so they don't do anything worse," Daniel said.

With a population of around five thousand Mexicans and Indians, Los Angeles was considerably larger than San Diego or San Luis Rey. Robert guessed a thousand small, inferior one-story buildings surrounded a central plaza. They had adobe walls and flat roofs of tar. Tar boiled out of the earth in several places near the city, and the city had the smell of stone coal. An unusual number of the buildings housed grog shops and gambling houses. On the way into Los Angeles, the Battalion had crossed the San Gabriel River, site of the final battle between Kearny and the Mexicans. Doctor Sanderson had inspected the mission at San Gabriel, declaring it to be unfit for human habitation.

Before they had gone far, the four men ran into some of the Missouri dragoons. A dozen of them blocked Robert, Daniel, Peck, and Bogart's way. "Get out of the way," Robert warned. He set his jaw and drew up his fists.

"You be the ones to stand back," a burly Missourian said. "We know who you are—you're Mormons. You're religious men, and we're not. You can't impose your will on us. We'll whip you if you try."

Daniel pulled Robert away. "It's not worth it."

Bogart was steamed at his fellow Missourians. He pointed to Robert. "You boys're lucky. This man was dern near the British heavyweight champion before he came to America. He coulda whupped up on all of you at one time."

Daniel pulled on Bogart's shirt. "Let it pass."

Robert strode a few steps away and then turned and gave the Missourians an icy stare. "You're right, Bogart. I could've whipped 'em all."

"I wonder what lies they've been spreading about us?" Robert said as he began walking again.

"I can't believe Fremont and his men would do such a thing to you Mormons," Bogart said as he peeked into a grog shop. It seemed that everyone in Los Angeles—the Californios, the Indians, and the Missourians—were prejudiced to the point they were not only spreading lies but stealing from the Mormon soldiers as well, just for spite.

"Let's find out," Peck said. He had his eye on a collection of Mexicans, Spaniards, and Californios sitting on a bench in front of a gambling house, waiting for it to open. Peck tapped a sunburned Californio wearing a wide *sombrero*. "Seen any Mormons around here?"

"Oh, yes, senor," the man said. He appeared to be in his thirties, the same age as Daniel and Robert. "Many Mormons arrived here only yesterday."

"Would you know one if you saw one?" Peck asked.

"Oh, yes, senor," the Californio answered. "They have horns under their hats."

Robert took off his hat and ran a hand through his brown hair and fixed a blistering gaze on the Californio. Peck noticed this and asked another question. "What else do you know about Mormons?"

The Californio took on an excited look and began talking in rapid clips. His English was decent, but his Spanish accent was deep. "All Mormon men have many, many wives."

Peck winked at Robert. "All of them?"

"Oh, yes, senor. All of them. And Mormons believe their women must remain pregnant, all the time, even into eternity, so they can send their babies to their own worlds."

Robert felt his teeth clench in frustration. Fortunately, he and Daniel had taught Peck and Bogart the truth about Mormonism, and these things the Californio were saying appeared not to bother Peck. "Mormons get to create their own worlds?"

"Oh, yes, senor. That is what they believe. That is what Joe Smith, their prophet, taught them. Joe Smith had many, many secret wives."

"He did?"

The Californio was wound up now, spinning his words like a top. "Oh, yes, senor. And that is not all. Before they came to the earth, Mormons lived on the moon, and some of them on the sun. Mormons wear funny underwear that they buy in their temples. They have Satanic symbols on their temple in Nauvoo, senor. Mormons believe Jesus Christ was married to three women—Mary, Martha, and that other Mary. Joe Smith received revelations from Satan through a peep stone. Mormon beliefs are mixed up with Judiasm and Christianity, Senor. Mormons don't even believe in the Bible. They have their own Bible, Senor, called the Book of Mormon."

"Mormons sound plumb crazy to me," Peck concluded.

"Oh, yes, senor. On their way to California, they killed many of my people in terrible battles. They ate the dead."

"Ate the dead?"

"Oh, yes, senor. Now all the Mormons in the world are coming to California. This is their promised land, senor. Brigham Young and the Mormons are on their way. The Mormons are invading. A shipload of them already arrived at San Francisco. If they can't convert us they'll kill us. They'll use their extra wives to populate. There'll be millions of them in just a few years. They'll steal everything we have. Mormons aren't even Americans. They're hardly human."

Peck had heard enough. Reports had preceded the Mormons to California all right, and Fremont had capitalized on it to affright the natives here. "Are you sure you'd recognize one of them?"

"Oh, yes, senor. By their horns."

"Who taught you all this?" Peck asked.

"Why the man who is going to be governor of California, Colonel Fremont, and his men."

Peck pulled Robert and Daniel to his side. "These two men have confessed to me that they are Mormons."

The Californio's eyes opened wide as saucers. "They have?"

"Want to see their horns?"

The man turned timid. "Oh, senor, this could be dangerous." He backed off a step or two.

Peck reached and took off the wide felt hats that Robert and Daniel were wearing. "These men are Mormons, but I don't see any horns." Peck ran his hands through Robert and Daniel's hair. "Don't feel any, either."

The Californio studied Robert and Daniel. "Perhaps they are new Mormons. Horns take a while."

"How long have you been Mormons?" Peck asked.

"Seven years," Daniel answered.

"How many wives do you have, Mr. Browett?" Peck asked.

"Two."

Peck turned to Robert. "And how many wives do you have?"

"Only one, but I miss her very much."

Peck turned his eyes back to the Californio. "What is your name, senor?"

"Torre."

"Well, Mr. Torre," Peck said. "You have been fed a pack of lies about

Mormons. I am not a Mormon, but by tomorrow I will be. I'm going to ask these two Mormons to baptize me as soon as possible. I have heard their doctrines, and they are nothing like what Colonel Fremont has told you. They believe in the doctrine of the creation, the creation of man, the fall of Adam of Eve, the need for a Savior, and the Plan of Salvation for example. And they believe in basic gospel principles like faith, repentance, baptism, and the Gift of the Holy Ghost. They believe in keeping their baptismal covenants—to obey God's commandments and serve Him to the end."

From the Californio's ashen expression, Robert sensed that Torre was slowly realizing that the rumors he had heard about Mormons were untrue.

Torre backed away another two steps. "I am sorry, then, my friends. I did not mean to offend you."

Peck laughed. "No offense taken. But perhaps you just helped me make up my mind about joining the Mormon Church."

8

April 5, 1847

Winter Quarters

THE SOUNDS OF SNAPPING HARNESSES AND creaking wagon wheels were unmistakable—Heber C. Kimball's six wagons were leaving Winter Quarters for the Great Basin, the first wagons of the Pioneer Company. Hundreds of Saints lined the ridge west of the city, near the haystacks, as the wagons headed west.

"I wish we were going with them," eleven-year-old Joseph said to his mother, Hannah. "Father will be expecting us."

The skies were cloudy, threatening more rain. Wilford Woodruff had intended to start the journey with Heber, but a heavy downpour that morning had caused Wilford problems. Other captains were loading wagons, preparing to leave later in the day, or within the next few days. The Pioneer Company, as organized by Brigham Young, would eventually consist of a hundred and forty-eight people and seventy-two wagons.

"Yes, he'll be mad if we're not there," Lizzy said.

"Oh, he won't be mad," Hannah countered. She carried her new baby, Robert III, in her arms. "Even if we leave by June, we might be there about the same time as your father and the other Battalion boys."

"How did you come up with that?" Joseph asked. "Father'll be released in July and it won't take that long for him to get to the Great Basin from California."

"How can Papa find the Great Basin if he's never even been there?" Lizzy asked.

"Brigham Young has never been there and he'll find it just fine," Hannah said. "He's been studying maps all winter. And he has those fancy instruments from England."

John Taylor and Parley P. Pratt had returned from their mission to England. With money contributed by the Saints in England, they had purchased scientific instruments for calculating latitude, elevation, temperature, and barometric pressure.

"But how will Father know for sure everyone will be in this Great Basin place?" seven-year-old William asked.

"He will know," Hannah said.

"Are we for sure going to leave by June?" five-year-old Thomas asked.

Hannah took another look at her new baby, wrapped in a wool blanket, clutched tightly to her breast. "Depends on a lot of things," she said.

"Like what?" William asked.

"Your little baby brother, for one," Hannah answered. "We need him to pink up a little better."

"Spring is here," Lizzy said. "We'll be able to eat better soon."

"We're a large family," Hannah said. "It's hard enough for some of the men to have to worry about getting their own families across the plains, let alone worry about the eight of us."

"Whatever you do, Mother," Joseph said sternly, "don't sell our wagon."

"Or our oxen," William said.

"We've got to meet Father this summer, we've just got to," Joseph said, almost to the point of tears.

"I can't wait," Lizzy said, dancing nervously on one foot and then the other.

"Don't you remember how tough it was across Iowa?" Hannah asked. "Think about all that walking, the dust, bad storms, cold nights, bad water, and the sickness."

"It'll be worth it," Lizzy said. "I want my Papa."

Elizabeth, little Moroni, Martha, and Harriet had wandered a ways out into the prairie, following the wagons, but now returned to Hannah's view.

"Exciting isn't it?" Elizabeth said.

"Yes," Hannah said.

"It'll be even more exciting when all the other wagons leave Monday or Tuesday," Harriet said. Tomorrow, Sunday, Brigham Young was to preside over a short session of General Conference.

"It's not fair that you've been assigned to a company and we haven't," Joseph said to his aunt with more than just a hint of spite. Elizabeth and Harriet had been assigned to a company to be led by Parley P. Pratt and Perrigrine Sessions, schedule to leave in June. Many other Battalion wives had their assignments too.

"Don't start that again," Hannah warned. "You know why we're not assigned."

"The baby will be fine by then, Mother," Joseph said.

"We'll wait and see," Hannah said. "I'll not lose a child on the plains."

"I want to travel with you, Auntie," Lizzy said.

"I know," Elizabeth answered. "But you're mother is right. The baby has to be healthy to make a big trip like that."

"There'll be room in our company, or one of the others, if things work out," Harriet said.

"We all need to say our prayers for the baby," Lizzy said.

"We do, every day," Elizabeth said with a warm smile.

"It won't be fair if Moroni gets to see his father this year, and we don't," William said.

"Yeah," Thomas said. "It wouldn't be fair."

9

April 9, 1847

Los Angeles, California

DANIEL FELT A PANG OF FEAR SWEEP through him as he contemplat-
ed the order Cooke had given him, a few other Battalion soldiers, and a few
dragoons: Go to Colonel Fremont's headquarters at the San Gabriel Mission
and retrieve Fremont's cannons, arms, horses, and supplies. Fremont had
returned to Los Angeles, but Daniel didn't know if Fremont would be with his
men or not.

"What if it turns out we have to fight Fremont's men to get them?"
Robert asked, reluctantly taking hold of the musket he had been issued in Fort
Leavenworth. He had killed buffalo, wild bulls, antelope, and deer with it, but
he had not fired a shot at a man.

Private Bogart gasped for breath as he considered the assignment. "Dern, I'd rather fight the Mexicans or Californians."

"Me, too," added Sergeant Peck as he stared at his saber. "Fremont's got mountain men with him, and Injuns, too."

"Well, we've got to do it, because Cooke ordered it," Daniel said as he mounted a horse he had purchased with his back pay. "And Cooke ordered it because it's what General Kearny wants." Daniel would not only ride the brown mare to the San Gabriel Mission, but he would ride out on it in July after his release from the army to find Elizabeth, Moroni, Harriet, and the main body of the Church.

The order to collect the cannons was all part of the unhappy dispute between General Kearny and Colonel Fremont.

"Dern, who is governor of California anyway? Kearny or Fremont?" Bogart asked as more than two-dozen men mounted up for the dangerous mission. The men led teams of mules so they could be used to tow the howitzers and cannon back to Los Angeles.

"In my mind, Kearny's the governor," Peck answered.

The San Gabriel Mission was only eight miles south, so the detachment arrived there in less than an hour. A little village stood just below the mission, between the mountains and the river. Near the mission buildings were long hedges of prickly pears, which protected the vineyards and orchards. Wheat fields surrounded the mission, too. Like most other missions, it was quite dilapidated. The capped buttresses gave San Gabriel a decidedly Moorish feel;

the Spanish cathedral had once been a mosque. Fremont and his men were camped in the trees near the orchards. Just as Peck predicted, there was an assortment of mountain men, emigrants, Walla Walla Indians, and a couple of tough-looking Delaware Indians. Though they looked feisty, they put up no resistance and began introducing themselves. Their leader carried a colorful name—"Hell Roaring" Thompson, who used foul language but showed the men where the cannons were.

"You men must be part of the Mormon Battalion," said one of Fremont's men, a young American that looked to be no more than twenty years of age.

Daniel felt a surge of uneasiness as he dismounted from his brown mare. Unsure of himself, he extended his right hand. "Sergeant Daniel Browett, Company E."

"Edward Kemble," the young man said. "I work for a Mormon—Samuel Brannan."

Daniel about fell over backward so complete was his shock, and he quickly swallowed his apprehension. "I didn't know Fremont had any members of the Church riding with him."

Kemble laughed and pointed to another soldier. "I'm not a Mormon, but this man is."

"Jesse Stringfellow," the other said, offering Daniel a handshake.

Kemble wore a big and friendly smile. "We've been in California since the end of July," he explained. "We came from New York on the *Brooklyn* with Samuel Brannan."

"We couldn't resist the idea of sailing to California around the horn," Stringfellow added.

"Until I enlisted with Fremont, I was working on a printing press for Brannan," Kemble said. "I'll go back to the same job soon, at the *California Star.*"

Peck stuck out his hand. "I'm a newspaperman, too. I report for the *Liberty Weekly Tribune.*"

Kemble looked at Peck's wornout uniform and his sergeant's stripes. "You from Missouri?"

"Yep, both me and Bogart here. But now we're Missouri Mormons. These Battalion soldiers converted us a while back. We were baptized two days ago."

Kemble looked impressed.

"We don't know much about Brannan," Daniel admitted as he scanned the trees where the California Battalion was camped. None of Fremont's men were offering any resistance. "Some things about him I've heard are positive, some not so positive."

Kemble and Stringfellow chuckled. "Oh, Brannan's had a long attack of Western fever," Kemble explained. "Samuel has been so focused on creating an independent state on the West Coast that it never occurred to him that the United States might have other plans."

Stringfellow nodded in agreement. "Brother Brannan might have joined the California Battalion with us if he had thought it would help establish authority in California under the banner of the Church."

Daniel felt confused.

"Brother Brannan thinks the Church ought to settle north of here, around the San Francisco Bay area," Kemble said. "He plans on crossing the mountains this summer to find Brigham Young and lead him to California."

California didn't fit in with Daniel's vision as a safe haven for his family. There was already too much anti-Mormon sentiment here. "I think Brigham Young will soon be headed for the West," Daniel explained, "but last we heard he's looking for a place near the lake of salt, within the Great Basin, where there are no other settlers."

Robert was watching the other Battalion members approach the howitzers with the mules they had brought. "Is there going to be a problem with us carrying out our orders—to take those howitzers back to Los Angeles with us?"

Kemble shook his head. "Nope. Colonel Fremont left word with us to turn them over to you, as per the order Colonel Cooke sent."

"Dern, does that mean he's gonna let Kearny be governor?" Bogart asked.

"Frankly, I don't understand your General Kearny at all," Kemble said.

Daniel forced a laugh. "And we don't understand your Colonel Fremont. To us, he seems awfully anti-Mormon." Underneath he felt a sudden upwelling of anger.

"I suppose he is, but he's treated us just fine," Stringfellow commented. "We think Kearny ought to go to Mexico and fight there, and leave California to be governed under John C. Fremont, as Commodore Stockton and the U.S.

Government intended."

Daniel really didn't want to argue against fellow Mormons, but he didn't want the facts to go unchallenged. Obviously, there was a lot of vagueness spewing forth from Washington D. C. Daniel said, "But our General Kearny has orders to be not only commander-in-chief of all military operations, but governor, too."

Daniel explained to Kemble and Stringfellow that Kearny possessed a letter from President Polk, dated the fifth of November 1846, giving Kearny that authority. Kearny had received the letter in mid-February.

Kemble countered, saying Commodore Stockton had official orders from the Navy Department to occupy and hold on to California if war broke out. Stockton had arrived in the bay of San Francisco way back in August. Washington had commissioned Stockton with authority to set up a government in California, after it had been secured, and Stockton still aimed to declare Fremont as governor.

"Fremont deserves to be governor, after all he's done," Kemble said.

"What's he done besides negotiate a bad treaty?" Peck asked. He was referring to the Treaty of Cahuenga. It was true: Kearny did not approve of its liberal conditions regarding prisoners, and paroles for Mexican officers and citizens.

"It wasn't a bad treaty," Kemble countered. "Fremont let Pico and Castro surrender with dignity and grace, something that a pure military man like Kearny wouldn't have done."

"Well, dern it all," Bogart said. "General Kearny wasn't pleased with it. He's a little put out with Fremont and Stockton."

Stringfellow snorted and looked grim. "Were you with Kearny at Pasqual and Mule Hill?"

Bogart hung his head as if he were a little ashamed. "Yep."

"Kearny would have died on Mule Hill after Pico routed you if you hadn't been rescued by Stockton's sailors and marines," Stringfellow said.

"I suppose that's true," Bogart admitted.

"Kearny's had it out for Fremont ever since 1843," Stringfellow charged.

"What happened back then?" Daniel asked. He still felt a slight revulsion at any mention of Fremont.

"Kearny allowed himself to be talked into letting Fremont take a mountain howitzer on Fremont's second expedition," Stringfellow explained. "Kearny regretted it later."

"But I'll tell you what's really peeved General Kearny," Peck said.

"What's that?" Kemble asked.

"When Kit Carson reported that Colonel Fremont had California under control," Peck said. "General Kearny sent two thirds of our dragoons back to Santa Fe. Then you know what happened at San Pasqual. We were outnumbered."

"Dern right, the general was steamin' mad after that," Bogart said.

"That bit of misinformation cost the lives of twenty-two soldiers, plus a lot more wounded," Peck said.

It was Kemble's turn to hang his head. "Well, Kearny's sure out to make Fremont look bad now. Kearny seems vindictive to me."

"But think of all of General Kearny's accomplishments," Peck asserted. "His conquest of New Mexico is truly remarkable as we think back on it, and I wrote newspaper accounts saying just that. He outfitted more than sixteen hundred men at Fort Leavenworth, barely took enough food to reach Santa Fe, and very capably established a civil government there. You'd have to admit that things haven't been going that good in California. First we received word that California was in the hands of the United States, and then we reduced our forces and had to fight the Mexicans at San Pasqual. By the time we got here, California was in the hands of the Mexicans again."

"I suppose that'd be Gillespie's fault," Kemble said. "He was too stern in Los Angeles, and the people didn't like him."

"Well," Peck said. "Gillespie was one of Fremont's top men. Fremont has to assume the responsibility for that."

"He assumes the responsibility," Kemble added. "But he still deserves to be governor. Commodore Stockton had the authority to make him governor. Fremont's caught in the middle. It's not fair that he's outranked by Kearny. When Kearny finally got to Los Angeles he was cranky, angry, weary, and wounded. He's taking it all out on Fremont. I met Stockton. He was generous to a fault, warm-hearted, and impulsive. Kearny appears to be quite frigid, grim, and selfish."

As Kemble defended Fremont, Daniel recalled what he knew about the explorer. In December of 1845, Fremont entered the Mexican province of Alta California ostensibly to map the west coast area. Although he made official contact with Mexican authorities, his movements around the province had always been a point of consternation to Mexico's northern regional commander, General Jose Castro. In particular, Castro had not cared for Fremont's contact with and sympathy for American settlers and emigrants. The Fremont party traversed as far north as Klamath before Fremont turned south upon hearing that a proclamation had been issued by Castro, aimed at driving foreigners out of the province. Fremont established a base camp in the Sacramento Valley a few miles north of Sutter's Fort and began to advise those who chose to confront the Mexican authorities. Word of Fremont's camp reached a group of settlers who were most vociferous in their dislike of the province's government. Ultimately, the group became known as the "Bear Flaggers," because they began a revolt, took the town of Sonoma, and raised their Bear Flag over the plaza. The Bear Flaggers evolved into the California Battalion and Fremont took over leadership. Fremont appointed Captain Gillespie as his adjutant. The Battalion was given legitimacy in July when it was recognized by the American military leader in California, Commodore Stockton. Stockton promoted Fremont to major and gave Fremont command over all the volunteer militia in California. After Los Angeles and San Diego surrendered, Fremont left Gillespie in charge of Los Angeles. His bumbling caused the locals to rebel, and that led to the battle at San Pasqual. Fremont's battalion really came into prominence when it accepted the surrender of the

Californios at Cahuenga Pass. The meeting between Pico, Castro, and Fremont had actually been arranged by a woman in Santa Barbara—Bernarda Ruiz—who was saddened by all the bloodshed in her country. There, Andres Pico, who inflicted the defeat on Kearny, surrendered to Fremont, thereby ending the conflict in California.

As Daniel listened to the friendly argument, he thought how the situation resembled a comic opera. He knew enough about Kearny to know that the man did not want to be bypassed in rank and authority by this mere young officer known as John C. Fremont. Fremont, after all, was just a lieutenant colonel in the Topical Engineers. Kearny was a brigadier general. Many older army officers, as well as West Point graduates, were insanely jealous of Fremont's rapid rise in the military. Fremont was just an explorer. But Fremont had a father-in-law who was a senator from Missiouri. Nevertheless, he wasn't a true military man and didn't really know the rules of the game. Daniel sensed Fremont wanted to be governor of California to further his personal political ambitions, but the same could be said of Kearny. The way Fremont saw it, Stockton had official orders from the Navy department to hold on to California if war broke out. Well, war broke out. Fremont had accepted a commission in the California Battalion from Stockton, and he had to do what Stockton said. In his letter to Kearny on January seventeenth, which he read to Kearny in person, Fremont committed a cardinal sin by telling a senior officer that he was not going to obey him. Kearny had given him a chance to take back the letter, but he didn't. Now he must live with it. Fremont was too proud, too filled with ego to consider his shaky position.

Kemble told Daniel and Robert about Yankee enterprise in Spanish America. He said Americans had been drifting into California on ships since the early part of the century. Mexican laws made it difficult for aliens to enter or live there, but Mexican citizens generally winked at the laws. In the late 1820s a second wave of newcomers began arriving in California. These were gaunt, leathery fur trappers who made it through the snowy Sierra passes, and some of them settled down as carpenters, masons, coopers, silversmiths, soap-makers, shipwrights, and millers. Most married pretty dark-eyed senoritas who smoked cigarettes in gold holders, rode like vaqueros, danced, sang, and played the guitar.

"Sam Brannan will want you Mormon soldiers to stay in California," Kemble said in a serious note.

"Not me," Robert said. "It's a nice place, but I've got a wife and six children waiting for me."

Daniel, Robert, and the two Missourians left to help hook the mules up to the howitzers.

"I know you come into Los Angeles once in a while," Daniel told Kemble and Stringfellow as his group began the arduous task of hauling the cannons and other items back to the pueblo. "Stop by. We'd like to get to know you better."

Kemble saluted. "Sure thing."

A few days later, Sergeant Peck was surprised that Colonel Cooke moved the Mormon Battalion farther away from town, a half mile below the pueblo. "What'd he do that for?" Peck asked Daniel as they strolled through town.

"Too many threats from the Missouri volunteers," Daniel answered. "Other than you and Private Bogart, we haven't made much headway with the Missourians. They still hate us."

In California, the established white inhabitants referred to themselves as *people of reason* to distinguish themselves from the Indians and Hispanics. Missourians had picked up on the term too, but had refused to include the Mormons in that designation. To them, Mormons were still known as "scoops."

Both Peck and Bogart had been baptized April sixth, the seventeenth anniversary of the Church. On that same day, Cooke had sent a wagon to the coast to load provisions from ships in the harbor. Since then, the Battalion's diet had been more balanced. The abundance of local leather had resulted in shoes, too. And a sutler traveling with a new force, the New York Volunteers, had arrived with wagonloads of clothing. General Kearny had sent word that the clothing could be purchased by soldiers at reduced prices. The news could-n't have been timelier: Robert and Daniel had just received some of their back pay, in gold.

Every Battalion member was blaming the Missouri doctor, George Sanderson, for the death of Private David Smith in San Luis Rey, too. Sanderson had a new supply of calomel and had not backed off his recommended dosages. Battalion members who had been left behind at San Luis Rey had rejoined the main body of the Battalion a week earlier.

Cooke had been nervous as a cat for the past month too, fearing that rumors of a Mexican invasion to retake Los Angeles might be true. Cooke sent Company C to guard the Cajon Pass, sixty miles away, took cannons away from Fremont's men at the San Gabriel Mission and brought them to the pueblo, and rejected a plea from the Battalion for discharge.

"You might think the war is over," Cooke had told the Battalion officers in a meeting as the petition was considered. "But the Indians are prowling, the Mexicans are restless, and we keep hearing there might be an army of Mexicans marching from the south." There were even rumors that the men at Cajon Pass had been attacked by Chief Walker and his party of Ute Indians, who were rumored to be in allegiance with the Mexicans.

Cooke then issued an order for the men to begin construction of a small fort overlooking the pueblo of Los Angeles.

"I suppose the rest of the Missourians will hate the Mormons forever," Peck admitted. "I've kept the news of our baptisms quiet. Otherwise, our own fellow soldiers might tar and feather us."

"Dern, I'd hate to be tarred and feathered," said Bogart.

Daniel threw his arms apart. "I don't suppose the Missourians hate the small handful of Mormon soldiers who act just as bad as the Missourians."

Peck laughed. "No, I guess you're right. We ought to hogtie those men and keep them from drinking and gambling."

Most of the Missourians and a small handful of Mormons were acting just as crude as the local Californios. One of the Mormons, John Allen, had already been excommunicated for his behavior. In Daniel's view, Allen had joined the Church merely to be able to join the army and get army pay. Allen was a tall proportioned man with a heavy beard. He was not only excommunicated, but Colonel Cooke had seen to it that Allen was drummed out of the service. Cooke ordered Allen's head and beard half shaved—meaning half shaved clean on one side but not the other. Allen had been brought to the parade ground under guard, the band formed, and the sentence of a court martial read to him. The fifers and drummers then played the *Rogues March* and drummed Allen out of town.

It was unfortunate, Daniel thought, that there were a few Mormon soldiers who were setting a bad example as they frequented the grog shops and gambling houses, tarnishing the good behavior of all the other men. Last night David Pettigrew and Levi Hancock had called a special Church meeting of all Battalion members and preached to them about the importance of keeping themselves unpolluted from the sins of the world. And last Sunday a Seventies Quorum meeting had been held, with Hancock condemning the stealing of public property, drunkenness, swearing, and all other sins.

Now that things were settled down, Levi Hancock had organized a Seventies Quorum. Daniel had been chosen as one of the quorum's seven presidents.

It was a hard thing for some of the weaker Battalion members to refrain from the worldly vices in Los Angeles. Brother Hancock had challenged Daniel and the other leaders of the quorum to teach correct principles to all the members of the Church in California. Things were different than they had been in Nauvoo. Here, there were grog shops and wine cellars all over. The Spaniards seemed to be an indolent race, in Daniel's opinion, spending all their time either riding, gambling, or drinking—despite the fact that they professed to be passionate Catholics. Every Sunday, right after their church services, they met for horse racing—which led to more drinking and more gambling. Their women, although fair and some beautiful, were also steeped in world iniquity. All the Spaniards seemed to treat Indians as nothing more than slaves. Indians could be seen daily working in the orchards and gardens, tending to the pear, apple, peach, coconut, and olive trees.

CHAPTER NOTES
    Edward Kemble and Jesse A. Stringfellow, both Mormons, enlisted in Fremont's California Battalion. Just as portrayed, the two men accompanied Samuel Brannan on the *Brooklyn*. Whether or not Kemble and Stringfellow were actually in Los Angeles at the time the Mormon Battalion members retrieved the cannons from Fremont is not known, but likely. Sources that cite Kemble and Stringfellow are: Bigler, David L., and Bagley, Will, *Army of Israel, Mormon Battalion Narratives* (Utah State University Press, Logan, Utah 2000); and Egan, Ferol, *Fremont, Explorer for a Restless Nation* (University of Nevada Press, Reno, Nevada) 1985.

10

End of April, 1847

Winter Quarters

HANNAH FOUND HERSELF IN Whitney's store again, this time needing meat—about the only thing left to eat in Winter Quarters after a long, drawn out winter.

"I promise, I'll find you some," Whitney said as Hannah scoured the store looking for anything to feed her children.

"How bad's the loss to the Indians?" Hannah asked.

"We think as high as five thousand dollar's worth," Whitney said with a sad shake of his head.

"My two oldest boys saw some Indians driving off two head of cattle night before last," Hannah said.

"I know," Whitney replied. "The Indians ignore the guards and Brother Brigham doesn't want them to shoot the Indians."

Now that grass had started the grow, the cattle had been turned loose, making the problems worse. Occasional cannon firing, military drills, and other conspicuous shows of force failed to deter the Omaha and Oto Indians.

"I still don't understand why they steal our cattle," Hannah moaned.

"To the Indian," Whitney explained, "the deer, the buffalo, cherries and plums from the trees, and things like strawberries are free. It's their mode of living to kill and eat. You have to feel sorry for them, they suffered during the winter worse than we did."

During the winter, the local Indians had been largely unsuccessful in their buffalo hunts and their efforts to grow and harvest corn last year had been a failure too. On some days during the winter, they stole two or three oxen a day from the Mormons. Big Elk, chief of the Omahas, on many occasions returned items stolen from the Mormon camps, but rarely returned stolen beef because his people were starving just as the Mormons were.

"And our men shoot their share of wild turkeys and small animals," Whitney explained. "The Indians considered wild game theirs."

"And they consider our cattle theirs too," Hannah said. "I've got a newborn baby at home. I need to keep myself healthy, for the baby's sake."

"I'll do what I can," Whitney said. "But Brother Brigham is taking a herd with him. Did you make the list."

Brigham Young was scheduled to depart on his long-postponed trip to the Rockies any day, without Hannah, and without a lot of other Battalion wives. "No, I'm not going," Hannah said. "Not with a new baby and six other children. I'd be too much of a burden for the other pioneers. But Elizabeth and Harriet are going."

11

May 10, 1847

Los Angeles

DANIEL HAD ALWAYS WONDERED WHAT a general looked like from three feet away. When General Kearny inspected the Mormon Battalion, he did it slowly and precision-like, as though he had all the time in the world. For a few seconds Kearny stood in front of Daniel, perfectly immobile except for a glint in his friendly eyes. The general had a long nose and smooth skin. He was tall and wide-shouldered, with a lean, sun-weathered face. If it weren't for his uniform, Kearny could pass for an ordinary soldier. In fact, that's the way he liked to be viewed. When Kearny had ridden into Santa Fe, the locals there couldn't tell him from any of the other soldiers.

The Mormon Battalion had early paraded for the general but now it stood in formation as Kearny prepared to address them. Soft, white clouds floated overhead; the breezes off the ocean were gentle. Yesterday, when Kearny arrived in Los Angeles, he had been greeted with a twenty-one-gun salute. Daniel, along with every other Mormon soldier, had been able to shake the general's hand.

Daniel felt a sigh of relief as Kearny began scanning the other Battalion officers with his intense dark eyes and then began speaking. Several townspeople were watching, the ladies all dressed up, anxious to talk to the three Mormon women who still accompanied the Battalion.

"You Mormon Battalion boys have accomplished something never rivaled in the history of military operations," Kearny began. "Napoleon may have crossed the Alps, but you boys have crossed a continent, mostly through an unknown region. You have come two thousand miles, all the way to the Pacific coast. You have created a new and useable east-west wagon road that others will follow. As foot soldiers, you walked. And part of the way you walked half naked, with most of your clothing traded for food. And with your shoes worn out. The few dragoons who came to California with me rode horses and mules."

These remarks made Daniel think of the times with crowbars, picks, and axes, he carved out a road over mountains which seemed to defy even wild goats, hewing passages through chasms of rock more narrow than the wagons.

Earlier, Kearny had repeated his admonition that his dragoons had actually won the battle at San Pasqual. After Daniel thought about it for a while, he had to agree somewhat. Kearny was rationalizing, to be sure, but the Americans had taken repossession of all of California. Andres Pico and his lancers—although they truly did decimate Kearny's dragoons—were nowhere to be found.

Kearny continued his address. "I am proud of the conduct of the Mormon soldiers. You deserve credit for your overall good conduct. The Mormon Battalion has not been guilty of anything derogatory to the character of a soldier."

Daniel's skin tingled and he felt more than a tinge of pride. Kearny was right. Overall, the Battalion had an almost flawless record. There had been a few instances when the conduct of some Battalion members would have caused Brigham Young to grimace, but compared to the conduct of the Missouri volunteers, the Battalion members truly were Saints.

"I am returning to the United States," Kearny announced. "I promise to represent your good conduct to the President of the United States, and to members of Congress." The general went on to make promises of access to better provisions and better clothing. He also made a plea for the men to re-enlist.

No thanks, Daniel said to himself. *I want to go home.*

"As you know, Colonel Cooke is accompanying me on the trip back to Washington D. C. If the war is still going when we get there, we will be able to be reassigned."

Word had been received of American victories deep within the heart of Mexico. Daniel expected the war would be over down there too, by the time the Battalion was released. Daniel knew the truth: Kearny was prematurely leaving California to escort John C. Fremont back to the Untied States so that Fremont could be arrested and tried for treason. Three men from each of the four companies of the Mormon Battalion in Los Angeles had been chosen to assist Kearny. Kearny had rejected Fremont's offer to go directly into Mexico and continue the fight against the Mexicans. Fremont had declared he had a hundred and twenty horses and sixty men to commit to the effort.

Kearny had chosen Colonel Richard B. Mason as his successor.

In Kearny's final remarks he introduced the Mormon Battalion's new commander, Colonel John D. Stevenson. Stevenson was commander of the New York volunteers who had just arrived in Monterey by ship.

Daniel felt a surge of uneasiness as Stevenson spoke to the Battalion for a few minutes. Stevenson stressed the need for the Mormons to re-enlist, adding that the new governor wanted them to re-enlist, too. Daniel gave a dire sigh. He had no intention of staying in California for any longer than necessary. In two months his military service would end. Earlier in the day, Daniel had visited with a group of Ute Indians who had been camping near town. They told of coming to California over the mountains northeast of San Francisco. Kearny and Fremont likely would follow that route to Fort Hall, on the Snake River, and from there follow the Oregon Trail back to the Missouri River. Somewhere, on that trail, Elizabeth, Harriet, and Moroni were coming the opposite direction, making their way west.

12

SINCE THE *VAQUERO* PRACTICALLY LIVED in the saddle, it was not surprising to Robert that the *vaqueros'* favorite pastime were tests of horsemanship. The *vaquero* was always ready to place a bet, take up a dare, or join in a competitive and dangerous game. Robert visioned taking up some of the *vaqueros'* skills when he returned to his family in the Great Basin, and dressing like them, too. California was part of the wild west and the Great Basin would be too.

This all became evident when the Mexicans at the pueblo celebrated St John's Day on June twenty-fourth. Not only were there games of horsemanship, but bull fighting and horse racing as well. The day was warm with light fluffy clouds drifting lazily in a blue sky, and the streets of Los Angeles were crowded with Mexicans, Mormons, Missourians, New Yorkers, Fremont's sol diers, Spaniards, Californios, and Indians.

"Dern, could you do that?" asked Private Bogart as a *vaquero* leaned down from the side of his bay horse at a full gallop and plucked a coin from the ground.

Even the *vaquero*'s wide-brimmed *sombrero* remained unfettered. Under the *sombreros*, each *vaquero* wore his hair parted in the middle and brushed back into a long braid that was folded up and tucked under his hat; or the braid was hanging down his back. Each *vaquero* wore a short-waisted jacket made of leather or cloth, and most of them were trimmed with fancy buttons along the sides and on the pocket flaps. Tight-fitting pants buttoned down the sides and were tucked into leather leggings, which covered their lower legs down to the ankles. Some wore leather sandals; others wore shoes. And all wore spurs that caused them to jingle and jangle as they walked. Every *vaquero* was bowlegged. Some of the *vaqueros* were Christianized Indians

Robert felt a surge of adrenaline, as though he were about to enter the ring to fight with his bare fists. "If I had lived all my life on a horse, I suspect I could," he said. "When I get home I'll try it, but not in front of this crowd." Other riders had plucked arrows and kerchiefs from the ground.

In a gruesome sport called *carrera del gallo*, a live rooster had been buried in the sand with only its head showing. The winning *vaquero* had swung back into the saddle waving the wing-flapping rooster in his hand, winning all bets along with whoops of approval from the crowd. It reminded Robert of Henry's stories about the games played by the men in Carthage, Illinois.

To Robert, the Spanish word *vaquero* sounded in English like "bucka-roo." Long before cattle came to California and Texas, cowboys rode the range in Spanish Mexico. They called themselves *vaqueros*, or cow herders, from *vaca*, the Spanish word for cow. Mexico's wide-open spaces had been ideal for raising livestock. Back in England, animals had been kept in pens. But here horses and cattle were allowed to wander at will, finding their own grass and water. Many of them had escaped to run free, creating enormous herds of wild horses and cattle. Huge cattle ranches dotted the landscape in California.

"I'd sorta like ta enter the ring race," Bogart mused. "That'd be the way to catch me a cute senorita."

"Better wait until you join up with the Mormons in the Great Basin," Robert said. ""There'll be plenty of cute little Mormon girls waiting for you. You can take one to the temple."

Both Bogart and Peck had plans to return to Missouri after the war, tell their parents about their conversion, and then leave to join the main body of Mormons in the Great Basin.

Bogart returned Robert's smile. The *la sortija*, the ring race, required a sharp eye and split-second timing. *Vaqueros* armed with short wooden lances, their bright-red sashes flapping in the wind, raced at a gallop toward a tiny golden ring hanging from a slender thread. The rider who managed to skewer the ring with his lance won it as a prize. He could then present it as a gift to a young woman he wanted to impress.

"Dern," Bogart said on second thought. "Makes me think of the battle we had with the Mexicans at San Pasqual. I can still see them lancers coming at me."

Bogart and Peck had described the battle to Robert in detail. Their wounds had entirely healed, however.

Robert's favorite game to watch was *colear*, or tailing the bull. In California, it was both a sport and a practical working skill to catch wild bulls. The coleador, the tailer, galloped up behind a bull, reached out from the right to grab its tail, passed the tail under his right leg, twisted it around the saddle horn, and then wheeled his horse sharply to the left, throwing the bull off balance and causing the stunned animal to crash headlong to the ground.

"I wish I had known how to do that at the San Pedro River in Arizona," Robert said as he remembered the attack of the wild bulls there. Tailing the bull required a certain knack. With the right leverage and timing, a small man on a horse could topple even the biggest bull. He stared wistfully at Daniel. "It would be nice to have a cattle ranch when we get home, and a big farm, too."

Daniel nodded his agreement. "They're starting the *paso de la muerte* competition," he said, pointing to a wide circle of spectators. It was the "ride to the death." *Vaqueros* were galloping alongside a wild horse—a *bronco*, the Spanish word for rough. One *vaquero* suddenly jumped from his mount onto the animal's back and rode until he was thrown, without benefit of a saddle, a bridle, or even a rope. Other *vaqueros* did the same to wild bulls, much to the amusement of the crowd. Several injured *vaqueros* were hauled away.

"I don't think that would be a good idea for our cattle," Robert said. "It would make the meat tough and the cattle wouldn't gain proper weight." He paused, realizing he was talking like his father, the butcher and cattle buyer, who had taught him the trade back in England.

The typical lariat was about sixty feet long and as thick as a man's little finger. The *vaquero* made his own lariat, cutting long strips of untanned cowhide, which he soaked and stretched until pliable. Then he braided the leather strips into a rope, which he stretched again, oiled, and softened, working it over until he was satisfied that it was ready to use.

Suddenly, and with great fanfare, a captured grizzly bear was dragged by long lariats into a special arena. Robert jumped away, frightened at the roaring beast. Five *vaqueros* had thrown lassos around its legs and throat, choking off its air. Soon it was released, with one leg tied. It faced a wild bull, and one of the bull's legs was tied. To Robert's amazement, the grizzly killed four bulls before it was mortally gored.

The celebration of St. John's Day was a wild thing compared to the calm celebration of St. Mary's Day three weeks earlier. On that day, the citizens erected four stages with altars in each corner of the town square. Mass had started at ten in the morning. Colonel Stevenson, the new commander over all armed forces in Los Angeles, ordered that one of the cannons be brought to the square to show the Mexicans they would be protected during the celebration. After the mass, the priest came out to the square to perform certain rites at each of the altars; a band belonging to the New York Volunteers played while a procession marched from corner to corner. As the priest passed, the

Californios threw costly garments on the ground for him to walk on. All the people showered down roses upon the priest's head. The cannon fired at intervals as the procession moved from place to place.

"What do you think Joseph Smith would have done if we had treated him like that?" Daniel asked.

"Told us to quit it," Robert said flatly. Joseph had preached against pomp and ceremony in the Church and had insisted that everyone treat him as just an ordinary neighbor.

All the Battalion boys had accepted the New Yorker, Colonel Stevenson, as their new leader without any hesitation. Stevenson had organized the Mormons into units to kill stray dogs. Seems there were as many dogs in Los Angeles as there were wild cattle and wild horses in the hills. Stevenson had also drummed John Allen out of town. Allen had been converted to the Church back in Fort Leavenworth, but not converted to the gospel. He had continued his drinking and raucous living. When Allen returned, Stevenson had him jailed, but Allen promptly escaped.

The day Allen escaped word reached Los Angeles about some of the details of the Donner Party. A large group of emigrants to California had been stranded in the mountains east of Sutter's Fort and several had died. There had even been some cannibalism. The only good news was that the route the Donner Party had taken over the mountains was the route Robert would use to find his family after his release next month.

A few days earlier, Robert and Daniel had worked on a ranchero, the

Isaac Williams ranch, trying to dispel the myth that Mormons were bad people. Robert, Daniel, and some of the other Battalion boys had met Williams a month earlier when Colonel Cooke had sent them to the ranch to help Williams defend against wild Indians. The Indians disappeared when the Mormons arrived. On this day, Robert, Daniel, and their two Missouri converts donated their labor all day, doing things the *vaqueros* typically did. Robert had tried his hand at taming a wild mustang. He helped a *vaquero* rope a horse by its front legs, throw it to the ground, and place a horsehair halter on its head. Then they tied the mustang to a tree to let him fall over, squeal with rage, and try to get free. The *vaquero* told Robert and Daniel that sometimes it took three or four days to calm the horse down. By then, the horse's neck was so sore from the rope that nothing could make him pull back, and his hind legs were sore, too. The *vaqueros* could now "sideline" the horse, tying a hind foot to its shoulder. When the horse submitted to this indignity without fighting back, the mustang was partly broken and ready for its first saddle.

Williams quickly took a liking to Robert and Daniel and invited them to help with the first cattle slaughter of the summer, which would take place shortly after the St. John's Day celebration.

Talking to Robert and Daniel made Williams curious about England.

"What did you do in England?" he asked Robert.

"Mostly butcher cows and pigs," Robert said.

"Are there lots of cows in England?" Williams asked.

Robert thought for a moment. He could remember his father going to the sale at Tewkesbury and bringing home cattle. And there were a lot of cows in the vicinity of his hamlet. He had slept beside their old milk cow on many a cold night when he was a boy, but he figured if he tried to lie down beside one of the animals they called cows on Williams' ranch the cow would be ten miles away before he got to sleep.

"There are cows," he said, "but you don't find them in bunches like you do here. There'd be no place to put them."

"A butcher like you ought to dirty his hands in our hide and tallow business," Williams said when the day's work ended.

Williams had purchased his ranch from his father-in-law, a Spaniard named Don Antonio Maria Lugo. In the early 1800s the Lugo ranchero had been part of the San Gabriel Mission and had been used to graze horses and cattle belonging to the mission. As early as 1810 Lugo had begun to accumulate lands that were to stretch from the San Bernardino Mountains to San Pedro. In 1841 he had been granted rights to what was to become the 47,000-acre Rancho Del Chino De Santa Anna, named after the patroness Saint Anne of the Fair Hair.

"I'll watch it from a distance," Robert said. "I try to avoid killing and skinning when I can. I'm sort of sick of it."

"Come back in two days," Williams said. "You'll see a sight you won't believe."

The day of the butchering, Williams' *vaqueros* drove more than a hundred wild bulls to a spot near the ocean.

"This will be different than anything you've ever seen," said Williams, who was mounted on the finest white stallion Robert had ever laid his eyes on. "We're interested in only two things—the hides and the tallow. The meat is almost worthless because there are so many cattle. You'll see the Indians jerk some of the meat, but most of it will be left to rot on the beach."

The only motive that induced foreign vessels to visit the coast of California was the hide and tallow trade, a fact that Robert now knew. The horned cattle herds of California were not exceeded in size anywhere in the United States.

Muskets did the killing, with the *vaqueros* taking dead aim at the bull's hearts or a spot right behind the ear. Indians leaped on the dying bulls with sharp knives and had the hides ripped off almost before the animals had quit breathing. Hides were stacked in piles, worth approximately a dollar each to the captain of the ship that lay waiting in the harbor. Tallow was rendered from the fat in large black kettles.

"Those are California bank notes," Williams said, pointing to the bales of hides. "We don't use coins here much. Bartering is our way of life."

"How many cattle will you kill this summer?" Robert asked.

"Probably two or three thousand," Williams answered.

"Aren't you afraid you'll deplete the herds?"

Williams laughed. "Not in the least. There're more than a million wild cattle in California. So many, in fact, that we're concerned they'll run out of grass sometime soon. Even if there weren't a market for the hides and tallow, we'd have to randomly kill thousands of cattle just to save the grass."

"Same with the horses?"

"I'm afraid so," the wealthy rancher admitted. "Just as the Indians did with the buffalo, Spaniards and Californios often ran herds of horses over cliffs just to get rid of them."

"What cliffs?"

"The ones that overlook rivers and the ocean."

"So if the fall didn't kill the horses, they would ..."

"You got it. Drown."

At mid-day, Mexican women brought a lunch consisting of jerky-dried meat and *pozole*, a soup made with hominy. The women's hair was pulled back smoothly and braided, and tied with a ribbon decorated with a silk flower.

Late in the summer afternoon a celebration was held at the ranch headquarters. A great pavilion shaded with green branches had been set up in front of the main ranch house. The inside of the pavilion was covered with white cloth adorned with ribbons and flowers. It had three sides enclosed and the fourth open for the men on horseback to congregate; there were plenty of sawhorses to keep the horses back. The ladies sat inside.

"Do you Mormons have festivities like this?" Peck asked.

"We had dances in Nauvoo, but not wild dances like the fandango," Robert answered.

Violins and guitars provided the music and there were three singers. The musicians and singers stood at one end of the pavilion. A master of ceremonies, called the *tecolero*, stood in the center of the pavilion to direct the dancing. Some were ladies-only dances, and the women would pick up the edges of their petticoats and circle the pavilion. When they were done the men dismounted, hung their spurs on their saddle horns, and entered the pavilion, hats in hand. Each man selected a partner and the dances varied, mostly the *la jota*, but also the *la bamba*, the *el Borrego*, the *el burro*, and the national dance of the Mexican people, the *el sarabe*.

"I've decided I like you Mormon boys," Isaac Williams said after the celebration. He offered a handshake to Robert. "You're not porch perchers like other men I've hired. If you don't re-enlist with the army, you could stay here and work for me."

"I've got a wife and children to get home to," Robert said. "Number seven should have been born in February." He began to think of Hannah's dream, and her fears. He prayed that both Hannah and the new baby were alive and healthy.

"Where's home?"

"I don't know."

Williams gave Robert a blank look. "You have a wife and seven children, and you don't know where home is?"

In the southwest, a very black and threatening cloud, which had been gathering for several hours, rose over the ranch—unusual for this time of year.

Rain discharged as though from a waterspout, sending those who remained scattering for shelter. There were brilliant and incessant flashes of lightning, and crashing peals of thunder. As the storm rolled through, the men sat in the veranda of the house and talked. Robert told Williams the story of how the Mormons were exterminated from Missouri and from Nauvoo. He concluded by telling Williams that his wife and children would end up somewhere in the Great Basin of the American West by the end of the summer, and that he aimed to find them.

"You're leaving soon?"

"July sixteenth. And we need horses."

"Pick one out. You can pay me after the army pays you."

As a rainbow formed a perfect and brilliant arch in the west, Robert combed through Williams' herd and picked out a sorrel gelding that reminded him of the sorrel that Joseph Smith had named Joe Duncan. The grass was wet. The air had a nice pungent smell, the smell that always came following a rainstorm.

"I've got a name for this here horse," Robert announced immediately.

"Let me guess," Daniel said, knowing his brother-in-law's unusual style of naming animals. "Name him after Thomas Sharp, the newspaper editor who helped assassinate the Prophet."

Robert laughed a good laugh. "Nope. The name's A. J.—I want to name the horse after Lieutenant A. J. Smith. The lieutenant rode us most of the way to Santa Fe. Now I'll ride A. J. all the way from California to wherever home is."

Daniel had his eye on a young but stout gelding. "What about calling this horse Chelt?"

Robert snorted in derision. "After Cheltenham, your hometown? A lame excuse for the name of a horse."

"It's my horse," Daniel retaliated. "I guess I can name it."

"The horse's name is George."

"George?"

"After Dr. George Sanderson."

"That way you can ride Dr. Sanderson out of town and I'll ride Lieutenant A. J. Smith out of town."

Daniel put a rope around the horse and admired its buckskin color. "I'll go for Sandy."

Robert quickly compromised. "Fine. Sandy it is. Dr. Sandy." And then in retrospect he said, "Too bad the horse ain't a black. You could ride the black-hearted Dr. Sandy out of town."

Daniel felt caught in the middle and he didn't like it. As an officer, higher Battalion officers such as Captain Jefferson Hunt and Lieutenant Dykes expected Daniel to not only re-enlist but to talk the privates in Company E into re-enlisting, too.

"I believe if Brigham Young were here he would counsel us to remain in the war against Mexico," Dykes said.

"But I have a new son I've never seen," Daniel argued. "All the men I've talked to want to go home to their families." He was thinking about the day he could saddle up Sandy and ride the horse out of town, toward his wives and little Moroni.

David Pettegrew argued on the side of Daniel. "Brother Dykes, I don't believe Brigham Young would counsel us that way. Through our Prophet we made a contract with the highest authority on earth. We agreed to serve one year. If one year won't satisfy the army, then twenty years won't either. I'm not re-enlisting."

It had been five days since Daniel and Robert had worked for Isaac Williams at the huge ranchero. Now it was June twenty-ninth. In just over two weeks—on July sixteenth—the Battalion would be mustered out of service. That is, unless officers like Hunt, Hunter, and even Captain Davis of Company E, got their way.

"But Colonel Stevenson has promised that we can elect our own lieutenant colonel," argued captain Davis. "And Governor Mason has said we can enlist for just eight months."

"But the army hasn't even given us the travel money they promised, and probably won't," Daniel said. "I don't trust them anymore."

Forty-seven-year-old Colonel Stevenson had just pleaded with the officers in a meeting, mustering all the oratorical skills he had acquired as a New York politician. In a stirring appeal, he claimed that until more troops could be transported from the United States, either around the horn of South America—like the New York Volunteers—or march overland from Fort Leavenworth, California was still vulnerable to a counterattack by the Mexicans. He said Kearny had given him orders to try to keep the entire Mormon Battalion, or at least a minimum of one company. Only a few hundred soldiers occupied California, and California was as large as all the New England states, plus New York and Pennsylvania.

"What if these rumors are correct, and California is invaded again?" posed Robert.

"It sounds too farfetched to believe," Daniel answered.

Kearny and Stevenson had been responding to the rumor that a Mexican general by the name of Anastacio Bustamente and been appointed commander-in-chief of the northwestern Mexican provinces, and, with fifteen hundred men, was on his way to California. The rumor had come from Abel Sterns, a long-time resident of Los Angeles, as well as from Andres Pico. They alleged that Bustamente had received six hundred thousand dollars from the Mexican government to fund the invasion. Locally, an American patrol had found horses concealed in a canyon, and someone at Santa Barbara had encountered twenty armed men displaying a Mexican flag. And several of the men living in Los Angeles had disappeared.

"You put all that together and it adds up to an insurrection," Robert concluded. "No wonder Kearny is nervous, and Cooke, too."

"You Mormon soldiers have been looked upon by the people of the United States with a jealous and suspicious eye," Stevenson said. "Your noble act of enlisting in the service of your country has done a lot to remove those jealousies and suspicions. Now think of it. If you re-enlist, and remain in the service of your country, in a few years you will be great and popular. Notwithstanding your families are in a peculiar situation somewhere out there in the wilderness, your country's cause requires your continued service in the army."

Stevenson's words hit Daniel hard. Afterward he told Levi Hancock, "I wouldn't re-enlist even if the men made *me* the lieutenant colonel. It still wouldn't be worth it." He figured a colonel's monthly pay was more than a hundred dollars.

"But it would be just until February," Captain Hunter said. "Besides, what if something happened to Colonel Stevenson or Governor Mason? This new Mormon colonel would be the top officer in all California."

Nevertheless, Stevenson's eloquence ignited an intense daylong debate between old adversaries that centered on who had the right to counsel the Battalion soldiers—officers such as Jefferson Hunt, or priesthood leaders such as Levi Hancock and David Pettegrew.

Daniel agreed with most of the other men. Why aid a government further that had permitted the Mormons to be driven from their homes in Missouri and Illinois? He had a few hard feelings toward men like George Dykes and Jefferson Hunt, too. At times they had been a little too harsh, treating him and the others more like soldiers and gentiles rather than like brethren in the Church. As a result, Hunt had lost control over a badly disunited group of Mormon soldiers. And there were nothing but bad memories of Lieutenant Smith and Doctor Sanderson. Daniel could not help but think how much better things would have been if Colonel James Allen had not died in Fort Leavenworth and had commanded the Battalion all the way to California.

In Daniel's view, Stevenson was a good man but had let the Missourians warp his thinking about Mormons. Stevenson had admitted in public that he thought Mormons were simple-minded, ignorant, and too much under the control of Brigham Young, or some master spirit. Brigham, he contended, wanted to get ballot box and military control of the entire country and impose Mormon will on the general populous. He didn't fear one company of Mormons, or even one Battalion, but he wanted the government in Washington to provide him with as many regular troops as possible. He also feared discharging the Mormons with their muskets still in their possession, but understood that had been part of the promise in their original signup.

The Mormons had been meeting since eight-thirty in the morning when Colonel Stevenson first spoke to them. The men had argued back and forth for more than three hours, and now a hot California sun beat down on them and on their tents. For a while the soldiers adjourned to a large tent where they agreed to form a committee to draft an agreement stating the terms of a possible enlistment. Captain Hunter, Captain Davis, and David Pettegrew were chosen as the committee. As soon as terms were written up, the men gathered and began arguing the pros and cons again. Two spirits were plainly manifest. Hunter, Hunt, Davis, and others still favored re-enlistment.

Pettigrew and Levi Hancock favored leaving California immediately after discharge to try and find the main body of the Church. So did men like William Hyde, Andrew Lytle, and James Pace. The meeting ended with only sixteen men saying they would sign up for six months.

"Six months, six days, six hours," mumbled Daniel. "I want to go home."

"Me, too," echoed Robert, who said he hated to see the division among the men. "But if some of them want to stay, that's their decision. They must not have six children like I do."

When the sixteen men presented their proposal to enlist for only six months, it was promptly rejected.

"I need you for longer than that," the colonel said sternly. "I'm not only worried about Indian violations in the vicinity of the San Luis Rey Mission, but the Mexicans, too."

PART TWO

The Release

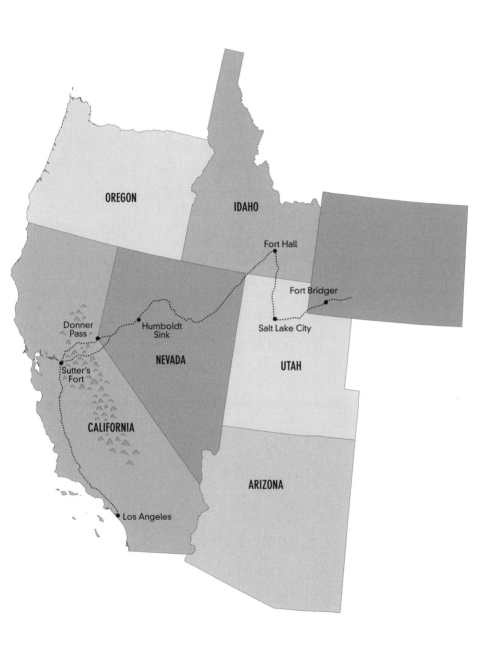

*The Mormon Battalin Route from Los Angeles to
Salt Lake City following their release.*

13

July 16, 1847

Los Angeles

ROBERT THOUGHT IT IRONIC THAT THE man assigned to discharge

the three hundred seventeen members of the Mormon Battalion was non other

than the despised Andrew Jackson Smith, now of the First Dragoons. For the

first time in a year there had been no roll call or guard mounts. The day had

been spent in preparation to leave the pueblo of Los Angeles. Now it was three

in the afternoon. The absence of music or a marching band made the moment

seem moving, even dramatic. There was an eerie silence.

Lieutenant Smith slowly marched up and down the lines of the assem-

bled Mormon soldiers. Company A was in front and Company E in the rear.

Company B had arrived the previous day from San Diego.

"Old A. J.'s said nothing so far," Robert whispered to Daniel. "Must have a dead rat in his mouth."

"I thought the New York volunteer band ought to be playing for us," Daniel whispered back.

Smith slowly strolled to the front. For a few moments he just stood there. Finally, he hung his head. His words were barely audible. "You are discharged," Smith said.

"Whoopee!" Robert screamed.

Let's go home!" Daniel yelled. He had been thinking while A. J. had meandered through the soldiers that it was impossible to return to a place where one has never been. The Battalion boys were going home to the bosom of the Church, but not returning.

Both men threw their wide brimmed felt hats in the air, and so did nearly everyone else. There came a unified cheer from all the men, three times.

"I'm glad Smith didn't try to make any kind of speech. I would have hated to laugh in his face on the last day," Robert said. Robert didn't regret leaving Los Angeles at all. He never did calculate on landing in such a bad place. With all the grog shops and gambling places Los Angeles had been as terrible as Santa Fe and New Orleans.

Eighty-two men had re-enlisted, succumbing to the pressures from Stevenson, Jefferson Hunt, and others. Daniel C. Davis had been elected captain. This time full uniforms had been issued. And they didn't have to march to San Diego—they were going by ship.

"I wish them best of luck, but I can't wait to get home," Robert said as the Battalion disbanded.

"I've never seen such pressure," admitted Levi Hancock. "It was as though a ball and chain had been hung around our necks. And I suspect it's not over."

The re-enlisted men were preparing to leave for San Diego for duty. Robert and the others were preparing to travel north, toward Sutter's Fort. But first things first. They had to wait for their pay. They had to pick up their horses, A. J. and Sandy, at the Williams ranch. They had to get organized for the trip north.

"Where do you think Brigham Young is taking the Church about right now?" Robert asked.

"He told us the Great Basin, but things could change," Daniel answered. "For all we know he's headed for the Bear River country, somewhere here in California, or Vancouver Island up in the British possession," Daniel admitted. "The truth is, we don't know for absolute certain. But I have faith the answer will be made known to us in a few weeks."

Daniel wondered if Brigham Young wanted the new Church settlement to be part of the United States, or if he wanted to create an independent theocratic state. There were good arguments for either.

The last few days had been a drag for Robert, despite all the festivities. Independence Day had been celebrated at Pueblo de Los Angeles with the Battalion parading at sunrise, the New York Volunteers playing "The Star

Spangled Banner" as the flag was raised, followed by nine cheers from the men. After the song, "Hail Columbia," the First Dragoons fired a salute of thirteen guns.

On July fifth, the Battalion had attended the funeral of one of the army regulars who had died in the hospital the previous night, the victim of continuous fighting among the Missourians. Others had died as well. Two days later one of the New York Volunteers and one of Fremont's men were arrested on charges of murder.

Another Catholic celebration had been held on the weekend, and the entire town was illuminated. Colonel Stevenson armed all the men because there was another rumor that the Mexicans would use the festival as an opportunity to recapture the town. Nothing happened. Robert thought it was another ruse to get the men to re-enlist. The festival continued uninterrupted and a huge bullring was erected. During the bullfights, Catholic priests, former officers in the Spanish army, and even Pio Pico—the last Spanish commander in the area—all attended. The bullfights continued until July twelfth. On the last day, several horses were gored. Even worse, a bull injured the six-year-old son of Captain Davis.

"Gather round for a few minutes," Levi Hancock said to the Mormon soldiers as they dispersed.

Robert joined a throng of other former Battalion members and heard brief speeches from Hancock, David Pettegrew, James Pace, Andrew Lytle, and Captain Davis. Thankfully, each man was brief. But Robert felt a loyalty to them. They, more than others, had at all times respected their priesthood.

"Let's get out of here," Robert said to Daniel afterward.

"I'm with you," Daniel replied.

The men were headed for a camp on the San Pedro River, three miles north of Los Angeles, where they planned to organize for the return trip.

As Robert thought back on his full year in the army, he contrasted his initial enthusiasm, patriotism, craving for travel, and adventure with how quickly he became bored with military life and how homesick he had become.

"Goodbye my good friends," Private Bogart said to Robert and Daniel.

Daniel accepted Bogart's handshake and embrace, and Peck's, too. "Any idea of when we'll see you again?"

"Look for me to ride into the Great Basin some day, looking for the Mormon settlement," Peck said.

"I suspect you'll lose your newspaper job back in Missouri when they find out you're a Mormon," Robert said.

Peck laughed a good laugh. "No doubt that's true."

If I were you, when I got back to Missouri I'd head straight north to Council Bluffs," Daniel suggested. "That'll be an active Mormon gathering place for two or three years, until everyone can recruit up and get to the Great Basin."

"Any pretty young Mormon women there?" Peck asked.

"Might be," Daniel said.

It frosted Robert when he found out that the army reneged on its promise to pay each Mormon soldier a transportation allowance.

"Must be A. J. Smith's doings, or Dr. Sanderson's," Robert said after he and Daniel picked up the sorrel and the black. Williams sold the two horses for a fair price, but it made a dent in the final payment of thirty-one dollars and fifty cents they each received. The price of horses in California had increased when the Mormons began buying so many. So did the price of salt and flour.

When Robert and Daniel reached the camp north of the pueblo, horror stories abounded. One Mormon soldier, Henry Standage, had gone to A. J. Smith to get his pay for working in the bakery, but Smith had refused. Standage finally had to go to Colonel Stevenson, who signed the order. Reluctantly, A. J. finally gave Standage the money.

The re-enlistment Battalion had left for San Diego. One of them, Henry Boyle, came to say goodbye to his friends in Company E. "It was a tough decision to re-enlist," Boyle told Levi Hancock as Daniel saddled his horse. "But unlike most of you, I don't have any relatives in the Church to return to. I'm going to stay in California for a while, then find the Church next year."

"I understand," Hancock said. "God bless you."

Five other men opted to take the southern route on their own, following the trail they had blazed through the Southwest in order to find Brigham Young and the main body of the Church. Four men made the decision to remain in California and seek work. Another six men had already contracted to build a mill for the rancher Isaac Williams. Two others bought tickets on a ship sailing to San Francisco.

Robert and Daniel opted to follow the counsel of Levi Hancock, the only Church general authority in the Battalion. At the San Pedro River camp, Hancock took charge and organized the remaining two hundred twenty-three men into companies of hundreds, fifties, and tens, following the ancient Israelite custom in the Old Testament.

"Good choices," Daniel commented as Andrew Lytle and James Pace were appointed captains of the two companies of just over a hundred men each. Jefferson Hunt, William Hyde, Daniel Tyler, and Reddick Allred were the four men appointed to lead the companies of fifty. Daniel was appointed a captain of ten, with Robert, Robert Pixton, and Levi Roberts in his group.

"Here we are, charging off again into unknown territory," Levi Hancock said. "None of us knows anything about the road north, but we're headed for Sutter's Fort. From there we'll head east through the mountains."

"And our final destination?" one asked.

As far as Robert was concerned, travel in the army had been bad and might get worse trying to find out where Brigham Young had taken his family. Robert had dreams he would never find the Great Basin, let alone a more specific place like the Bear River Country, a fact that preyed on his mind. From all indications the Great Basin was a large place, and it might be like a tiny ship in the vast ocean trying to find a particular tiny island.

"We don't know, but I have faith that it will be made known to us,"

Hancock replied. "Let's just stick together." He repeated his opinion that they would find Brigham Young somewhere near the Bear River Country, perhaps within five hundred miles of the Great Salt Lake.

Jefferson Hunt promptly made the motion that the entire group follow a well-established route along the Pacific Coast to San Francisco. The road had a name—*El Camino Real,* an old Spanish road connecting the California missions. Hunt, a Kentuckian, still imagined California would become the ultimate destination of the Mormon migration and harbored hopes yet of forming a new Battalion of soldiers with him in charge.

"I propose that all of us go that route," Hunt said in the meeting.

Hancock shook his head in opposition. Robert knew why. Hunt wanted to see the new governor of California, Colonel R. B. Mason, and lobby Mason into giving him a military appointment as commander-in-chief.

When it was discovered that another route was shorter, the other three companies of fifty voted to take that one. It would take them directly north, through the old Pio Pico Ranch in the San Fernando Valley, the Tejon Pass, the rugged mountains of the Sierra Madre.

"If we can find the Walker Pass on that route, it'll get us to the Great Basin a lot quicker," said one soldier.

"But that route takes us through a long central valley in the dead of summer, and that valley is about as bad as a desert," Daniel countered.

"I hope there's no buffalo tea there," Robert said, remembering the *jornada* just northeast of Santa Fe. So far he hadn't seen a single buffalo in

California, but he'd seen plenty of other wild game, including bears.

He put A. J. into a lope and it was a pleasure to see how the sorrel ate up the ground. With such a horse under him he could soon make his way through the mountains and up through the central part of California, and then make it all the way to the Great Basin. Trouble was, the former soldiers had a herd of cattle and the men could move no faster than the animals. Robert resigned himself to the fact that they would move no more than ten or fifteen miles a day and that it would take clear to October to find his wife and children.

14

August 24, 1847

Consumnes Valley, California

ROBERT'S HEART JUMPED TO HIS THROAT. Suddenly now, despite all the wild speculations of where Brigham Young had led the Church, Robert knew where Hannah and his children were—the Great Salt Lake Valley.

"Do you think we can get there by the first of October?" he asked Levi Hancock.

Hancock had just conversed with a member of the Church by the name of C. C. Smith, who had traveled to a place called Green River, somewhere between Council Bluffs and the Salt Lake Valley. Smith had traveled there with Samuel Brannan, who was still in the Salt Lake Valley trying to convince Brigham to bring the Saints to California. The ex-soldiers were now in the

Cosumnes Valley, some fifty miles south of Sutter's Fort. Around twenty Mormon families, including those of Thomas Rhodes and Martin Murphy, Jr., had settled here.

Levi's face carried a slight smirk. "If Samuel Brannan convinces Brigham Young that this is our future home, then we don't need to go any farther."

C. C. Smith smiled too. "Brother Brannan wasn't having much luck when I left. I wish Brigham would listen. California's a nice place, as you can tell."

Robert had to agree that the area looked tempting. Smith's farm was surrounded by magnificent oak groves, large expanses of streamside forests, and rich bottomland soil. The Cosumnes floodplain was a haven for tens of thousands of migratory waterfowl, songbirds, and sand hill cranes. Smith showed the Battalion boys catches of salmon that came from the river.

"What's the Salt Lake Valley like?" Daniel asked.

"Dry," Smith answered. "I talked to the people at Fort Hall along the Snake River, which is nearly two hundred miles north of the Great Salt Lake. They say nothing will grow there except sagebrush."

Robert grew impatient. "Sagebrush or not, if that's where Brigham's taken my family, then that's where I want to be. Let's get going. Can we make it by October? What's the road like?"

The ex-soldiers had sent scouts up the Kings River two weeks earlier to try and find Walker Pass. The pass had been named after Joseph Walker, a trapper and guide. They failed to find it, so Hancock and the other two groups of fifty had continued north.

"You're not far from Sutter's Fort," Smith answered. "You can buy sup-plies there, and shoe your horses, too. From there the road is good until you hit the mountains. Rough going there. Then you've got a desert to cross and it's the worst time of year to try it. The creeks will be down and there're places where there's no water at all. Most of the time you'll follow the Humbolt River. Once you get to Fort Hall you turn south. They say the Great Salt Lake is about ten days away from Fort Hall. You have a chance to get to the Salt Lake by the first of October, but you'll have to make good time every day."

Robert forced a smile. Smith had crossed the deserts of the Great Basin, but Robert and the Mormon Battalion had crossed the *jornada* on the Santa Fe Trail and survived, and the desert country between Santa Fe and San Diego.

Thomas Rhodes had arrived in California the previous October, settling between the Cosumnes River and Dry Creek with his large family. When the ex-soldiers camped near his farm the next day, Rhodes was most occupied let-ting two of his sons tell about how they helped rescue members of the Donner Party who had been stranded in the mountains the previous winter. The boys told a grisly tale about survivors who ate the flesh of those who died. The boys, John and Daniel Rhodes, were in the first rescue team and John returned sev-eral times into the mountains to bring out the stranded emigrants.

Robert also learned about John Sutter and his need for laborers. Sutter, a Swiss emigrant, had purchased nearly fifty thousand acres at the junction of two rivers, the Sacramento and the Feather, and the site dominated three important routes: the inland waterways from San Francisco, the trail to California across the Sierras Nevada, and the Oregon-California Road. Sutter needed carpenters, hunters, blacksmiths, farm workers, and herders.

"You boys ought to work there for a few months, save up, and start your farms near here," Rhodes suggested. "My prediction is that Brother Brannan will convince Brigham to bring the Saints to California. Here's where our future is, not the deserts of the Great Salt Lake."

Robert blinked and blinked again. In Smith's opinion, Brannan stood no chance of winning Brigham over. But Rhodes was suggesting that the entice-ment was too good to pass up. Robert closed his eyes, his thoughts a swirling tempest of fear and confusion. What Rhodes was saying was true. Of all the places he'd seen since leaving Council Bluffs, California was the best of them all, especially the area around Rhode's farm. The weather beat Nauvoo and England, too. No winter snows to contend with, perfect temperatures most of the time, and plenty of water.

"No, thanks," Robert finally retorted. "I think I'll make my course the Great Salt Lake. If we find Brigham on his way to California, I'll gladly follow him back."

Daniel placed a hand on Robert's shoulder. "My sentiments exactly."

Rhodes made a prediction. "Word is that Brannan is on his way back to California. You'll likely meet him on the trail somewhere."

15

August 28, 1847

Sutter's Fort

"ANY OF YOU MORMON BOYS LOOKING for work?"

The man who posed the question to Daniel was tall, slender, had a long, narrow nose, and sharp features. "My name's James Marshall," the man said as he thrust forward a hand. He was cleanly dressed and looked to be about the same age as Daniel, or in his mid to late thirties.

Daniel was barely inside Sutter's Fort, a frontier trading post with adobe walls eighteen feet high. The fort had shops, houses, mills, and warehouses.

Daniel accepted the handshake. "Not me, but there are a lot of us former soldiers who might be." Daniel suspected by the time it was all over, perhaps two or three-dozen Battalion boys might make the decision to stay in

California.

"I especially need carpenters," Marshall said in a pleading voice. "And Captain Sutter needs blacksmiths, millers, bakers, gunsmiths, and men to make blankets."

"You must work for Mr. Sutter," Daniel said, venturing a guess. There were several Californios milling around dressed in white shirts and pantaloons. Large *sombreros* shaded their heads. None of them looked like carpenters, though. Neither did any of the mostly naked Indians.

Two cannon guarded the entrance near where Daniel stood. They looked like they had been taken off ships at either Monterey or San Francisco. Inside stood a large house with good shingles. At diagonal corners stood two-story blockhouses.

"Yep," came the answer. "I've been working for Captain Sutter since April. Now I have a contract with Sutter to build a sawmill up yonder, on the American Fork of the river in a place the Indians call Coloma."

Marshall said that John Bidwell, a New Yorker who had been a member of the first wagon train from Missouri to reach the Pacific Coast, had written up his contract. Samuel Kyburtz, the fort's general manager, had witnessed the signing. These were facts that Daniel had no interest in, and no interest in the job, either.

Daniel scratched his head. "Seems I've seen you before."

"Probably in Los Angeles," Marshall replied. "I served under Fremont in the California Battalion. But I was discharged right after you Mormons arrived there. You may have seen me around in your first few days there. When I got back to my place up here, all my horses, mules, and cattle had been stolen during my absence. I've got to work for a spell, to recruit up again, and make a new start. I want to restock my ranch."

"Sorry to hear that," Daniel said. "Who stole from you?"

"The danged Indians, I'd suspect. I don't suppose they all just strayed away."

Daniel cringed at the prospect Indians would wreak havoc on the settlements here. It was another reason not to stay in California. He hoped there were no bad Indians where Brigham Young had taken the Church. Daniel said, "Well, I'm a carpenter myself, but I'm going to use my talents to build me a home in the Salt Lake Valley, where my family is waiting." He didn't mention the fact that he had two wives.

"I met a Mormon named Captain Jefferson Hunt a few days ago," Marshall said. "Sutter tried to hire him but he seemed in a hurry, too."

Daniel laughed. "Captain Hunt's on his way to see our leader, Brigham Young. Hunt wants to recruit another Battalion of Mormons to serve under him, and then come back to California as part of an occupation force. I guess he wants to be a big military leader all his life or something."

Marshall turned to go. "Let me know if you change your mind. All you have to do is tell Mr. Sutter. He'll pay you very well. Sutter counts his horses, cattle, and hogs by the thousands. Work for a year or even six months and you'll earn enough animals to stock your own ranch."

Marshall said Sutter was in a desperate situation. Sutter's imprudent speculative behavior had left him heavily in debt, short of capital, but also short of experienced, reliable workers.

Everyone's situation was desperate these days, Daniel concluded. Money was scarce and so were competent laborers. Sutter, a big shot, owed a lot of money to the Russians for his purchase of the property surrounding the fort. Marshall was in financial distress caused by the neglect of his Feather River ranch property during the war with Mexico. But Daniel's own situation was precarious, too. He hadn't seen his wives and child for a long time. He had walked all the way from Council Bluffs to California. His clothing, including his garments, had worn out. For all these reasons Daniel's mind was set.

"No thanks," Daniel said politely. "But I'll pass the word along to the other men. We're leaving tomorrow."

Marshall rode away and Daniel and Robert spent an hour or two at the fort. While at Sutter's Fort the Battalion boys were having the blacksmith shoe their horses, mending trail equipment, getting information about how to get over the mountain passes, and buying provisions. Toward evening, Daniel and Robert returned to camp.

Hancock had set the camp near the William Johnson ranch near Sutter's Fort. Johnson was an American sailor who had settled on the river in 1845. He had remained a bachelor for nearly two years but had married a survivor of the Donner party—a member of the Church named Mary Murphy. Johnson openly complained they weren't getting along. Mary's mother, Lavina, had been converted to the Church in Tennessee by Wilford Woodruff. Lavina had moved to Missouri and then to Nauvoo. When the Church began its western exodus she had agreed to cook and wash for the Donner party as a means of getting her large family west.

Johnson lived in a small two-room house, half constructed of logs and the other half made of sun-dried bricks. Livestock pens made of poles and pickets surrounded the modest home. Several calves were kept in the pens, bawling for their mothers who had been turned loose for forage in the trees. The soil of Johnson's bottomland looked fertile. Johnson's ten-acre wheat field had produced thirty bushels to the acre, but he refused to sell much of it, saying he and his wife needed it all to survive. The Battalion boys bought a hundred pounds for eight dollars. He had a field of corn, too, but it didn't look promising. The ground was too dry and Johnson hadn't irrigated the corn. Poor as the settlement was, it represented the only evidence of civilization in the immediate area. Johnson had nothing to offer the men except milk and cheese.

Daniel's wondered how many might stay in California. Some needed the money and others were suffering from the summer effects of ague fever in their blood, a carryover from Nauvoo. Luckily, Robert's health was fine and so was Daniel's.

A party of Indians was gathering acorns nearby. If acorns were all Indians and Californios ate around here, Daniel figured he'd be better off someplace else. Johnson told the men that the Indians dried and pulverized the acorns into mush. To them, acorns were the "staff of life," much as wheat and corn were the staff of life for the white man.

"Where'd the Donner Party get stranded from here?" Daniel asked as Johnson unfolded the story to him and the ex-soldiers. Members of the Donner Party had run out of wheat and corn and everything else.

"You'll pass nearby," Johnson said. "By now the snow's melted enough you're apt to find the bones of my wife's mother. A lot of people died up there. It'll be a mournful sight."

16

September 5, 1847

Sierra Mountains

DANIEL STARED AT THE MUMMIFIED FLESH of pitiful human beings and groaned audibly. For several minutes he stood immobile, gasping for breath, taking stock of what must have happened the previous winter to the Donner Party. No one, he surmised, could grasp the true horror of what must have been a desperate fight for survival. Most of the bones and skulls had been ravaged by wolves and scattered over the landscape.

"Let's get them buried," said Robert, who was already digging in the soft earth beneath the towering mountains. Jacob Kemp Butterfield was the first to help him and then the other men started to help too.

A nineteen-year-old soldier named Henry Bigler slowly shook his head.

"If ever there was such a thing as witches and hobgoblins, it'd be in these mountains. The work of the devil has been on these poor Missourians."

As Robert and the others dug, Daniel continued to stand still, so complete was his shock. If emigrants could die in great numbers like this, scores of them, what were the chances deaths may have occurred among the Mormon immigrants between Council Bluffs and the Great Salt Lake? How many died even before the trip began? Was Elizabeth alive? Harriet? Moroni? His mother, Martha? His sister, Rebecca?

Johnson had told Daniel that the Donner Party set out from Independence, Missouri, in May of last year, which would have been just three months before the Mormon Battalion left Fort Leavenworth. Technically, that didn't make them Missourians. They merely gathered, recruited up, and departed from there. By the time the Donner Party crossed the deserts west of the Great Salt Lake and approached the Sierra Mountains, it was late in the season and their provisions were running low. Gambling that they could make it through the mountains in late October, they pressed onward—but snow began to fall. Soon terrible winter storms brought heavy, deep snow, trapping the eighty members of the party. Although they had come two thousand five hundred miles in seven months, they had lost their race against the weather, despite the fact that they were only a hundred a fifty miles from their destination—Sutter's Fort. Realizing they were stranded, the main body of the party erected cabins along the lake that Daniel could see, and another group made a camp of tents back along the trail. Over the next four months the men, women, and children of the party huddled together in cabins, makeshift lean-tos, and tents. Their cattle had all been killed and eaten by mid-December and the people began eating bark, twigs, and boiled hides. Attempts to cross the mountains mostly failed, but one group of seven finally reached Sutter's Fort. Their arrival caused an outcry of alarm, and rescue attempts soon followed. By early February, the first rescue party reached the lake encampments. Not everyone could be taken out and since no pack animals could be brought in, sustaining supplies were few. Many people had already died and some of the survivors left in the camps had begun to eat the dead. Johnson had told Daniel that about half of the survivors resorted to cannibalism, having held off for as long as they could after their food was gone.

"Let's get out of here," Daniel pleaded. Earlier in the day, swarms of yellow hornets had stung men and mules. But burying California emigrants was far worse than the sting of hornets.

"Help us dig," Robert said.

"I can't bear to look," Daniel said. He turned his head, mounted his horse, and slowly rode away. "I don't want to ever be here again."

Robert and the other Battalion boys kept finding bodies and kept digging. A cabin yielded several skeletons. He found a woman's hand, partly burned; those fingers that had not burned had dried into mummified flesh.

"Any of this the work of Indians?" Jacob Kemp Butterfield asked.

Robert thought Jacob was talking to himself but answered anyway. "I don't see any arrowheads lying around, or any arrow or hatchet wounds. I'd say it was just plain starvation and cannibalism."

A separate location of dead bodies proved Robert's point. Some had been cut up—men and women with their legs cut off, others with ribs sawed out of their bodies. One skull had been sawed open and the brains taken out.

"Let's get our job done and get out of here," Jacob said.

17

WHEN ROBERT RAKED THE BEEF, BEANS, and biscuits onto his plate, such a crowd of possible tasks rushed into his mind that he was a minute or two responding to Daniel's suggestion that Daniel had heard a noise. Robert had been thinking about whether or not to butcher one of the cattle, try to shoot a deer or rabbit, or hunt for mountain grouse that had fluttered up during the day. The birds had a dark and glossy plumage with a small tuft of feathers on their heads. He reckoned they would be good eating.

One thing for certain—Robert was trying to erase the thought of mummified bodies of the Donner Party out of his mind.

Robert was one of the Battalion boys traveling in the James Pace group.

The ex-soldiers had made twelve miles through thick Sierra Mountain forest during the day. When they left Sutter's Fort a few days ago, they had traveled almost due north to Johnson's Ranch on the Bear River, and then struck east to the mountains following a trail blazed in 1844 by the Stephens-Murphy-Townsend party. It was the trail the Donner party had tried to follow and the route General Kearny and Colonel Fremont had taken; Captain Jefferson Hunt and his group had taken it too. Now Robert was camped in the top of the Sierras at what explorers had named Soda Springs. The Lytle group was a few miles behind. At one summit Robert had counted nine small lakes, surrounded by fairy-like stands of trees. From that summit the men had rolled huge rocks down the mountain that made tremendous crashing sounds below. The lakes had no outlets, sparkling clear water, and plenty of fish. Travel in the mountains had been difficult. The horses and mules had been forced to leap from crag to crag, climbing in some places over perpendicular precipices of smooth granite rocks. One of the mules, heavily packed, fell backward and rolled against a large rock. The men thought the mule may have broken a leg, but it emerged unscathed.

"I hear something," Daniel said again as he hunched over the evening campfire eating the last of the huckleberries he had found during the day. He expected another cold night in the mountains; this morning a slight frost had been perceptible on the grass.

Robert glanced up to see what Daniel could be so aroused about. Robert had yet to set up the tent—the same one he had slept in since Fort Leavenworth. Robert Pixton, Levi Roberts, John Cox, Richard Slater, and Jacob Kemp Butterfield were now traveling in his mess.

"It's a man on a horse," exclaimed Butterfield.

Robert's eyes locked onto a horse and rider emerging from the trees, coming from the east, the direction the Battalion boys would be going in the morning. The rider wore an expensive-looking felt hat and was otherwise well dressed so Robert immediately ruled out an Indian.

"My guess is that you boys are from the Mormon Battalion," the rider said as he dismounted. The man had sharp features, a dark but well-trimmed short beard, and wavy thick black hair. Two mules loaded with a bedroll and provisions trailed behind the man's horse.

Captain James Pace reacted quickly. "We are, and who might you be?"

"Samuel Brannan, president of the Church in California."

Robert had used his forefinger to capture the absolute last drop of honey off his plate, which had dripped off his biscuit. Honey was just as sweet licked off a finger as it was when eaten on good sourdough biscuits made from Hannah's recipe. Soon a large crowd of the Battalion boys had gathered around Brannan, asking questions, searching for information about Brigham Young and the Saints. Still savoring the honey he had purchased at Sutter's Fort, Robert injected a question of his own. "What's a man like you doing riding in here all alone anyway?"

"Oh, I've been riding with some other men," Brannan explained. "I struck out early this morning. I'm a little more anxious than they are. I'm trying to get home; they're just trying to find you."

Robert had seen Indians on the trail several times during the day.

Brannan's answer seemed strange. White men didn't survive in Indian country riding alone. "You like biscuits, Mr. Brannan?" Robert held up the last sourdough biscuit.

Brannan's mouth watered as though he were going to get one. "Sure do."

"You're sure to ride into a mess of Indians if you ride alone. You do that and you'll not live to enjoy another biscuit." Robert bit into the biscuit and began to devour it. Brannan's eyes lowered in disappointment.

John Cox picked up on the conversation. "What other men?"

Brannan took on a hard look, which made Robert even more suspicious. "Former Battalion members," Brannan said, his eyes locked on Robert's chewing of the biscuit. "From the detachment that wintered at Pueblo."

Robert decided to test Brannan. "Name them."

Brannan shrugged his shoulders and gave the look of someone who did not enjoy being doubted. "Gilbert Hunt. I believe he was a corporal in Company A. William Gribble of Company D, and there was Lysander Woodworth, Henry Frank, and Jesse Brown. Oh, I guess I might mention Captain James Brown, too."

Brannan colored when he mentioned James Brown, a fact that Robert noted with curiosity. But Robert recognized all the names.

"I just came from the Salt Lake Valley," Brannan said.

Robert's ears picked up several notches and his skin began to tingle. "Did you happen to see my wife and children? Her name is Hannah, Hannah Harris. I'm Robert Harris. She would have been traveling with my sister,

Elizabeth Browett."

Brannan shook his head no. "I was too busy talking with Brigham Young to get to know all the pioneers very well. But none of those names ring a bell."

Robert was persistent. "What about Thomas Bloxham? Edward Phillips? John Benbow? Thomas Kington?"

"Sorry, no."

Brannan was terribly low in spirit and disinterested in names. But he told what seemed to Robert an incredible story. Brannan had left Sutter's Fort in April with five other men with the goal of seeking Brigham Young's counsel and guiding the Saints to San Francisco. Brannan had encountered the last of the Donner relief parties on the way through, even meeting the man accused of living on human flesh for several weeks, a German by the name of Louis Keseberg. At that time of the year the snow depth in these very mountains had measured from twenty to an incredible hundred feet. Crusted snow conditions had enabled Brannan and his companions to cross the Sierra Mountain passes with their eleven head of horses and mules, a distance of forty miles, in less than two days. Brannan sent two men south to locate an easier pass across the Sierras and then continued east with three men until he found Brigham Young and the Pioneer Company in a place called Green River. Brigham became annoyed with Brannan's talk of San Francisco and sent him back along the trail to help guide the Pueblo sick detachment to the Salt Lake Valley. Brigham said he would stop there because the Saints didn't have the means to make it to California. Brannan's main purpose for making the trip was to guide Brigham and the pioneers through the Sierra Mountains to California.

"Sounds like you weren't successful," James Pace concluded.

"Brigham Young is a stubborn man," Brannan charged. "But I won't give up my efforts. Brigham is going to find it near impossible to farm the parched ground of the Salt Lake Valley. I predict he'll be forced to bring the Church to California, but it's too late this year. You'd have to be coming through these mountains about now to make it. That's what happened to the Donner Party. They arrived at the Sierra Mountains too late in the year."

"Did you bring us any letters?" Pace asked.

Brannan shook his head again. "No."

Robert grimaced. "What about Captain Brown—does he have letters from our families?"

"I suppose he does," Brannan said, sounding disinterested.

"How far behind is he?" Daniel asked, openly anxious for any news about Elizabeth and Moroni.

"I suspect he'll be here sometime tomorrow."

Robert and the other members of the James Pace group spent the evening quizzing Brannan about the Salt Lake Valley and the road leading there. Brannan told them that they wouldn't be able to purchase any supplies until they arrived at Fort Hall on the Snake River, and that they would encounter a lot of dangerous "Digger Indians" along the trail that followed the Humboldt River and sink, a desert area.

"You'd best travel in a larger group," Brannan warned. "Else the Diggers will try to kill your horses, mules, and livestock. They're a desperate people and have nothing much else to eat."

Brannan described the trail: after the Donner camp and the lake now named after the ill-fated party, the ex-soldiers would travel northeast to Alder Creek, from there to Dog Valley, follow the Truckee River south, and then east to Truckee Meadows. After that, they'd have to endure the "forty-mile desert," where there were only occasional hot springs, and then follow the Humboldt River through more deserts. The traveling would get easier, Brannan said, when they would follow the Raft River north to the Snake River, and from there to Fort Hall.

"You're one to warn about Indians," Robert told Brannan, still wondering why this Church leader would even think of traveling alone.

The next morning Pace assigned one of the men, David Rainey, to accompany Brannan until they located the other company of returning soldiers, who were under the leadership of Captain Lytle. "Tell them that Captain Brown will soon be here with mail and news from Brigham Young."

Brannan was gone and Robert was glad.

Daniel pressed the letter from Elizabeth to his nose and sniffed it, hoping to catch the scent of the woman he loved more than life itself. He loved Harriet, too, but in a different way, perhaps out of duty. With childlike eagerness he clutched the letter to his breast and looked for solitude among the willows and trees in the Truckee Meadows where the Pace Company and the Lytle

Company had come together to greet Captain Brown and the men who had traveled with him. It was already evident that they were telling a much different story than Samuel Brannan, but Daniel ignored those details for the moment.

As he trekked to the shade of a tree, Daniel noted the disappointed look on Robert's face. "No letter from Hannah?"

"I guess not," he said. "I can't understand it. Why would you get a letter, and not me?" Robert just looked at Daniel sadly, as though he had not expected to be let down like this. Brown's mailbag had been stuffed with letters, but none for him.

Daniel was as perplexed as Robert. He waved the letter as he sat under a tree. The herd was in sight and so were the horses and mules. Several of the men had received letters and they began to read them. "Maybe this will explain it. Or maybe Hannah's letter is in here, in the same envelope."

Robert followed every little movement Daniel made, from the tearing open of the envelope to the pulling out of the letter. There were several pages. Daniel sorted through them before he began reading, trying to make out Elizabeth's handwriting. "Sorry, mate. Nothing from Hannah."

Hiding his disappointment, Robert sat beside him.

The first words of the letter stunned Daniel. "Oh, no!" he exclaimed.

"What'd she say?" Robert asked.

Daniel gasped and for a few moments he was unable to form any more words. He didn't want to think about what the letter said. He tried blocking it out of his mind. But Moroni was dead. He had died of canker way last November, about Thanksgiving time.

Daniel looked at Robert, angry with his brother-in-law for a moment though he knew it wrong to be. Robert had a whopping total of seven children, all living, all healthy. It had taken ten years for Elizabeth to conceive. Brigham Young had given her a blessing while they were still in England, promising that she would be a "mother in Zion." Willard Richards had cautioned her that the blessing might mean that she would have only one child. One child! Now that one child was dead! Why had the Lord taken Moroni? Moroni was only fourteen months old when he died! Daniel had not seen his little boy take his first steps or hear his first legible words.

"What's wrong? What's happened?" Robert asked.

Daniel began to sob. Tears rolled down his reddened cheeks. He rose to his feet and slowly walked in the opposite direction of the rest of the men. "It's Moroni," he stammered. "He died."

Robert followed in temporary silence. He reached out and took Daniel by the shoulder and then drew him into an embrace. "I guess we should have stayed in Council Bluffs. We should have stayed with our wives."

Daniel felt an impulse to agree with Robert, but grief had so overcome him that he lapsed into silence again for a few moments. Weariness overcame him and he slumped against the tree. Being away from his family, marching all the way to the Pacific, and being part of the Mormon Battalion had suddenly gotten a lot harder. All his life he had been careful to control experience as best he could, but when he left Elizabeth in Council Bluffs some things had been taken out of his control. The death of Moroni would never be forgotten in the pleasure of anything else. He regretted being in California, in the tops of the mountains. Yes, he should have stayed with his wives and provided for them and for Moroni. He should have let some other man enlist in the Battalion, taking his place. He began to dwell on all his mistakes. Not only was his little boy gone, but Elizabeth was probably more grief-stricken than he was.

"You'd better read the rest of the letter," Robert said.

Daniel wiped his eyes, began reading, and then stopped again. The words were blurry so he wiped at his eyes again. He read some more. "Elizabeth and Harriet are in the Salt Lake Valley with Brigham Young. But Hannah didn't make it. She's still on the Missouri."

Robert looked paralyzed. "What about my new baby?"

Daniel drew a deep, painful breath. "Hannah had a boy. She named him after you and after your father. His name is Robert Harris III."

Robert tried to mask his true feelings about Hannah not being included in the Pioneer Company of Saints that had made it to the Salt Lake Valley. Right now it was almost too much to deal with the loss of Daniel's son. After all, Hannah and his seven children were at least alive. Moroni was buried underneath the dark moist soil in a temporary Mormon settlement called Winter Quarters, a burial spot Daniel might never see.

But the burn of disappointment was there. To a man, everyone camped here in the Sierras felt that Brigham Young and the members of the Twelve had in essence made a contract with members of the Battalion: If they would enlist, the Church would get their families to the Great Basin the following summer. In Robert's mind it was that simple. He had done his part, enlisted over the protest of Hannah, and marched two thousand miles to California. Since Hannah wasn't in the Salt Lake Valley with his children, he now had to face the dismal fact that he had to travel another two thousand miles to find her in Winter Quarters. If it weren't for the reality that Daniel's grief was far worse than his own, he would be snarling with frustration.

"I guess we're in a pickle now," Robert finally said. "Your wife is in the Salt Lake Valley and mine is still on the Missouri." Robert couldn't understand why Elizabeth had chosen to leave Hannah. Elizabeth had always been a second mother to his children. Joseph, Elizabeth, William, Thomas, Enoch, and Sarah Ann had never known what life was like without their aunt to assist them in little things by making bread, sewing and mending clothes, administering herbs when they were sick, and telling them stories. Robert tried to picture the scene when Elizabeth and Harriet left Winter Quarters with the Pioneer Company, and how Hannah must have felt being left behind. He supposed he now knew the reason for no letter. Only the men whose families were in the Salt Lake Valley received mail. He wasn't the only man whose wife had not made it.

Daniel just nodded, still lost in his grief.

Robert's vision of the Salt Lake Valley improved as he listened to Captain James Brown's report, which sharply contrasted that given by Brannan. Brannan's opinion of the valley was sour: It froze every month of the year, the ground was too dry to sprout seeds, and it was no place for an agricultural people like the Mormons. The Saints could not possibly eke out a living there. Brannan had constantly touted California to Brigham Young, where clover and wild oats grew year-round up to the belly of a horse. Brannan claimed that John Sutter, owner of Sutter's Fort, had expressed his wish that the Mormons settle near his fort. For several days Brannan had traveled with the Saints, trying to paint a bleak picture of the Rocky Mountain region of the Great Basin, telling them that he had seen more timber on the Green River, where they were traveling, than he had seen anywhere on the route since he had left California.

Captain Brown, on the other hand, contended that Brigham Young was optimistic—that the ground could be watered by irrigation, that there would be an adequate growing season and sufficient timber, and that the Saints could prosper the Kingdom of God on earth there. The only thing Brannan and Brown agreed on, it seemed, was the fact that with winter coming on, the Saints in the Salt Lake Valley wouldn't have enough food to live comfortably.

"Brigham's not coming to California, boys," Brown stated with an emphatic nod of his head. "You can get that out of your minds, despite what Sam Brannan may have said."

Brown had already disclosed the fact that part of his mission was to collect the pay of the Battalion detachments to Pueblo. None of the sick men who had been sent back by either A. J. Smith or Cooke had been paid. Brown was on his way to see the new governor of California, Richard Mason, and collect the money. Brown said the army owed around five thousand dollars to the Church as compensation to those soldiers.

Brown said that Brannan had joined Brigham Young, Wilford Woodruff, Orson Pratt, and eleven other men on an exploring expedition of the Great Salt Lake and the valley shortly after the arrival of the Pioneer Company. Although Wilford Woodruff called the lake "the eighth wonder of the world," Brannan had cursed the desert country, constantly comparing it to the lushness of California and couldn't understand why Brigham wouldn't listen to him. Instead, Brown said, Brigham had gone so far as to to strike a stick in the ground at a particular location and state during a mass meeting that a temple would be built there. He further asked the assembly, "shall this be the spot or shall we look further? I want all to freely express their minds."

Brown shook his head in disgust. "Sam never said a word, but I knew the whole thing was giving Brannan spells of lightheadedness. Brigham insisted that the valley was fine with him because it was where the Lord wanted the Saints to be, and he was satisfied with it and would be even if the location were nothing but barren rock. Brigham made the motion that the Saints locate right there, and that they immediately lay out a city. The motion carried without a dissenting voice. Still Sam didn't say anything, but he sure worked over Brigham every chance he could get until we left for Fort Hall."

"Sounds like Brother Brannan really got under President Brigham Young's skin," Levi Hancock said. He had been traveling with the Lytle group.

"I suppose he did," Brown added. "Brannan had been coaxing Brigham since the time he found the Saints at Green River. Finally, in the valley of Salt Lake, he told Brannan that the Saints had no business in California and that the Gentiles would be there soon in great numbers. The Gentiles, Brigham said, within five years would make California a place no better than Missouri or Illinois for the Saints to prosper and to be left alone."

"That apparently didn't satisfy Brannan," Captain Pace remarked.

"No, it didn't," Brown said. "Brigham finally had to get quite direct with him. He struck his cane in the soil and said that he was going to stop right there, that he was going to build a city there, and a temple, and build up a place for the Saints to build the Church up."

Brown continued to unfold his story. Brannan hung around the Salt Lake Valley until early August, constantly bantering Brigham Young. At the end of July a three-hour meeting was held there, discussing the Mormon Battalion. Brigham lamented Dr. Sanderson's use of chemical medicines and stated that he would be cursed for his crimes against the Battalion men. During the meeting, Brigham instructed Captain Brown, Samuel Brannan, and others to go to California, to find the Battalion, and to tell the former soldiers where the Saints had settled. Brown left the valley on the ninth of August, four weeks after the Battalion's discharge in Los Angeles, and when the ex-soldiers were still traveling north in central California. Brannan's pride was damaged when

Brigham Young placed Captain Brown over him for the trip.

"I guess Sam Brannan felt he should be the one to be giving me orders since he had the position of President of the Church in California," Brown said. "I'd hate to be one of the members of the Church living under Sam's leadership here in California. If there's not a lot of dissatisfaction and contention I'll eat my hat."

Robert had to agree. He had picked up on that point in talking with a few Mormon settlers at New Hope.

At this point the ex-Battalion soldiers who had wintered in Pueblo and were traveling with Captain Brown took over the conversation. For them, the trip from the Salt Lake Valley had been tense but comic. Brown and Brannan had been snuffy toward each other the entire trip—from the valley north to Fort Hall, and from Fort Hall west to the Sierras. At their camp three days earlier, tension between them erupted to the point of fisticuffs and near gunplay. Brown wanted to get an early start that morning, but Brannan insisted on eating breakfast first. Brown said he would leave anyway and take all the horses because they belonged to the government and were under his personal care. Both men went for the horses and that's when the fight commenced. They pounded on each other with fists and clubs until they were separated and then they both ran for their guns. The men separated them again and prevented them from using their weapons.

"So that's when Brannan struck out alone?" Pace asked.

"After the fight he retained his stubbornness and began cooking his own breakfast," Captain Brown said. "So we left him there."

"He showed up here with a horse and two mules, so you must have given him the horse," Pace said.

"Yep," Brown acknowledged. "I let him take one of the horses."

Henry Bigler laughed. "He must have finished his breakfast in a hurry. It wasn't long until he passed us. I tried to talk him into rejoining us but he insisted on traveling alone. It's a wonder the Indians didn't get him."

Captain Brown spit in the campfire. "That man has a bad attitude. He belittled Brigham Young the entire trip. He belittled Church doctrines, too, especially polygamy. He believes that polygamy makes a woman a slave worse than the Negro."

At this point Robert noted that Daniel finally perked up a little. Daniel had never treated Harriet with any less respect than Elizabeth and neither had any of the other Mormon men who had additional wives, in Robert's opinion.

The subject turned to two letters from Brigham Young that had been carried by Captain Brown. Already there had been considerable discussion over them while Robert and Daniel had been grieving about Moroni and poring over Elizabeth's letter. The first, directed to the Saints in California under the presidency of Samuel Brannan, summarized the trials of the Mormons and made it clear that Salt Lake was to become the headquarters of the Church. The tone of the letter gave Brannan only a mild endorsement but did designate him as president of the Church there. The letter was more of an epistle. It said that Orson Hyde was now the presiding elder in Winter Quarters, how-

Winter Quarters had been organized, that the mission in Great Britain had solidified once again, and that the Pioneer Company numbering less than five hundred souls had left Missouri in early April and had arrived in the Salt Lake Valley on the twenty-fourth of July. Brigham said that crops had been planted there, that the soil was excellent, that living conditions were better there than they had been in Illinois or Missouri, that the city was being laid out, and that Brigham was planning to return to Winter Quarters right away.

Right away? Robert asked himself. Would he find Brigham Young in the Salt Lake Valley or Winter Quarters? He wanted to confront the Church leader and personally ask him why Hannah and his children had been left behind. Robert did not relish the thought of traipsing halfway across the continent to find them and then turn around and bring them to the Salt Lake Valley. He felt a flash of annoyance and he was certain it would stay there until he could give Brigham a piece of his mind.

In the second letter, Brigham Young had crafted a careful defense of his treatment of the Battalion members' families. The Prophet said that it was "hardly to be expected" that "every one of your families" would have been able to travel to Salt Lake, but that some of them had. There was no definite list but Robert knew from Elizabeth's letter that Hannah had not made it. Robert could see disappointment written on the faces of more than two-dozen other men who were in the same predicament.

The second letter also carried instructions for the Mormon Battalion veterans. When the letter was read again for the benefit of those who had been gleaning the contents of letters sent from their families, it contained a decided preference to have the men gather to the Salt Lake Valley.

Robert felt that his head would burst. Salt Lake Valley was nowhere near Hannah and his children. The only thing Robert liked about the letter was Brigham's surprising grasp of western geography. At least he now knew the certain route to Fort Hall and to the Salt Lake, and the route from there back to Winter Quarters. The men were counseled, for example, to avoid the Hastings Cutoff, a shortcut that avoided Fort Hall on the Snake River altogether. There was a lack of water on that route. For a few minutes the men discussed these things and then the conversation turned back to California.

"A few of the men have already decided to stay in California," Levi Hancock admitted.

"Shall we go back and get them?" David Pettegrew asked.

Robert held his breath. He didn't want to be the one to go clear back to Los Angeles and get the six men who contracted to build a mill for rancher Isaac Williams. Or even back to Sutter's Fort, where a few others had stayed.

"No," Captain Brown answered. "Willard Richards actually dictated this second letter. Although Brigham Young signed it, Brigham's intentions are a little different. The situation is quite destitute in the Salt Lake Valley, as you might imagine. There is no economy, very little money, and hardly enough food to sustain the people that are there."

"So what are you saying?" Pettegrew asked.

Robert was confused so he tensed a little. He said a prayer in his heart that he wouldn't be required to stay in California just to help Brigham's Salt Lake economy. He had a goal in mind and one goal only. That was to get to Hannah's side before winter and it would take some doing. If he averaged twenty-five miles a day he calculated it would take him until late November or early December to make it.

"I'm saying that there's a clear need for some of you to remain in California and labor here, and then bring your earnings to the Salt Lake Valley in the spring," Brown said.

"To follow the counsel of the Prophet, who should continue on and who should go back and work?" Hancock asked.

Brown referred to the second letter, tracing a line with his finger. "Says here that men who do not have families ought to be the ones who go back. I interpret that to mean those who do not have children. I suppose that your financial needs ought to be considered, too."

Hancock hung his head. "Brother Brown, we're all just about out of money. If we based our decision on that, we'd all go back to work. I hate to see us split up. I feel we all either go back, or all stick together at least to the Salt Lake Valley."

Robert stole a quick glance at Daniel. As of last November, Daniel was childless again. As the men broke out into a discussion about who should continue on and who should go back and seek employment at Sutter's Fort and other places, Robert wondered how Brigham's counsel would affect his brother-in-law. Brown said those who stayed and worked should do so for only one year and then proceed to join the main body of the Church. After consider-able discussion, with Daniel remaining decidedly quiet, the men decided a good decision would be to have half the men go back and half continue onward. Brigham's letter stated that the Lord would be with those who chose to turn back.

"What about you, Brother Harris?" James Pace asked. "There's a scarcity of provisions in Salt Lake. We can't stay there for the winter."

"I'm not staying in California and I'm not going to Salt Lake," Robert said. "I'd like to drop down into the Salt Lake Valley and see my sister for a day or two. But I'm headed for the Missouri. I'm going to spend Christmas and the winter with my wife and children."

Pace continued the query. His wife and children had not made it to the Salt Lake Valley either. His aim was to head for Winter Quarters on the Missouri, too. "And what about you other Battalion boys?"

One by one, more than two hundred ex-soldiers expressed their choices. When it was done, about half voted to continue on and half voted to return to Sutter's Fort. All except Daniel. He remained in his silence and grief and refused to say one way or another.

That night the California sky was heavily seeded with stars, barely seen through the tall trees that surrounded the dozens of campfires of the Battalion boys. With his head on his saddle, not sleeping, not even wanting to, Daniel was still lost in his mourning over Moroni. He was genuinely furious over his enlistment in the Battalion and wished he could reverse time and start over again, beginning with his arrival in Council Bluffs more than a year ago. From time to time he would quiver as he lay there on the ground, his eyes popping with hatred. He didn't hate Brigham Young, Jesse Little, Orson Hyde, Wilford Woodruff, or anyone else who had talked him into enlisting. He hated himself for giving in, for leaving Elizabeth and Harriet. Life had stepped out of line. It was unfair and it was too bad.

One time when he quivered and moaned, Robert surprised him. "You've got a decision to make, you know," Robert said.

Daniel stalled for a few seconds. "I know."

"Where do you think Moroni is right now?"

Daniel hadn't thought of deep things such as that. He was just swallowed up in the tragedy of death, not its reality, and not the religious doctrine of the matter.

"Aren't you going to answer?" Robert asked in the darkness.

Daniel took in a deep breath and released it.

"Maybe it's not such a big change," Robert said. "The spirit world is right here on earth, that's what we've been taught. Moroni's still around. You haven't lost him, in an eternal sense. You know that, don't you?"

Daniel finally spoke. "Yes, I know that."

"You've still got a life to live and two wives to take care of. You're still young, only thirty seven. You can have another child, maybe two or three, or even a dozen."

Daniel's vision of Moroni was swimming again. The memory of the boy was burned deep in his mind, the blue eyes, the thin blond hair, the fair skin, his laughter, his bouncy personality. For an instant he let himself drift back to the day Moroni was born, recalling every detail, the sound of Moroni's first cry, the happiness lit on Elizabeth's face, and how proud he had been to finally become a father. A dozen children could never replace Moroni.

"Are you coming with us in the morning, or staying here in California?" Robert asked in a whisper.

"I don't know."

"Well, you just can't stay here in the mountains all alone."

"Maybe that's what I'll do."

"You know what you need to do, don't you?"

Daniel fell silent again.

"Roll out of your blanket and get it done. Take a few steps down the mountain, find you a good spot where you can see the stars, and say your prayers."

Daniel had not expected this reversal of roles. For the past eleven years ever since he had known Robert, it had been Robert who needed the spiritual uplift. Without saying another word, Daniel rose off the ground and walked downhill in the darkness.

CHAPTER NOTES

The Battalion met Captain Brown at Truckee Meadows, site of today's Reno, Nevada.

18

ROBERT EXPECTED DANIEL TO MAKE the decision to press on to the Salt Lake Valley, but he didn't. He threw his lot with the men who were returning to Sutter's Fort.

"What do you want me to tell Elizabeth?" Robert asked when he found out.

The morning air was brisk, so he shivered as he talked. Daniel had been gone so long during the middle of the night that Robert had fallen to sleep on his grassy couch again, and when he awoke Daniel was separating his belongings from Robert's and packing one of the mules. Most of the other Battalion boys were up too, doing the same thing. Provisions were being split up, with those continuing on taking the most. Campfires had been built. Robert Pixton was fixing breakfast the same as he had done since Fort Leavenworth. It would be another frugal breakfast of bread and bacon. Pixton, too, told Robert he was returning to Sutter's Fort.

"Tell her that I'm following the advice of our Prophet," Daniel answered mournfully. His eyes were still red and he looked forlorn, like a man who had lost just about everything. "I have no children. If anyone should follow Brigham's directive to work in California, it's me."

Robert was struck with the realization that he would have to get along without Daniel for the first time in thirteen years. With the two groups scheduled to separate tomorrow, Robert found himself regretful, nostalgic already for things he hadn't particularly thought of but now hated to think of losing, like Daniel's close companionship. Daniel and his mother had moved next door to the Harris family butcher shop in Apperley, England, in 1834. Daniel had fallen in love with Elizabeth almost at first sight. Daniel and Elizabeth had been married at the same time as Robert and Hannah, in a double ceremony in the little Methodist Church there in Apperley. The two men had stuck together like glue through their eventual conversion to the Church, their journey across the Atlantic and up the Mississippi to Nauvoo, five and a half years in Nauvoo, and a year in the Mormon Battalion.

The cattle were grazing among the trees, snipping at the short grass that grew there.

Robert let the reality of the situation settle over him. "Elizabeth will be sorely puzzled."

"I know."

"She'll be hankering to start over. She'll want another child."

"It'll have to wait for a year." Daniel pressed a letter into Robert's hand. "Give this to her. I hope it'll help."

Robert began to feel a heavy heart for both his sister and Daniel. The Spirit had spoken to Daniel during the night, and hard, he concluded. But that wouldn't totally mitigate Elizabeth's disappointment. Robert began thinking about what he could tell her to salve over the reality that her husband had delayed their romantic reunion for another year. He wouldn't have much time to talk to her either, because he planned to stay in the Salt Lake Valley only a day or two and then strike out for the Missouri. He hoped Daniel's letter was a good one, worded just right.

From the depths of a heavy heart Robert joined a quick meeting with the men who were continuing on, about a hundred. Pace recommended that those who were going to hurry on to Council Bluffs travel in the advance group. Pace also suggested that the men travel in small groups to take advantage of the trail's limited resources. Once they descended out of the mountains and hit the desert along the almost-dry Humboldt River, grass would be sparse. It was September, the dry part of the year, and immigrants and their livestock heading from Fort Hall to California would have used up most of the grass anyway. Levi Hancock objected to the further fracturing of the two main companies, but the men overruled him.

Leading a mule, Pixton sauntered up to Robert. "Will you do me a personal favor?"

"Yes, certainly," Robert answered.

"Deliver Coop to my wife," Pixton said. "She needs the mule more than me." Pixton was a British convert, too, but not among the United Brethren. He had only one child in Nauvoo. He had given the mule the name of "Coop" because his wife's maiden name was Cooper.

Robert patted the mule on its rump. "It's a nice fat mule, Brother Pixton. What if we run out of food and we have to eat this mule before we get there? Food's apt to be scarce in the early winter about the time we hit the Platte River."

"Now's not the time for jokes," Pixton said rather seriously.

"You're right, I'm joking," Robert said. "I promise this lop-eared mule will be delivered to your wife." He jerked on the mule's halter. "Come on, Coop. You and me are going to find the Missouri together."

The men began saying their goodbyes. Of Robert's new mess, Daniel Browett, Richard Slater, John Cox, and Levi Roberts were turning back to Sutter's Fort. The others, Hiram Judd, Jeduthan Averett, and Edward Bunker were striking out for the Missouri with him.

"We've been messmates ever since Fort Leavenworth," Robert said to Richard Slater, another English convert. "I'll miss you."

"Give my love to Ann and my children," Slater said as he embraced Robert. Slater was staying in California despite the fact he had four children back in Winter Quarters.

"Same for me," John Cox said. He had five children. John had been a boyhood friend with Robert in Deerhurst, England, and was about the same age as Robert. Like Robert, John had been converted to the Church by Wilford Woodruff. His wife, Eliza, was a sister to Levi Roberts.

Levi Roberts was mounted on the horse he had purchased in Los Angeles and a lead rope led to a mule packed for the return to Sutter's Fort. Like Robert and John Cox, he had been converted by Wilford Woodruff, too.

"I can't believe you brethren aren't going back to your wives and children, like me," Robert said to Levi.

A tear came to the eye of Levi Roberts. He had packed his mule, readjusted the packs with great care, and now was unpacking the same mule. "I've been up all night. One minute I decide to be included in the half that stays in California, but another minute I want to go back to Harriet Ann and the children."

Nearly a hundred men had decided to turn back, among them Henry Bigler, Henderson Cox, and Ezra Allen. Ezra's mule, "Old Jenny," let her air out as the men stood there. In their consternation of what to do, he hadn't tightened the pack enough. Her pack had turned, and her burden, instead of being on her back, was suspended under her belly. Ezra turned his attention to it.

"Well, I'm not wavering," Robert said. "I'm taking this here mule and delivering it to Sister Pixton. But the real reason I'm going home is to see Hannah and my seven children."

Levi wiped his eye and gave Robert a mournful look. "Guess I'll go with you, then."

Robert smiled. "Good choice, brother. Let's get out of here."

"Not without saying goodbye to me," said Daniel Browett.

This was the moment Robert regretted. "This is hard," he said. Tears began to well up inside him.

Daniel drew Robert into a tight embrace. "You've been the best friend I've ever had, next to Elizabeth."

Both men sobbed in plain sight of the other men, all two hundred of them.

"You take care of yourself," Robert stammered through his tears. "Stay out of sight of the Indians."

"I will," Daniel promised. "Tell Elizabeth and Harriet that I love them."

"Don't get any wild ideas about staying in California for any longer than a year," Robert said.

"Look for me coming into the Salt Lake Valley late next summer with a string of livestock," Daniel said. "You find a good spot for our farm and ranch there."

"Partners forever," Robert agreed, finally breaking their embrace. He stared into Daniel's blue eyes for a long time.

"Why are you staring at me like that?" Daniel asked.

"I don't know," Robert answered. "Suddenly I wish you were going with me. I'm not liking this idea of you returning to Sutter's Fort."

"Follow the Prophet," Daniel said, a reference to Brigham Young's wishes.

"You might be better off this time to follow me and find Elizabeth," Robert said wistfully. "I feel uncomfortable about all this."

Daniel wiped his eyes and laughed a little. "Go on; go back—either decision is a good one. Tell Elizabeth to watch for me. I'll be in her arms in about a year."

Robert and those pressing onward toward Fort Hall and Council Bluffs were anxious so they were the first to leave. Robert's goal was to make it to the Salt Lake Valley by October and to Winter Quarters—an additional eight hundred miles—by Thanksgiving and certainly before Christmas. "I'm riding A. J. Smith out of California," he said in a joking tone to Daniel. Robert now had two mules loaded with provisions, the tent his mess had slept under, the musket the army had issued him in Fort Leavenworth, and cooking gear. One of the mules was his own, and the other now belonged to Sister Pixton.

Daniel still had packing to do but he stood still as a stone as he watched Robert and the other men begin to disappear through the trees and down the hill. He suddenly felt sentimental. "And I'm riding old George Sanderson back to Sutter's Fort," Daniel said, referring to his buckskin horse, Sandy. When he could no longer see Robert, he turned to Richard Slater. "I hope we've made the right decision."

"Me, too," Slater said. "I'd hate to die in California."

CHAPTER NOTES

It is from Robert Pixton's family history that we learn Pixton gave the mule to Robert Harris and asked Robert to give it to his wife. Levi Roberts had originally planned to return to Sutter's Fort and work, but changed his mind and went with Robert Harris. Pixton also tells us who was in Robert Harris's mess at the time the Battalion boys split up: Daniel Browett, Richard Slater, John Cox, Levi Robert, Hyram Judd, Jeduthan Averett, and Edward Bunker.

The Levi Hancock journal states that the Battalion men passed through the remains of the Donner Party on Monday, September sixth, and Tuesday, September seventh. Although members of the Kearny-Fremont party had previously come across these remains, and buried some of them, Robert and Daniel's group also buried some of the remains as well. Hancock states that Captain Brown came into their camp on the eighth of September.

In 1847, emigrants, explorers, and others traveling in the area referred to the river that traversed northern Nevada as both the Humboldt River and the Mary's River. The author has chosen to refer to it in this book as the Humboldt.

Men who decided to stay in California include: George Adair, Ezra Allen, James Reddick Allred, Rueben Allred, James Barger, Henry Bigler, Jacob Kemp Butterfield, Orson Billings, Robert Bliss, John Borrowman, Daniel Browett, James S. Brown, Richard Bush, Alvin Calkins, Robert Collins, William Coray (and his wife, Melissa), Henderson Cox, John Cox, William Coons, Daniel Dennett, Joseph Dobson, James Douglas, Israel Evans, Levi Fifield, William Garner, Ephraim Green, Levi Hancock, Orrin Hatch, Benjamin Hawkins, Shadrack Holdaway, Jonathan Holmes, William Holt, Timothy Hoyt, Wilford Hudson, Sanford Jacobs, William Johnson, Zadock Judd, William Kelly, Jesse Martin, Orlando Mead, Samuel Miles, Miles Miller, David Moss, William Muir, James Park, George Pickup, Ebenezer Pierson, Robert Pixton, Samuel Rogers, Richard Slater, James Sly, Azariah Smith, Alexander Stephens, John Stoddard, William Strong, Jacob Trueman, Edward Wade, Thomas Weir, John White, Samuel White, Ira Willes, Sidney Willes, and Francis Woodard.

19

WHEN ROBERT AND THE CAPTAIN PACE group camped at a spring on the other side of Truckee Meadows they found a party of California immigrants getting ready for their attempt to cross the Sierras. Daylight was about to disappear. The late afternoon September sun cast long shadows.

"Are you men Bear Flaggers?" the leader of the party asked Captain Pace as the Battalion boys approached. He introduced himself as Chester Ingersoll and his camp consisted of more than three-dozen curious men, along with their wives and children.

In the background, away from the camp, mules were braying and oxen were bawling as though they were about to die. Robert temporarily concluded that the feed wasn't adequate, although the grass had looked good to him. There were other noises, too, children playing in the meadow, and the metallic sound of axes biting into the pitchy, resonant trunks of cedar trees for fire-wood. He could also smell salt pork bubbling with freshly picked wild onions in blackened kettles over crackling fires.

"No, we're not Bear Flaggers," Captain Pace laughed as he dismounted. "We're Mormon soldiers returning from the war with Mexico."

Ingersoll had a deeply tanned weather-beaten face with a full beard, but he seemed to pale a little at the answer. "Mormons? All of you?"

"All of us," Pace answered. "We enlisted at Council Bluffs on the Missouri, got outfitted at Fort Leavenworth, and walked all the way to Santa Fe and from there to Mexico and to San Diego. We were released from the army in Los Angeles in the middle of July. Now we're trying to find our families."

Ingersoll relaxed a bit. "Is the war over? Is California secure?"

"There were still rumors that the Mexicans might mount a counterattack from the south, but I doubt it," Pace explained. "The area around Sutter's Fort seems peaceful and safe."

Robert and the other Battalion boys dismounted, not knowing if Pace intended to camp near the immigrants or push on for a few more miles. Pace passed along the latest news of the war that he'd heard in Sutter's Fort, that there had been major American victories deep within the heart of Mexico. Doniphan had won skirmishes in El Paso and Chihuahua. General Scott had invaded Mexico City. News of an imminent American victory was expected soon. Pace explained that the Bear Flag Revolt happened in June of last year.

The revolt, he said, took place when a few dozen American settlers stormed the home of General Mariano Vallejo, who was in charge of Mexico's military district of Northern California. The Americans demanded his surrender. To their surprise, Vallejo invited them in for a drink to discuss terms of surrender. A lengthy session resulted in the inebriation of most of the arbitration committee, but it marked the beginning of the end of Mexican rule in California. Pace told of Kearny's battle at San Pasqual, the surrender of the Californios to Fremont, and the relatively peaceful occupation of California by the Mormon Battalion and other American forces.

Robert wondered why Ingersoll seemed so ignorant of these war details since Kearny and Fremont had surely crossed paths with the Ingersoll group, and so would have Captain Hunter and his advance party. As Ingersoll continued to relax, he admitted that indeed he had talked to both parties, and that he knew more than he let on. Ingersoll invited the Mormons to camp nearby and to return later in the evening to exchange information. Ingersoll was just as curious about the trip over the mountains to Fort Sutter as Pace was interested in the trail to Fort Hall.

When Robert and the Battalion boys followed Pace a few rods beyond the Ingersoll camp to make a camp of their own, Robert saw why the immigrant's mules and oxen were making such a fuss. Three oxen and two mules were bleeding from wounds of some kind.

"What's wrong with them animals?" Pace asked the men of Ingersoll's party as the Mormons rode by. The men had long hair and matted beards, and their clothing was soiled and worn.

"We pulled arrows out of 'em this morning," one of the men said. "At least they're still alive. We've lost livestock almost every day since we started to follow the Humboldt."

Robert gasped. He hadn't taken Brannan's warning very seriously, and he hadn't figured on losing A. J. to Indians, or his mule, or Sister Pixton's mule, either. He had made a promise to deliver the mule to Sister Pixton and he aimed to keep his word, Indians or not. He had seen plenty of Indians between Sutter's Fort and here, but they had not bothered the Battalion boys and had not stolen or shot up any of their animals. Perhaps it was due to the fact that the Battalion boys looked like seasoned veterans, were riding horses and mules instead of pulling wagons, and every man was armed with a musket.

"The Diggers along the Humboldt are the worst Injuns I've ever seen," Ingersoll explained that evening around a campfire as the immigrant party and the Battalion boys exchanged information.

The men said the Indians were called Diggers because they mostly lived by digging up roots, but that some pioneers called them Goshiutes, Piutes, and Washoes. The Diggers had been a source of irritation to the travelers, constantly attacking them from the willows and bushes along the Humboldt River. Ingersoll used words like "emaciated" and "wretched" to describe them.

"Worse than the Plains Indians?" Robert asked. Ingersoll's party had encountered the Northern Plains Indians whereas the Mormon Battalion had encountered the Southern Plains Indians along the Santa Fe Trail.

Ingersoll fouled the warm evening air with his cursing. "The Plains Indians at least knew the value of a horse, but the Diggers don't. They eat every horse and mule they steal. They ain't got brains enough to see the value of ridin' one." He went on to say that he sort of admired the Indians he'd seen on the plains and talked about their noble stature, their horsemanship, and their teepees. "The Diggers must live in holes in the ground, or in the willows," he said. "I never once saw a teepee or any kind of house since we left the Raft River."

"They're holed up like wild animals," a woman said.

"If it weren't for eatin' our mules and oxen, they'd have nothing to eat but roots and grubs and rodents," said another woman, not hiding her disgust.

"And they eat about everything raw," a woman said. She said she saw a Digger campfire only once. The Diggers had been cooking in a pot made of stiff mud, but the pot fell apart during the cooking.

"I gave a Digger woman some raw bacon and she ate it down right in front of me," said another woman.

Robert got the impression that the sole employment of the Diggers was to obtain food. Every member of the Ingersoll party referred to them in contemptuous, loathing, and ridiculing terms. And for good reason. Every time they camped the Diggers shot arrows into their livestock, hoping to either kill them or render them useless so that the whites would leave them behind.

When Ingersoll told stories of how the first trappers and explorers into the region had conflicts with the diggers, Robert began to feel uneasy. The story of Captain Joseph Reddeford Walker's experience with the Diggers was especially distressing to Robert. Walker led an expedition through the Humboldt River area on his way to California in 1833. Diggers began appearing from the willows and high grass in front and on the rear, soon surrounding Walker's men. Soon the Diggers made signs that they wanted to smoke with the whites, but Walker realized it was a ploy to allow more Diggers to catch up. There were already more than a hundred Digger men. Walker told his men to fight, and this they did by horseback, leaving thirty-nine dead Indians when it was all over. Walker's men had muskets, the Diggers just bows and arrows.

"Ever since then, travelers along the Humboldt have had troubles with the Diggers," Ingersoll explained. "Walker either had to fight or be killed, but the Digger's haven't forgotten it. It was a tragic affair, but I suspect the Injuns ain't never gonna forgive the white man."

Another member of the Ingersoll party, a young man who had a mouthful of yellow teeth, took an even dimmer view of the Diggers. "They ain't much more'n an animal, anyways. The sooner they're all dead, the better." He described the Diggers as small in stature, ill formed, with ugly features and hairy bodies, naked except a grass breechcloth, and feet that were thick and hardened like animal's hooves. The Diggers were armed not only with bows and arrows, but with pointed sticks and sharp flint knives. He said the Indians were so destitute that they regularly opened the graves of the dead whites for the purpose of stealing their clothes and mutilating the bodies.

Robert trembled a little, hoping he and the returning Mormon soldiers would not have any serious encounters with the Diggers on the way to Fort Hall. He and the others were armed with muskets, they were all former soldiers, and there were no women and children among them. But they couldn't run from the Diggers. The Diggers occupied the only water on the trail and the river represented their home, teepees or not.

Robert found the members of Ingersoll's party to be short of temper and taut of nerve, but for good reason. They were running short of food, their wagons were in bad repair, and they had lost not only mules and oxen to the Diggers, but milk cows and beef cattle, too. They were bone weary from travel—all the way from Independence—and were desperately longing for the ordeal of the journey to be over. Most were weak from sickness and from an improper diet. A few days here in the Truckee Meadows would do them good. Considering the plight of the Ingersoll party, Robert wondered how Hannah and his children had fared if they had made the trip to the Salt Lake Valley.

The immigrants were just as interested in the trail over the mountains to Sutter's Fort as the Battalion men were in the trail leading to Fort Hall.

"We heard there are still dead bodies up there from the Donner Party," one immigrant, a mother of three children, said in an unsure voice. The immigrants had learned of the Donner Party from newspaper accounts and knew that Kearny and his Mormon escorts had buried some of the dead but not all of them.

"Don't know," Captain Pace admitted as Robert listened. "We buried some more of them, but there still might be bodies up there somewhere strewn around that we don't know about."

"Well, at least the winter storms won't get us," the woman said with a sigh of relief.

"Where you headin'?" Captain Pace asked.

"Lots of possibilities," Ingersoll said. "Somewhere around Sutter's Fort, Sacramento Valley, or maybe even San Francisco."

"You've got your aim just right," Pace said. "That's the best part of California we've seen."

Ingersoll's suspicion of the Mormon soldiers had mostly dissolved. "California's gonna be part of the United States, thanks to you soldiers," he predicted.

Robert remembered Jesse Little's map that Little had displayed in Council Bluffs just before Company E enlisted. True to Jesse's prediction, the size of the United States was going to jump by more than a third with the addition of California, New Mexico, and Arizona because of the assumed victory over Mexico, and all of Oregon Territory by virtue of a treaty with England. For a moment Robert thought about what future history books would say about all this.

"And I suppose you're headed for the Salt Lake Valley," another woman said.

"Yes, ma'am," Paced admitted.

"Your leaders have settled in the wrong place," the woman's husband said. "Crops can't grow in the Salt Lake Valley." She said that the commander of Fort Hall, a man named Grant, had been telling everyone passing through the fort of Brigham Young's mistake.

"Well, our group is on its way to the Missouri River in Iowa Territory," Pace explained. "Our families are still there. Then we'll make the trip to the Salt Lake Valley. By this time next year I have confidence that our people will be growing their second crops there."

One of the women gasped. "You mean you have to cross the plains and then cross them again?"

"That's the way it is," Pace said.

Ingersoll scanned the Battalion boys and their assortment of cattle, mules, and horses. "Grass is scarce between here and Fort Hall, and timber, too. There's not enough timber to make a snuff box and not enough brush in some places to shade a rabbit."

Robert gulped. He had not liked the *jornada* northeast of Santa Fe, or the desert country between Santa Fe and San Diego. He wished the Lord would have taken the time to make the new areas of the United States and the Great Basin country a little friendlier.

When Robert rolled up in the same wool blanket he had bought at Sarpy's at the beginning of the trip, his mind began to race. Above him the moon appeared like a ball of fire. It was shining with a dim and baleful light that seemed to struggle downward through a thick bank of smoky vapor that over-hung the high ridge of the Sierra Mountains that stood to the west of the camp. Fires lighted by Indians were visible on the mountains and in several places in the valley, a few miles distant. All this caused new fears to take hold of him. He dwelled about the route to Fort Hall, the desert land he'd have to cross, and the Diggers he'd have to encounter. Trekking over country he'd never seen before was nothing new, but with the Battalion there had always been pilots who sort of knew the route. Now the Battalion boys were on their own. He had to find Elizabeth in a Great Basin location known as the Salt Lake Valley. He wished he were going to "Pleasant Valley," or "Heavenly Valley." The word "salt" meant nothing more than desolation to him. With all his might he prayed that Hannah was there, despite the lack of a letter. He hated the thought of riding a starving mule across the plains during the beginning of winter weather just to reach Winter Quarters.

He had been both amused and impressed by the pioneers he'd just met. Some of them seemed cruel and selfish, hard-tempered and hard-tested by their ordeal so far, but at the same time compassionate and generous. Mostly he was impressed by their determination to get to California and not let the hellish trail get the best of them, despite the hardships they'd encountered. He concluded that there was a measure of bluff, bravado, and impatient know-everthingness in these American pioneers, and it affected the women and children as well as the men. Ingersoll's party, just like the Mormon Battalion, was pushing boldly into the unknown with a certain amount of conceit and gall that would see them reach their goal.

Robert wondered how much Ingersoll or any of his party really knew about California, or if they knew anything at all at the outset. They were true Americans, wanting to go directly west under their own power and authority, and in a way they could afford. There was no single word to describe these wilderness travelers. They were mostly from places in the East like Virginia, New York, or Kentucky. They were from among the prosperous and the poor, the intelligent and the stupid, the educated and the ignorant. They were the religious, the proper, the solid-citizen farmer, and merchant. They were the sacrilegious, the lawless, and even the feckless youth. Several were the rudest and most ignorant of the frontier population, like the Missourians. They knew little about this western country and its inhabitants. But to a man, these Americans felt that their country was not filled out, that America was like a great, gangly adolescent boy, teetering on one foot on the banks of the Mississippi and the Missouri, destined by fatiguing muscles to lose his precarious balance and come crashing down westward. Robert concluded that the mood for expansion must be everywhere in America, and that Americans must see little need for boundaries or even have the thoughts of boundaries. Even without the treaty with England, they would have continued to settle in Oregon Territory. In a way, however, Americans were no different than the Mexicans. As for Mexico, they took the land now known as California and New Mexico from Spain didn't they? The Mexicans couldn't even control things at home, let alone all those millions of empty miles to the north and west. For these American settlers, the land and its treasures were there for the taking, just as their fathers had taken.

Brigham Young and the Church were in the same mold. Practically the only difference was that Brigham hopefully had selected a portion of this new country that no one else wanted. Brigham had bit off a big chew, almost matching the exodus of the Children of Israel. Getting forty or fifty thousand Saints across the American wilderness to the Salt Lake Valley would be no easy task.

Chester Ingersoll's party had come farther than Brigham, but with far fewer people. Ingersoll had followed the California Trail as it snaked its way like a great recumbent vine across hundreds of miles of dreadfully dry country. But Ingersoll was not done. He still had not reached Sutter's Fort. In contrast, tomorrow the Battalion boys would strike east following the Humboldt, its stinky water, and its lurking Digger Indians. Ingersoll would strike west, over the Sierras. Robert couldn't imagine trying to take covered wagons over the trail he'd seen. Ingersoll's party had to conquer the Elephant, and the Elephant would put up a fight. If Ingersoll truly understood the travails of the Sierra Summit he might turn back. Donner Pass, for instance, was roughly a thousand feet above the starting point at Donner Lake, and this distance had to be climbed in less than two miles. Previous immigrants had to dissemble all their wagons to make it over the top. Wagons had been lost over narrow ledges, crashing thousands of feet below. Three days of travel up there might only yield ten miles. The Ingersoll men doubtless had felt their spirits lifted when they first saw the Sierras. The fresh breath of the forest might be animating for them. But Robert felt that their rush of excitement would fade quickly as they tried to traverse the country where the Donners had wintered. That was true even if they took the new route through Roller Pass. Even there, wagons would have to be unhooked and then rehooked to the combined efforts of two dozen mules or oxen to pull them up the thirty-five percent grade. But Robert reckoned they would make it; others had done it and the Ingersolls seemed just as determined. It would be worth it when they finally descended into the Sacramento Valley, the place Daniel had headed for.

With his head in his saddle, Robert gazed at the stars above his head and wished that he was already in Council Bluffs. He hated the thoughts of returning to the desert country with its dryness, its sparse vegetation, its blinding dust storms, and fierce winds. The Humboldt would be bad, but there was no other option. It was a much maligned route, but it made travel from the Truckee Meadows to Fort Hall possible. Apparently there was no water at all if a man took a direct route to the Salt Lake Valley. Ingersoll had found the Humboldt not bad at first, and terrible by the time it had sunk into the earth—which must be a true characteristic of rivers in the Great Basin. There was no place for a river in the Great Basin to empty into the Atlantic or the Pacific. Robert hoped the desert would bring a few moments of rare beauty and a few hours of restful tranquility. But he knew the reality of desert travel, too. The desert destroyed; the desert killed. He had learned that on the *jornada* and in the wild country beyond Santa Fe. He still remembered the battle with the bulls on the San Pedro River and the struggle it had been to get from Tucson to San Diego.

Finding Hannah and the children was not going to be an easy thing. According to Ingersoll, the Battalion boys would first follow the Truckee River east until the river turned north toward Pyramid Lake. Goodbye, and end of good water. From there Robert would have to cross the "forty-mile desert" where the only water boiled out of the earth was too hot to drink. Next would come the terrible sink where the Humboldt River disappeared into the earth, creating a mud lake, an ocean of ooze, a sea of slime ten miles long and four or five miles wide. The water there was undrinkable, a strong solution of tepid moisture laced with bitter salts and tasting like rotten eggs. From there the water would get better gradually, but the threat of Diggers worse. They would come to places described as Granite Point, Big Meadows, the misnamed Thousand Springs Valley, Chicken Springs, Rock Spring, Humboldt Wells, Goose Creek, City of Rocks, Cassia Creek, and finally the Raft River. The Raft River emptied into the Snake River and the Snake would lead the men to Fort Hall. The Battalion boys had not found anyone who knew one solitary thing about the route that led from Fort Hall to the Salt Lake Valley. The Oregon Trail—the route wagons followed from Fort Bridger to Fort Hall—didn't go near the Salt Lake Valley at all. After a short visit with his sister, Elizabeth, he, along with the other Battalion boys, would have to find their way from the Salt Lake Valley to Fort Bridger. The trail from Fort Bridger would be well worn but there was a far greater problem. He would be traveling in a harsh part of the United States in the wrong time of the year. He would be lucky if he wasn't frozen in his tracks or buried in the snow by then. He thought of Daniel as the lucky one in this respect. The weather at Sutter's Fort during the winter would be tolerable, and Daniel was probably there already, employed as a carpenter, making money. What little money Robert had left in his pocket would be long gone by the time he reached Winter Quarters.

20

Sutter's Fort

September 1847

"WHAT IF CAPTAIN SUTTER WON'T HIRE US?" Robert Pixton asked as he fixed dinner in the same campground the Battalion boys had camped in a few days ago just outside Sutter's Fort.

Daniel harbored no fears in that respect. Work was available. What he feared was loneliness. He missed Robert already, but he missed Elizabeth and Harriet worse. His mind was already playing tricks on him. More than ever he saw himself living with his two wives, starting a family all over again, and being a husband and a father. He feared Indians, too. He had seen plenty of them during the return trip over the mountains. Last night, at camp, the mules and horses had been greatly alarmed, breaking their picket ropes and running in all directions. Daniel and the others got them all back, but it had been a frightful night. There were plenty of Indians around Sutter's Fort, too. Some were well dressed, but most were nearly naked. They had tried to trade dried meat and roots for white man's clothing. Either that or they were trying to discover what they could steal.

"He'll hire us," Daniel said with a chuckle. His conversation with James Marshall was keen on his mind. "He needs workers worse than a duck needs feathers." Daniel had been one of three men chosen to ride over to the fort and talk to Captain Sutter.

On the way out of the Sierras, the men had passed the grave of a small child, buried in the mountains by California immigrants. Wolves had broken the grave open and scattered not only the feathers of a pillow she had been buried with, but the girl's remains as well. The men reburied her. The Battalion boys also passed by the grave of Battalion member Henry Hoyt, who had died while traveling in the group behind Daniel and Robert. His grave, too, had been decimated by wolves. The men reburied Hoyt high on the side of the mountain, under a sprawling oak tree.

When Daniel saw Captain Sutter at the Fort, Sutter was strutting his forty-four-year-old portly body around like a red rooster. He was giving orders faster than a Missourian could hate a Mormon. The orders had to do with the wheat harvest. The fort was a beehive of activity. Leather tanning, distilling, blacksmithing, and construction were going on under Sutter's watchful supervision.

"Mr. Sutter, we'd like a word with you," Daniel said.

Sutter wheeled, acting slightly distracted. But a huge smile suddenly graced his face. His Swiss accent was pronounced. "Tell me mine eyes aren't deceiving me. More Mormons, ya?"

"Yes, sir," Daniel answered. "More Mormons."

"You'f decided to take me up on mine offer?" Sutter asked. "You vant to verk, ya?"

Daniel returned the smile. "Yes, we want to work. Thirty of us returned. The rest of our Battalion boys are on their way to the Salt Lake Valley, but we're staying here until spring."

By now Daniel had learned that the other Battalion boys that had stayed behind had already been working in Sutter's tan yard, at the shops at the fort, putting in foundations for a gristmill on the lower American River, and making shoes and boots. One, Ezra Allen, was working in the fort's bowling alley.

Sutter's smile faded. "Only until spring, ya?"

Will that make a difference?" Daniel asked. "You don't want us?"

Sutter turned apologetic. "I vant you, I vant you. Any of you be carpenters, ya?"

Daniel replied, "Why yes, I am, and some of the others, too."

"Goodt, goodt," Sutter said. "Finally I kin finish mine gristmill."

"Gristmill?"

"Ya, up da river at Brighton; a large one, of four run of stones. Already I half ze sum of twenty-five *thousand* dollars invested in it. Ya?"

Daniel gasped out loud. "Twenty-five *thousand?*" The total sounded far-fetched to him, but he had no reason to disbelieve Captain Sutter. To him, twenty-five thousand dollars sounded like the gross national product of the United States of America. Daniel thought of the gristmills in Nauvoo, wondering how much money they had cost. After all this settled over him, Daniel said to Sutter, "Sure, I can help finish your gristmill."

Sutter's eyes seem to dance with happiness. "You kin kume and see me first ting in da morning. I vill hire all of you. Ya?"

Daniel left Sutter's presence feeling certain warmth for the man. He knew only a few facts about the Swiss emigrants. Johann "John" Sutter was from near Bern, Switzerland. With the financial aid of his mother-in-law he had opened a dry goods store in Burgdorf. For some reason he accumulated a lot of creditors and had mounting debts. Facing debtors' prison he secretly obtained a passport and slipped out of Switzerland. One step ahead of the police he crossed into France, made for the seacoast, and took the first ship to America, leaving his wife and five children behind. Sutter hoped to succeed in business here so that he could send for them. For five years Sutter skipped around the New World, trying his luck in New York, Westport, Santa Fe, and eventually the west coast. By way of the Sandwich Islands and Alaska he arrived in San Francisco in 1839—known then as Yerba Buena. Hardly thirty persons lived there. At Monterey, the capital of Alta California, the governor gave Sutter permission to settle along the unfamiliar Sacramento River. Within a year Sutter returned to Monterey for his papers of Mexican citizenship and a title to his chosen lands. He established his "New Helvetia" where a tributary stream, the American River, entered the Sacramento River. In 1841 Sutter received title to eleven broad leagues of land. Bold in his dreams, he purchased from the Russian Fur Company on credit two establishments called Fort Ross and Bodega. He hired several people, including a trusted American, John Bidwell, in 1843. That year he applied for additional land in the name of his oldest son and began making plans for his family to join him.

"Yah," Daniel answered. "We'll be back in the morning. We need work."

Daniel's meeting with Captain Sutter at the fort yielded good fruit. Just as James Marshall of the California Battalion had a contract to build a sawmill at Coloma, Daniel Browett of the Mormon Battalion now had agreed to finish building a gristmill at a river location known as Brighton, twenty-five miles away. Although the foundations had been laid, Sutter previously had limited access to skilled carpenters—and Daniel had that skill. And Sutter promised to hire every Battalion boy, some at the sawmill, some at the gristmill, and some at the fort. Each man was to receive a dollar and a half a day, paid in the spring either in the form of cash or trade for livestock and provisions.

"Why that's around forty dollars a month," exclaimed a happy Robert Pixton, who began counting and recounting on his fingers. With Sutter so willing to pay a dollar and a half a day, Daniel couldn't figure out why so many loiterers hung around the fort, sponging off Sutter. Worse, the loiterers were all drunk. It seemed to be the daily condition of Missourians and these loiterers, too.

"That's more than seven times as much as I was paid as a private in the army," added Israel Evans, "and almost as much as the captains were paid." Israel had been a private in Company B.

"How about helping me on the gristmill?" Daniel said to Evans. He explained to the men that a three-mile race had to be dug so that waters from the American River could be diverted. The gristmill itself was to be built of planks eventually supplied from Marshall's sawmill. Sutter also wanted to export planks to San Francisco and Monterey where homes and fences were being built at a rapid clip.

"Sure thing," said Evans.

Jesse Martin and Ephraim Green, old messmates with Evans, volunteered to work on the gristmill, too. So did Ezra Allen, Henderson Cox, and Jonathan Holmes. Ezra had been the Company C musician. Cox had been a private in Company A and was only eighteen. Holmes had been a private in Company D.

Daniel smiled. He could see himself returning to the Salt Lake Valley in a year with more than a hundred dollars in cash and a herd of horses, mules, and cattle. Sutter had also agreed to let the men live in some of his adobe huts, and furnish the men with provisions, too, but they had to do their own cooking. The Battalion boys' horses and mules would be pastured with Sutter's livestock free of charge and corralled every night by Sutter's *vaqueros*.

"But doesn't Sutter already have a gristmill?" said young Henderson Cox.

"It's not big enough to grind enough flour to meet the increasing demands of food here at the fort," said Daniel.

"How many more people does Sutter expect around here?" Henderson asked.

"He thinks the non-Indian, non-Hispanic population will begin to swell to perhaps twenty thousand people within five years," Daniel responded. "He thinks this is the best part of California and that immigrants will flock here."

More Battalion boys began volunteering to work with Daniel: Henry Bigler, Azariah Smith, and William Johnstun. Bigler and Smith had been privates in Company B, spending time in San Diego, and Johnstun had been a private in Company C.

Daniel held up a hand. "You can't all work at the gristmill—Sutter needs men to work in his tannery, the bakery, and he needs blacksmiths, too." A few men, including John Cox, said they wanted to see San Francisco and try to get a job there.

The conversation with Sutter had given Daniel a new perspective on California, and he could now see it almost the same way Sam Brannan saw it. It was huge in land mass and huge in resources. California was bounded on the north by Oregon, on the east by the Rocky Mountains, on the west by the Pacific Ocean, and on the south by Mexico. It extended seven hundred miles from north to south and from east to west by nearly the same distance—to as yet undefined borders—making for an incredible land area of around four hundred thousand square miles. It would dwarf his native England, and, in fact, all of Great Britain—which included Scotland and Ireland. There were great mountains here, such as the Sierras. Who knows what great mineral wealth might be there? There were mighty rivers, too, like the Colorado which the Battalion had followed in the southwest, the San Joaquin, and the Sacramento which flowed in front of Sutter's Fort. Great valleys held the prospect of being inhabited by thousands of people, even hundreds of thousands.

While it was true that the old missions, presidios, and practically anything connected to the Spanish rule and even the Mexican rule were in shambles, under American rule California would revive quickly. Immigrants would begin to pour in, swelling its current population of ten thousand non-Indians to double and even triple within a few short years. Like the Mormons that had already settled here under Brannan's leadership, immigrants would find California full of wild horses, wild game like elk and deer, and so many wild cattle that could be used for beef that it made the mind go bungled. The soil, without irrigation, yielded vegetables, grains, and fruit of nearly every kind—grapes, apples, pears, peaches, figs, oranges. Vicious winters tore at the mountains, but the valleys remained pleasant even in months like December and January. The temperatures in San Diego, Los Angeles, and here along the Sacramento were agreeable year around. The Hispanic people were, for the most part, now rabidly pro-American. They were a pleasant people, too. The deportment of the women toward strangers was queenly. Their dark eyes exuded a grace and warmth. Most of them puffed *cigaritas* with gusto, but Daniel thought it amusing and didn't harbor bad feelings toward them.

Indians were another story. Daniel had bad feelings about Indians.

Work on the millrace had progressed nicely in Daniel's opinion. Sutter had picked a spot near his rancho on the American River where the men were building a dam. The idea was to get a good fall of water with the dam and then dig a millrace that would end up four miles long. The diverted water would also be used to irrigate a large tract of good farming land. From this part of the river, Sutter had plans to ship the flour by steamboats and launches to places like San Francisco and Benicia.

Aside from a few men who were working as leather tanners and shoemakers at the Fort, most of the Battalion boys were digging the millrace. On this day, a familiar figure dressed in buckskin rode out of the willows on a horse.

"Can you boys spare a few hands?" the man said.

Daniel had the overall responsibility for the millrace and the gristmill. He took on a puzzled look for a moment, and then recognized the man on the horse. It was James Marshall, the man who had the contract with Sutter to build the sawmill.

"Depends on who's asking," Daniel said, appearing a little agitated. Fewer men meant a tougher time meeting Sutter's deadlines. Marshall already had five Mormons working for him—W. H. Willes, Sidney Willes, Ebenezer Persons, Alexander Stephens, and James S. Brown. They had been offered work by Sutter when the men first passed by the fort, and had not been in any of the groups that had met Sam Brannan or Captain James Brown in the Sierras.

"It's a request from Captain Sutter himself," Marshall said.

Daniel drew a deep breath and then let it out. "He's the boss. Take who you want."

"Just need five more men," Marshall declared. "Sutter wants the sawmill built as soon as possible. The five Mormons that I have are my best workers. I'd like five more, and Sutter gave me permission."

Suddenly Daniel understood. Boards from the sawmill were needed to construct the gristmill. No boards, no gristmill. It was that simple. There was no growth of timber in the vicinity of Sutter's Fort that was suitable for conversion into lumber—Daniel had seen that the first time he laid eyes on the area. The trees growing there were crooked and too brittle for boards. The nearest source of a suitable supply was the Sierras, and Daniel had been to the tops of the Sierras once.

Daniel didn't have all the Mormon workers. Some were building a boat for what Sutter called his New Helvetica ferry and others were making shingles out of California cedar.

"Any volunteers?" Daniel asked his men.

There was stone silence.

A non-Mormon, Charles Bennett, raised his hand. "I'll go," he said. Bennett was a recent arrival from Oregon. Marshall raised no objection.

"Need four more," Daniel said.

Henry Bigler threw his shovel aside and raised his hand. "I'll give it a go."

Azariah Smith, William Johnstun, and Israel Evans also volunteered.

"How far's the millsite?" Daniel asked as the men left to gather their belongings and their horses.

"Two-day trip from here, maybe three depending how the mules are loaded," Marshall said. "First I've got to take these men back to the fort. We're gonna pack up with provisions, enough for a month or two. Come up and see us sometime."

Out of habit, Daniel saluted Marshall. After all, Marshall had been a member of the California Battalion. "Will do," Daniel said.

CHAPTER NOTES

There is a notation in the John Sutter diary, recorded on 21 September 1847 that reads: "Employed more carpenters to assist Brouett [sic] on the Grist Mill." From this the author assumes that Sutter hired Daniel Browett to build the gristmill and that Sutter assigned additional carpenters from the former Battalion soldiers to assist him.

21

THE HUMBOLDT RIVER ROUTE was proving far worse than Robert ever imagined; he was feeling the most profoundness of solitude and desolation of his life. The stagnant sink smelled worse than rotten eggs, even worse than dirty soapsuds. Its only redeeming factor was the ducks and geese that had speckled its surface. Big Meadows had at least provided good grass for A. J. and the other animals, but most of the pools of water had been covered with a yellow slime and smelled almost as bad as the sink. He and the other Battalion boys adopted a simple water rule—drink it if you see snakes and frogs living in the water, avoid it if you don't because it's poison. They adopted a hot springs rule, too—don't let the dogs near it. One of the dogs had rushed into a pool thinking of a cool drink, but soon was boiled to death. Robert felt lucky that Duke was still alive. Sometimes Duke would hold up a foot and complain of the hot sand.

Traveling along the Humboldt was pure misery for Robert, the same monotonous scene day after day. The clouds of dust—composed of light clay and volcanic ash—were suffocating. The reflection of the hot sun on the light soil burned his eyes. Bogs and swamps caused A. J. to sink up to his belly in a sickening alkali mud smelling of sulfur. The horse refused to eat grass in the miry river bottoms. The only vegetation was sagebrush, willows, and a few sunflowers. In Robert's mind, the awful profoundness of the solitude here rivaled that of the deserts in the Cimarron and north of Tucson.

"I suppose Chester Ingersoll was right about the Humboldt," said Levi Roberts as he trudged along on his mule.

"Why's that?" Robert asked as the sun poured out its scorching rays. The reins in his hands felt as though they had been fried to a crisp.

"Ingersoll said that the devil designed the river in the middle of the night," Levi explained. "And when he woke up the next morning the devil was so ashamed he hid his face."

Robert laughed. Instead of a river three hundred miles long, it actually covered more than a thousand miles if one added up all the meanderings.

Ingersoll had been right about the Diggers. Last night all the mules had been greatly alarmed, some breaking their picket ropes and running in all directions.

Already a few Diggers had been seen emerging from the willows. Two or three were dressed in white man's clothing, either given to them by immigrants or found by digging up graves. The second day three Diggers approached camp wanting to trade salmon trout for tobacco and powder—if the Battalion boys read the Indians' sign language just right. They turned the Indians down; they had no tobacco and didn't want to give up any gunpowder. The next evening several Diggers came to camp with ground rats tied to their waists. One held a roasted rat at arm's length, offering to trade it for something. The Digger made signs with his teeth and tongue, that it was delicious, but neither Robert nor any of the other Battalion boys yielded a jot. The Diggers disappeared where they came from. There were plenty of places for the Indians to hide in the willows.

This evening's trouble began when a Digger stole one of the men's fish hooks. He followed, threatening to shoot him if the Indian didn't give it up. Then another Digger stole Robert's knife and hid it in the sand near the campfire, waiting for a chance to dig it up and make a running escape. But Levi Roberts dug it up instead, and chased the Indian out of camp with Duke nipping at the Digger's heels.

"Better watch the animals closely tonight," Captain Pace warned. Sentinels had been posted every evening but so far not a mule, horse, or beef had been lost to the Diggers. As a captain, Pace was proving to be a good leader. Robert figured he probably learned some of those traits while serving on the Nauvoo police force.

Morning proved a different matter.

"I can't find A. J.," Robert complained.

"I'm missing a mule," Levi Roberts said.

"My mule has two arrows in him," said William Hyde.

Look at that poor beef," added David Pettegrew. "He's about to collapse."
The animal had six arrows sticking in it.

This all led to one disturbing conclusion. The Diggers had struck. Robert
found A J. in the willows, the victim of an arrow. Robert quickly pulled it out
and dressed the wound. And then he retrieved his mule and the mule that
belonged to Sister Pixton.

"Don't die on me, A. J.," Robert told the horse. "I need you to get me to
the Missouri."

"Give me a blessing, Brother Browett," Robert Pixton pleaded. The work of
cutting a millrace on the American River had come to almost a complete halt.
Many of the men had taken sick with the bilious fever. The hard work had
stirred up the men's blood; the old Mississippi River bilious fever symptoms
were resurfacing. The Nauvoo ague was back again, striking not only Pixton
but also several of the other men who worked for Daniel Browett.

Daniel took a vial of consecrated olive oil from his pocket. "Sure thing,
Brother Pixton. I thought California was supposed to be the place where there
was no sickness." There were fewer swamps here, although there were some.
The exact location of the gristmill was a fairly good one, but the work was
hard. The men had to build a dam across the river and divert the water into a
hand-dug millrace.

"I don't know about that," Pixton said. "It's the same fever that's come upon me every summer since that first year in Nauvoo."

The ague hadn't hit Daniel but he considered himself lucky. The other men had been so sick they hadn't been able to help each other with a drink of water. The men had had lain in the hot California sun to keep from making a chill. Daniel wished Elizabeth were here to care for the men, but she wasn't. He wished he had some quinine to give to them, but he didn't. A least Sutter had given them plenty of provisions, especially beef, flour and squash.

As an employer, Sutter was good to work with. He seemed like a patient man most of the time. At other times, however, he exhibited a little impatience. Daniel told himself that if he had Sutter's debt, he'd be impatient, too. Sutter owed more than thirty thousand dollars to the Russian-American Company dating back to the original purchase of the land along the American River.

With the availability of a reliable workforce—the thirty Mormons— Sutter had begun other enterprises, too. Now he had a tannery, where he expected to process hundreds of hides from his cattle that roamed the countryside all but untended. Two of the Battalion boys were making boots and shoes. Others were employed as blacksmiths. James Marshall and his helpers were building a water-powered sawmill in the mountains, where yellow pine was abundant.

"I wish I hadn't stayed here in California," Pixton said, wiping the tears from his eyes.

The remark made Daniel feel the same way. Elizabeth and Harriet were crossing the plains, expecting to meet him in the Salt Lake Valley. His longings for them were getting worse each evening when he was alone. "You could have the fever out in the desert along the Humboldt River just as well as here," Daniel said. "You'll be fine in a few days."

Daniel remembered when Robert, Brother Pixton, and several others had come down with the bilious fever, or ague, a year earlier while in Fort Leavenworth. Daniel had run out of quinine a long time ago, but he'd hadn't run out of consecrated oil for blessings.

Pixton was well enough to ask a pertinent question. Sweat was pouring off his brow. "What's happening at the sawmill? When do we get lumber?" Actual construction on the gristmill depended on boards sawed at Coloma.

"I'm going there tomorrow," Daniel said. Sutter had asked him to make the trip. With bad weather not too far away, there was an urgency to get the sawmill in operation and there was pressure to get the Brighton gristmill done. "I'll find out firsthand."

"Can you take me?" Henderson Cox asked.

"You can go," Daniel said. "I don't want to travel in the mountains without an escort, not with all the Indians."

"How about me?" Ezra Allen asked. Daniel had known Ezra in Nauvoo. Elizabeth had nursed Ezra's wife and daughter back to health two years ago.

"Okay, it'll be the three of us," Daniel said.

The sawmill site was on the South Fork of the American River, fifty miles from the fort. Marshall had told Daniel that the road was an old Indian trail. The trail led Daniel and his two companions methodically up the river through a narrow canyon; in some places the hills on both sides were very steep. When the canyon began to widen after two days, Daniel knew he was near Marshall's project.

"When you get there, coax your horses up the mountain and take a look at Coloma," Marshall had said. "It sits in a pretty little valley."

That's exactly what Daniel did. "Get up, Sandy," he said to his horse. Everytime he dug his heels into the horse Daniel thought of George Sanderson, the calomel doctor after whom Daniel and Robert had named the gelding. He'd ridden Sandy out of town at Los Angeles, and now he was riding him out of Sutter's Fort all the way to Coloma.

The little valley was indeed picturesque. It was only about a quarter of a mile wide and a half-mile long. On both sides were low rounded mountains broken here and there by narrow ravines and gulches down which small streams rushed and tumbled to the river below. The mountainsides to the south of the river were rather densely forested with groves of olive-colored oak, cedar, redwood, balsam, ash, and pine trees of the yellow and pinion variety— perfect for logging. The valley floor was covered with oaks, sparse growth of greasewood and chaparral, and with occasional clumps of trees.

"I can see the boys down there working," Ezra Allen commented. Just like at the gristmill site at Brighton, a millrace was being dug along the river.

The South Fork of the American River made its way into the little valley through a canyon to the southeast. From his perch on the mountain, Daniel guessed the crystal-clear river to be around fifty feet wide here. It was rushing and roaring over its rocky bed, tracing a winding course through the valley floor to the base of the mountains on the northeast. A luxuriant growth of grass, interspersed with wildflowers, carpeted the valley.

"If all California were like this, and Brother Brigham knew about it, maybe he'd bring the Church here," Ezra said.

"Perhaps," Daniel said. "But perhaps not." But he could see why Marshall had chosen this valley for the site of the sawmill. The tree-clad mountainsides offered a plentiful supply of accessible timber suitable for lumber. The strong, rapid current of the river would afford ample waterpower to operate the sawmill. Below him, Marshall and his men were building the diversion dam. It was being built across a northward bend in the stream so that water could be diverted through a depression to the left of the south bank of the river, in what looked like an old riverbed. Once completed, the diversion stream would have sufficient fall to turn the mill wheel.

"We gonna stare at this or go down and see our brethren?" young Henderson Cox asked Daniel.

Daniel nudged Sandy down the mountain. "Patience, Henderson, patience."

The Coloma community consisted of several people in addition to the Mormons hired by Marshall. The entire Wimmer family was there: Peter, his wife Elizabeth Jane, and three children. A double log cabin had been built; the Wimmers live on one side and the hired men lived on the other. Marshall lived in a small cabin on the mountainside, not far away.

Peter Wimmer was in charge of several Indian laborers. When Daniel and his two companions arrived, Wimmer was supervising them in lining both sides of the mill race with heavy plank to prevent the loose sandy soil from filling it again. Indian herders were caring for a flock of sheep, numbering around forty.

"Good to see you Brother Browett," Henry Bigler said when Daniel rode into the work area. Bigler had been out hunting for game to help feed the crew. The other Mormon workers were snaking felled trees down the mountainside with ox-teams. Azariah Smith was making wooden pins for the mill, and helping to bore and mortise the timbers.

"Nice big deer you've got there," Daniel said to Bigler. The deer, a four-point buck, was strewn across the back of Bigler's mule. A domestic Indian was Bigler's hunting companion.

"The men get tired of mutton and fish," Bigler said. "Until a few days ago, we didn't even have salt. Sutter finally sent us some flour, salt, and pumpkins. We've had plenty of peas though, and the supply of sugar and coffee has been good."

Mrs. Wimmer cooked a fine meal, in Daniel's opinion. She cooked by a log-heap and the meal consisted of deer liver, deer steaks, peas, bread, and boiled pumpkins. She fed the white men only; the Indians ate in their own camp. The pitch-rich wood from her fire put out a lot of smoke.

"It's startin' to get cold at nights," the Wimmer woman said as they ate. "There's gonna come a time when I'll have to start cookin' inside."

The men ignored Mrs. Wimmer, for it was just woman's talk. But she persisted. "You've got to stop long enough to build me a chimney."

The workers paid no attention so Daniel asked a question. "Have any problems here with wild Indians?" he asked Bigler. Daniel wondered if the Indians claimed the ground where the men were working. Daniel had had no problems yet with Indians at the gristmill site, but wanted to avoid them if he could.

"Yes, some," Bigler said, talking with a mouthful of pumpkin. "Our mill Indian workers woke us the other night, repeating the words, *'malo hinty, malo hinty.'* That means 'bad Indian, bad Indian'."

Daniel immediately felt a chill. "So were there bad Indians around?" he asked, his curiosity piqued.

"The mill Indians claimed they could see 'em, but we couldn't," Bigler said. "We could hear 'em, but not see 'em."

"So what'd you do?"

"Well, we realized we'd been careless. The night passed without an incident, but the next day we sure enough took stock. Most of the men had left their rifles below at Natoma and we only had four. Mine is in good working condition 'cause I use it for huntin'. But the others needed repair, and we were short on ammunition."

Daniel took on a worried look. "Are you still short?"

Bigler's look was serious. "Next day we commenced to molding bullets and cleaning the rifles," Bigler said. "They're in first class order now, and we had the others brought up from Natoma. And we've put guards out. The bad Indians have left as far as we can figure."

After supper one mill Indian strolled near the Wimmer cabin smoking tobacco.

"That's old Charley, we call him," Bigler said. "He's a good worker, but he believes we're working on a fairy tale."

"What do you mean?" Daniel asked.

"Listen to this," Bigler said. "Hey, Charley. We do good work. We build big mill, mill saw big boards, all by itself. No hand sawing when mill is done."

"Damned lie," the Indian said. He puffed on his tobacco and strolled away.

Bigler laughed. "He thinks it's a lie. He doesn't believe in the white man's magic, but he likes the money Sutter pays him."

22

October 1, 1847

City of Rocks, California Trail

NOT EVEN THE FANCIFUL SHAPES IN the City of Rocks could take Robert's mind off the fact that even with a healthy horse it would take until Christmas to get to the Missouri at the pace they were making. With A. J. still wounded, he rode his mule and didn't mind it as long as each step drew him closer to Hannah and his children. He hoped he wouldn't have to eat his mule before he got to Winter Quarters. There might be nothing else to eat on the prairie in November. He certainly couldn't eat Sister Pixton's mule. He had made a binding promise to deliver the mule to her.

Robert had renamed his riding mule "Digger," after the loathsome Indians that had killed his horse. It was a half-lazy mule and it gave him no little pleasure digging his heels into the mule. All the mules evidenced much stiffness and exhaustion from following the Humboldt. Robert hated the Indians that had shot an arrow into A. J., his horse. A. J. still limped, but in a few days Robert figured he could ride him again. He couldn't imagine eating a horse, but then he couldn't imagine being a Digger either. He hated the Diggers but he knew he shouldn't. After all, they were a fallen Nephite people known as Lamanites. They were just as much his brothers and sisters as the boys in the Battalion, or the Saints in Salt Lake Valley. He just shook his head day after day at the realization that they had fallen into a deeper crevice than he'd ever imagined. The Indians along the Humboldt had fallen so far that they truly were not much more than animals, a fact that he regretted. They lived in huts made of willows and grass. They ran around virtually naked. They collected flies for winter food storage. And they had shot his horse with the intention of eating it.

"That formation looks like the castle above Ledbury in England," said Levi Roberts. Ledbury was a hamlet where Wilford Woodruff had baptized many former members of the United Brethren congregation.

Captain Pace pointed to another formation. "And that looks like the cupola on the capitol building in Springfield, Illinois."

Yesterday the Battalion boys had passed through Goose Creek, where more Diggers had come out of the thick willows wanting to trade gunpowder for an antelope ham. Robert had been the first to run the Indians off. The day before that the former soldiers had camped at Rock Spring, where springs rose on the west side of the trail from under a ledge of rocks. Indians were seen here, too, but not on top of Flatiron Mountain as one would have witnessed on the plains between Fort Leavenworth and Santa Fe.

Emigrants had many names for the rock formations they were now in: Pyramid Valley, Chapel Rocks, Cottage City, and Monumental Rocks. "With a little fancying you can see just about anything you want to imagine," Robert said to his companions. "That there looks like a thatched cottage in Apperley, my home town."

"And that one looks like my mother-in-law," another said. "Short and squatty."

The men had seen hardly any life along the Humboldt and it wasn't much different here, either. There were no animal sounds and no hum of insects to disturb the tomb-like solemnity.

When they entered the City of Rocks not too far from Granite Pass, two cone-shaped rocks rose triumphant from the valley floor to a height of four to six hundred feet. "Those look like my two sisters," another had said. "Tall and authoritative."

Robert made no comment about his two sisters. One was dead, a victim of ague in Council Bluffs. The other was in Salt Lake Valley, still mourning the loss of her only child, and waiting for a husband that was still in California.

The Battalion boys found emigrant names carved on some of the rocks. Dwarf cedars dotted the mountains and hills. "We'll camp here for the night," said Captain Pace when he saw a grassy vale between the rock formations. A few men began gathering the dead limbs of the cedars for a fire.

When the horses and mules had been unsaddled and unpacked, and put out to graze, Robert cradled his musket in his arms.

"Where you going?" Levi asked.

"I'm gonna make certain there're no Diggers hidin' in the rocks," he said. "I'm not gonna lose Sister Pixton's mule, or mine neither."

"You da best verkers I've ever had," a smiling Captain Sutter said to the Mormon workmen when a group of them came to the fort for provisions.

"Thanks," Daniel said as he stuck out his chest just a little. The compliment made him feel better about staying in California. He suspected that by now Elizabeth and Harriet had made it into the Salt Lake Valley.

When the Battalion boys had passed by Sutter's Fort in August, Sutter was just beginning to recoup his losses from the army occupation and the effects from the war with Mexico. All the army volunteers had not pulled out until late September; Sutter was now attempting to suppress the painful year that had just passed. Carding, spinning, weaving, wood cutting, brick making and the building of a lime kiln, and a new bake oven could not absorb all his energies. Sutter's heart was set on his Brighton gristmill and sawmill at Coloma.

"Ven you finish the gristmill?" Sutter asked Daniel.

"I promise before Christmas," Daniel replied.

"Oh, you vonderful," Sutter exclaimed.

Daniel knew Sutter was already bragging to Mariano Vallejo, his California rival, that his three Mormon shoemakers made the best shoes in the state, that his two Mormon tanners supplied more than enough leather, and that the hands at both the sawmill and the gristmill were "the best people I've ever employed." He now had fifteen hundred hides to export.

"How long you been here in California, Captain Sutter?" Daniel asked.

"More than five years," Sutter said with his heavy accent. "If I would have had you Mormon workers, by now I would have made a fortune. Too many of the past workers have been bad people, but you are good people. Thank you for being good people."

"You're welcome," Daniel said.

"If you Mormons stay long enough, I'll soon be out of my difficulties," the captain of the fort said.

Daniel understood. Slowly but surely, Sutter now would be able to pay off his debts and build his empire.

CHAPTER NOTES

City of Rocks is located in southern Idaho, south of the small villages of Elba and Almo, and east of Burley. The author has visited there, following the route the Battalion boys took home. It is known today as the California Immigrant Trail.

23

October 6, 1847

Fort Hall

ROBERT HADN'T SEEN THAT MANY beaver in rivers and creeks as he had traveled the Humboldt, Raft River, and the Snake, so he figured that either they were all trapped out or that the trappers had made a bad decision to locate Fort Hall where they did. But he was glad to be there. And he was glad that all three groups of the Battalion boys were there, too. Captain Jefferson Hunt's group had been the first to arrive, just a day ahead of the Pace group. And the Lytle group had just pulled in.

"I'll take a slab of that bacon," Robert told Commander Grant's wife, a part Indian. Robert figured she was not a Digger, so he decided not to blame her for the arrow that had been shot into A. J. She was much too attractive to be a Digger, dressed not in buckskin but in fashionable eastern wear. She spoke good English, too, apologizing that there was not much left in the way of fresh produce like lettuce and onions because of the lateness of the season.

"We had lettuce out of our fields just a month ago," she said with a helpless gesture.

"That's all right," Robert said. "At least you've got bacon and flour." His mess had run out of flour when they reached the Humboldt Sink. He relished the thoughts of making more of Hannah's sourdough biscuits for he had saved just a pinch of sourdough. He guessed Grant's wife to be either Shoshone or Bannock, the two prevailing tribes of the area.

Robert couldn't decide whether he liked Commander Richard Grant, or not. Grant was tall and angular, and looked more like an Indian than his wife. A former Canadian and mountain man, he dressed in buckskins, carried a knife, and had a full beard. Grant cursed to the men when some of them asked about Fort Bridger, dredging up old wounds between him and former competitors within the Hudson's Bay Company. But the next minute Grant was treating the Battalion boys in a gentlemanly manner, offering provisions at a remarkably fair price. He even had a few potatoes to sell, good ones, too. There was no corn left, but a few turnips were available. Peas were long gone.

"Have all the pork you want," Grant told them. "I don't fancy it myself. It's the worst insult to a true mountain man. Pork's not a food of the mountains; it's the food of towns and settlements. Lots of *mangeurs de lard* pass through here."

Robert looked puzzled, not knowing French.

The Indian woman laughed. "French for lard eaters," she said.

Grant seemed impressed with the travels of the Battalion, the fact the ex-soldiers had walked all the way from Council Bluffs to California. "You men've got the hair of a bear," he said in a complimentary tone. "I hope you slung lots of Galena pills at them Mexicans."

Robert understood that terminology. Galena lead from England was the preferred lead of the mountain man. Not one of the Battalion boys brought up the fact that they had not been in an actual battle.

"Brigham Young must be buffalo witted," Grant said as he began talking about the Salt Lake Valley. "I'd advise you boys ta go back ta California, or up ta Oregon. You'll never raise a tater where Brigham's taken yer people. Or wheat or lettuce. There's no shinin' time down there. *The Great Salt Lake* ain't worth a green frog pelt. Brigham's bobbled the buffalo chip all right."

Robert grimaced again. Grant had poisoned Ingersoll's mind with the same logic. All the way to Fort Hall Robert had tried to imagine what the true nature of the valley would be, and what kind of farm he'd eventually own when he settled there. Right now it didn't sound too promising.

Grant seemed angry that the Battalion boys purchased none of his whiskey, rum, or other alcoholic spirits. "Waugh! Spring loose for some of this medicine water," he coaxed. "It'll tide ya over."

A few of the Battalion boys had discovered the fort's guest register. Abner Blackburn, Robert Bliss, and Nathaniel Jones signed it before Grant erupted, cursing with colorful mountain man language. "You don't all have ta sign; I'd have to buy a new book. You ain't all got the ability to write, do you?"

When Grant had calmed down, Robert picked up the Fort Hall diary and thumbed through it. Samuel Brannan had signed it on his way through. A year earlier the man who had pioneered a trail from the Sierras to Oregon had signed it—Lindsay Applegate.

"How far does this go back?" Robert asked Grant as he flipped towards page one.

"The Hudson's Bay Company was on the earth before Christ," Grant said in a sacrilegious tone. "Look for yourself, but don't write any more names."

Later in the evening, as the Battalion boys made camp among the willows and trees that lined the Snake River near the place where the Blackfoot River and the Port Neuf River emptied into the Snake, Robert had a clear understanding of the history of Fort Hall. Hudson's Bay Company had established the fort in the bottoms of the Snake River in 1834 through the efforts of a young businessman from New England by the name of Nathaniel Wyeth. He had brought three thousand dollars worth of goods to trade at the Mountain Man Rendezvous that year, but the company, being in financial difficulties, refused to accept Wyeth's goods. Seeing no other way out of his difficult situation, Wyeth moved a little farther westward and began construction of a trading post that he later named after the oldest member of the New England trading company that had financed Wyeth's enterprise. Hudson's Bay Company retaliated by building a trading post of their own near the junction of the

Snake River with the Boise River, naming the post Fort Boise. Its purpose was to simply put Fort Hall out of business. They did precisely that by using the almost limitless resources of the great English company to outbid Wyeth in the payment for furs and underbid him in the sale of goods to the Indians. Wyeth sold out to the Hudson's Bay Company in 1837 at a thirty-thousand-dollar loss. The English flag thus flew over Fort Hall until last year when the United States gained possession of all land south of the forty-ninth parallel by a treaty with England. Richard Grant had been commander of the fort since the year Wyeth left, and still worked for the Hudson's Bay Company. The fort was losing money on the declining fur trade, but was doing a big business with emigrants on their way to the Willamette Valley in Oregon, and to California.

The fort was built of unburned adobe brick in the form of a square with towers at the corners. Its walls were about twelve feet high, and so were the walls of the two-story houses inside. Commander Grant's horses numbered around two hundred, a mixture of brood mares, geldings, and a few stallions.

The Battalion boys weren't the only ones camping near Fort Hall. In addition to Oregon and California emigrants, there were some Shoshone warriors holding a dance around a scalp they had taken from the Blackfeet. The emigrants were worried about rumors that the Blackfeet, Crows, and Sioux had banded together to kill all the white people they could. Robert wondered why the Diggers weren't included in that group.

Robert now knew the route to the Salt Lake Valley. In the morning he would follow the Portneuf River south about twenty-five or thirty miles until it forked. He would take the right-hand fork, a marshy river or creek that wound another thirty or thirty-five miles through a pretty valley. Then he would have to strike out over a mountain pass, but not a bad one, and it would lead to the Malad River and the Bear River. The trail would be faint, used by former mountain men and by the Indians. But it would eventually lead to the Salt Lake Valley, the place where Commander Grant and Sam Brannan said nothing would grow. In ten days or less he would see his sister, Elizabeth. And he would find out the real reason Hannah had been left behind.

CHAPTER NOTES

Although around a hundred Mormon Battalion men passed through Fort Hall on the way to the Salt Lake Valley during the fall of 1847, only four actually signed the register: Nathaniel Jones, Abner Blackburn, Reddick Newton Allred, and Robert S. Bliss. The Hunt, Pace, and Lytle groups were in Fort Hall about October 5th and 6th. As portrayed in this chapter, Samuel Brannan signed the register too, either on his way to meet up with Brigham Young on the Green River, or on his return trip to California.

In those days, the correct spelling of the Portneuf River was "Port Neuf." The river winds through Lava Hot Springs and McCammon before joining the Marsh Creek near Inkom, and then dumping into the Snake River near the old Fort Hall site. Several descendents of Robert Harris currently reside in the area. The author of this book was raised in McCammon. My grandfather, Joseph Memorial Harris, homesteaded near McCammon. His father, Robert Joseph Harris, homesteaded near Portage, Utah. Robert Harris helped settle the Portage area in 1869 when he established a farm at Woodruff, Idaho, near Portage. It is believed that Robert named the settlement after Wilford Woodruff. After Robert Harris and the Battalion left Fort Hall, they traveled past the future settlements of McCammon, Woodruff, and Portage on their way to the Salt Lake Valley.

24

October 15, 1847

Near the Salt Lake Valley

ROBERT TRIED TO PICTURE THE SALT Lake Valley in his mind, but the closer he got the farther from reality he realized he was. He'd heard of startling contrasts, not knowing which to believe: Was the soil rich and black, or poor and alkaline? Was the grass tall and green, or short and brown? Were the mountains inviting, or the deserts forbidding? Were the Indians friendly, or hostile? Were they like the Diggers on the Humbolt, or like the Plains Indians on the Santa Fe Trail? Was the Fort Hall commander right about the bad growing conditions, or was he wrong?

Robert had long ago concluded that the American continent was a land of strange contrasts. He felt lost here; for certain it wasn't England and it wasn't Illinois. If Hannah were here, he'd force himself to get used to this strange country and like it. But if she weren't, he decided to wait to adjust another day. As the lake of salt came into view for the first time, shimmering to the west, he concluded that the lake was a joke of nature just as the Humboldt sink had been, and just as the deserts in New Mexico and Arizona had been. The Great Salt Lake—the name itself was an aura, strange and mysterious, much like the Dead Sea in the Bible. The lake of salt lay silent, moody and withdrawn, uniting a raw sense of desolation with a haunting sense of loveliness. Three rivers, alive with fresh water, dumped into the lake, only to become enmeshed with the lake's salty brine. The Bear River of the north dumped into the Bear River Bay, the Weber River found its way to the lake farther south, and a third river—named the Jordan by the Mormons—emptied into the lake a few miles southwest of the Salt Lake City settlement.

At Fort Hall Robert had learned of the bizarre folklore connected with the lake of salt—maelstroms ravaging on its surface, great vents opening on the bottom of the lake to drain its water horribly into the bowels of the earth, appalling monsters bellowing on its surface and making forays upon its shores, noxious vapors rising from its surface to bring instant death to birds flying above, and corrosive salts burning those who dared swim in its waters. There was an island in the lake. It, too, had its own folklore—mysterious white Indians once lived there; so had gigantic Indians, riding on elephants.

Robert felt uncomfortable with all these stories and began to wonder if

Brigham Young had been in his right mind to settle near the lake. Spaniards and mountain men had explored it, but avoided it. Now the Mormons had fled to it despite the salt waters and the blazing deserts of the lake's own making. The Donner Party had made a mistake in crossing its desert; had Brigham made a mistake settling here? The lake was everywhere bulwarked with mud morasses and salt marshes. It looked uninviting, certainly a stark contrast to the lush Sacramento Valley where Sam Brannan was still whimpering, upset that the Mormons were not settling there.

Commander Grant had described the waters of the Great Salt Lake as both grayish green and leaden gray. His wife had described them as bright emerald. Others had called them sapphire and turquoise, and even cobalt. Robert decided they were all correct, depending on the time of the year, the weather, and the vantage point from which the waters were seen. Under a clear October sky, the lake seemed serene enough today, but Robert imagined what the lake might be like on a cold, windy day in the winter or spring—with smashing four-foot waves, twisting and tilting under the surging green brine.

The view to the east was better. Robert crossed several streams rushing from the mighty ramparts of the Wasatch Mountains. The mountains were not only massive but also towering, their snow-capped peaks glistening in the brisk October air. Innumerable peaks like pyramids stretched toward the Heavens. On the opposite side of the valley, west of the lake of salt, rose a lesser, parallel range of mountains. Was this the great valley of promise, held in reserve by the hand of God as a resting place for the Saints? Where Zion could finally be built, far away from the enemies of righteousness?

To tired eyes accustomed to the dry emptiness of the Humboldt, the remoteness of California, the bleakness of the San Pedro River country, and the barrenness of the Santa Fe Trail, the peacefulness of the surrounding mountains gave Robert pause for soul-searching reflection. If it were not for the fact that Hannah and his children were not here, he would be home. With all his might he began to wish that the message in Hannah's letter were not true, that at the last minute there had been a change in plans and she were actually here. The valley had withheld its secrets for centuries, undiscovered until Jim Bridger first looked upon it in 1824. Was the Salt Lake Valley holding another secret—his wife and family? Where might the valley be hiding Hannah and Elizabeth? He shuddered to think that his family might be camped in a wagon box up one of the canyons he was passing. He preferred to think the Church, because Hannah was the wife of a Battalion volunteer, had already built her a cabin.

The sun's brilliant orange ball was slowly disappearing into the lake of salt when Robert and the other Battalion boys saw their first Mormon settler. The man had been herding cattle near a creek and he was waving his hands to attract their attention.

"You must be more Battalion boys coming down from Fort Hall way," the settler said. Robert figured he was getting close to the Salt Lake settlement. Captain Jefferson Hunt and his men had beat Robert's group into the valley by a few days, and so had a small group led by P. C. Merrill.

"And you look like Perrigrine Sessions," Robert told the man. It was a stroke of good luck to see this Mormon. Perrigrine was the oldest son of Patty Sessions, the midwife. If anyone knew where Elizabeth might be, it would be Perrigrine or Patty.

"That's right," Perrigrine said. "And who might you be?"

Robert felt slighted that Sessions didn't recognize him. After all, he had shaved the night before and even bathed in a creek. Perhaps it was his Californio clothing that made him unrecognizable, and his Mexican-style hat. "I'm Robert Harris. Elizabeth Browett is my sister."

Sessions squinted at Robert. "Oh, yes. Sorry. I believe I met you a time or two in Nauvoo. I suppose you're looking for your sister."

"I am, and my wife, too," Robert said as he crossed his fingers.

"Your sister was in my company," Sessions said. "But not your wife and children. We were one of the last companies to leave Winter Quarters. We've been here only three weeks. You'll find Elizabeth and Harriet Browett somewhere in the valley, probably at the fort."

"They've built a fort already?" Captain Pace asked.

"Yep, and a good one too," Sessions said. He went on to say that the pioneers laid the stockade out on August second and worked throughout the month to enclose the ten-acre fort. "That's probably where you'd find women without husbands, inside that fort."

Robert tried to hide his disappointment. No Hannah. And no children.

He still clung to the faint hope that they had joined a company that left afterward, but it was faint, indeed. The trek back to Winter Quarters with Captain Pace and the other men was becoming a distinct reality. For an instant Robert let his eyes drift to the west where the sun had disappeared, toward California. It had been a pleasant autumn day and the men had made twenty miles. Last evening they had camped at a place called Fort Buenaventura near the confluence of the Ogden and Weber Rivers.

"I suppose Brigham Young by now is tired of hearing complaints," Robert said out of the side of his mouth. "But I'd like to ask him why my wife and family didn't make it."

Sessions chuckled. "If you want to register a complaint with him, you'll have to do it in Winter Quarters."

"What?"

"Brother Brigham left Salt Lake several weeks ago. So did Wilford Woodruff and several of the other brethren. They're going to winter on the Missouri again and lead more companies of Saints to the valley next spring."

"Shucks, and I do so want to give him a piece of my mind."

"It'll have to wait."

"How far to Salt Lake City?" he asked Sessions.

"A good twelve miles," Sessions answered. "You're welcome to camp here. Good water in the creek."

For a moment Robert entertained the thoughts of pushing on, with or without the other men. But a night with no moon would make the trail hard to follow. And it would be difficult to locate Elizabeth in pitch darkness.

Robert dismounted. "I think we ought to accept Brother Sessions' invitation and camp here for the night," he told Captain Pace. Pace had already learned from Sessions that his wife had not made it either.

Pace dismounted and stood next to Robert. "We accept your invitation to camp here with you. Would you be so kind as to tell us about the trail from here to the Missouri?"

Captain Pace seemed edgy the next morning, but Robert knew that could be said of him, too. With the chance of finding their wives and families in Salt Lake reduced to a sliver of hope, the conversation turned to the trip back to the Missouri as the men hurried toward the new Mormon settlement. They were riding in the shadows of the mountains. It was early; the sunlight had yet to peek over the Wasatch Range.

"It won't be any picnic getting to Winter Quarters, boys," Captain Pace said as the trickle of horses and pack mules struck out. "We've got to get through the plains before the snow is too deep and the temperature too cold. Indians might know how to survive in that country, but not us."

Sessions had given the Battalion boys a detailed description of the route between Winter Quarters and Salt Lake. Just like Brigham Young's Pioneer Company, Sessions had followed the trail west just north of the broad, silt-clogged Platte River. He had described how it rose almost imperceptibly through the Nebraska prairies and onto the grass-covered High Plains. Past

Fort Laramie the trail climbed gradually through an undulating landscape covered with sagebrush and bunch grass toward the snow-capped ranges of the Rocky Mountains. It crossed the Continental Divide at an unprepossessing place called South Pass, a beautiful but wind-swept upland between the mountains. Sessions said that a beaver trapper had discovered this broad, flat corridor through the Rockies in 1812. After crossing South Pass, the Mormon wagon companies had come to Fort Bridger. Sessions described crossing the beautiful Bear River, trailing southwest through Echo Canyon, and then following the Donner Trail through Emigration Canyon into the Salt Lake Valley.

"What'll we do for food?" Robert asked Pace.

Sessions had already told the men that they would be lucky to get few, if any, provisions from the destitute Saints in Salt Lake and that they ought to make a beeline to Fort Bridger and try to obtain provisions there. Sessions said that all the pioneers had reached the valley behind schedule, making it late for planting crops. Most were lucky to plant potatoes and barely got enough seed back for next year's plantings. It had rained that first day that Brigham arrived in the valley, a good omen, for many had convinced them that it never rained there in the summer. The Saints had planted buckwheat, corn, wheat, and beans too. Everything had shot right up through the rich soil. Brigham Young had already exhorted the Saints to faithfulness and industry, offering them fifty cents a bushel for corn, a dollar twenty-five for wheat, and twenty-five cents for oats. Robert could see hundreds of acres of winter wheat. The Saints had found good timber, too, up the canyons, and used it for the fort.

"We might have to make do with what we bought at Fort Hall," Pace said. "Make your visits short. We'll leave in the morning shortly after sunrise."

"Where'll we meet?" Robert asked the captain.

"At the fort," Captain Pace said.

Robert began seeing tracks. The Indians here in the valley were Great Basin Utes. Most of them still traveled on foot and had already been labeled as "diggers" for their propensity to live off ants, grasshoppers, crickets, roots, seeds, and weeds. He wondered how the Mormons were getting along with them.

"Come on, A. J.," he said as he kicked his horse in the ribs. "Let's see what the Great Salt Lake City looks like."

Robert had heard in Fort Hall that the Salt Lake Valley was a good hundred miles long and forty miles wide. Right now it seemed two or three times that large. He began to see evidence of a city in rough form: streets laid out in exact north-south east-west quadrants, large city lots laid out so that all streets had equal frontage, crude log homes, plowed fields, irrigation ditches, and evidence of a meager harvest. There was evidence, too, that former Battalion boys were here—soldiers who had been in the sick detachment and sent to Pueblo. They had built small Southwest-style adobe homes and corrals out of dried mud. Wagons had been converted into temporary homes, too. A bowery for worship services had been erected in the center of a public square. He could see a gristmill, granaries, a store, a school, and even a cemetery. Dogs barked, cattle lowed, and sheep bleated all around. Blacksmiths were hammering out

wagon repairs. A whole new sound of industry and a budding sense of excite-

ment dented the daunting silence of the sprawling valley floor. It was the

sound of new life and a new future for the Saints.

With winter coming on, Robert wondered how the Saints would fare.

The newly arising city looked promising but bleak, but he knew that it was

probably just as bleak in Winter Quarters. Perrigrine Sessions had said the city

had already been laid out large enough to accommodate six thousand people,

that the soil—although at first it had broken many of the plows—was deep,

rich, black, and mixed with sand. Brigham Young had already established a

system of land distribution: properties were assigned to obedient followers of

the faith, a reward for commitment and endurance. With Hannah not here

and no idea as to when he could bring her across the plains, Robert wondered

if any of the choice locations would be left. Brigham already had his, right next

to the temple plot. So did other members of the Twelve.

Robert and the returning soldiers weren't the sunburned, weather-beaten

novelty he thought they'd be, even with their California ponies and Californio-

style clothing. People here were too busy trying to figure out how to survive

the coming winter. Captain Jefferson Hunt and his men had been here for a

week. Sessions had said Hunt was sorely disappointed that Brigham Young had

left for Winter Quarters again; Brigham was the only person in the Church

who could approve of Hunt's enlistment scheme. So a frustrated Hunt volun-

teered to lead a small party back to California to obtain seeds and animals for the new Salt Lake Valley settlers who faced the winter with a declining food supply.

The Saints the Battalion boys saw were friendly enough though, and tried to answer questions about the soldiers' families as best they could. One man said there were more than two thousand Saints in the valley.

Where was Elizabeth? Where was anyone he knew? An old neighbor? English converts? Former United Brethren people? He wondered what he could say to her to express his sorrow over the death of Moroni. Would she be in deep depression, angry over the loss? Or by now would she have bounced back? Regrettably, she had two personalities. Most of the time she was happy, vivacious, and upbeat. For a year she had been a beast to live with following the realization that Daniel had been asked to take a plural wife. But when she decided to accept the doctrine, Harriet had become her absolute best friend. He wondered, too, how she would take the news that Daniel had stayed in California to work. There would be no in-between; she would either support it enthusiastically or fly off the handle.

The fort was built of hewn timber with walls of sun-dried bricks surrounding ten acres of ground south of the temple lot. It had been built in three sections, all enclosed. Along the walls, strewn together, were adobe houses. Each house had a porthole for defense against Indians. Robert hoped Elizabeth and Harriet occupied one of the houses. Not far from the fort Robert could see a camp of Indians.

"You have an Elizabeth Browett here?" Robert asked a man at the fort.

"Oh, yes, she's here," the man said. He identified himself as Joseph Noble, a leader of fifty in the same company Sessions had been in. "She was in Asa Barton's ten. She'll be anxious to see you. Are you her husband?"

"No, her brother," Robert responded.

Word was now spreading throughout the fort that a new group of Battalion boys had arrived. Some of the settlers began congregating on the dirt streets, looking for someone they might know. Others were congregating at an old military tent, provided by the Battalion boys from Pueblo, that was being used for the first school in the valley.

"Robert!"

The voice was recognizable and it sent chills down Robert's spine. He spun his horse around to see Elizabeth running toward him with Harriet following. He jumped off A. J. and swooped Elizabeth into his arms.

Elizabeth gave him a long embrace and then drew herself back, asking the inevitable question. "Where's Daniel?" Her anxious green eyes were scanning the other Battalion boys and the city blocks to the north where they had entered the city.

Robert drew on his courage. He didn't want to do it, but it was up to him to give Elizabeth the bad news. There was no sugar coating the pill. "He stayed in California. Brigham Young sent word that he wanted half of us to stay there and work for a year. Because he had no children …"

Elizabeth cut him off. Tears welled up in her eyes and spilled down her cheeks. "No! No! This *can't* be true!"

Harriet began to sob, too, and the two women held each other for several seconds. Harriet finally said, "We feared this might happen. We know about Brigham's letter."

"We camped last night with Brother Perrigrine Sessions," Robert said. "He told me that Hannah is still back at Winter Quarters. Tell me it's not so."

Elizabeth merely stared at the ground but Harriet answered. "Yes, it's true. Sorry. She got left behind."

"But why?" Robert queried, realizing now that they had exchanged disappointing information. "I thought the Battalion families would be given top priority."

"*None* of the company captains wanted to be *burdened* with all your children," Elizabeth said in a bitter tone.

Harriet took a different tone. "It was a difficult trip for us as adults. Hannah has a newborn. It would have been a risk."

Robert snorted in derision. "I expected her to be here." He tended to agree with Elizabeth's version of why his family had been left behind. He had already seen a few children less than a year old among the Salt Lake City settlers. They had made it across the plains. Hannah could have done the same thing in his view, provided she had the help the Church should have given her. "I wish she were here," Robert said three times.

"Maybe she'll come next summer," Harriet said.

"You can winter with us," Elizabeth said. "We need *someone* to take care of us."

Robert shook his head. He hadn't said anything about Moroni yet. He feared that if he did, Elizabeth would be worse. "I'll be headin' out tomorrow at daybreak. There're several of us Battalion boys that're in the same fix." He pointed to the other men on horseback, still looking for the slim possibilities that their wives and children had actually made it, but struck with the probability that they would have to continue on to Winter Quarters.

"But it's the middle of *October*," Elizabeth said dejectedly. "Winter's almost here. You'd *die* trying to reach the Missouri."

There was a definite chill in the air, and a cold wind was blowing from the west. Robert shivered at the burden he was facing, to reach Hannah by Christmas. "My mind's made up. I want to be with Hannah and the children."

"Bah!" Elizabeth countered. "Stay here and take care of your sister. There're bad Indians out there. I need protection."

Robert cast a glance at Harriet, who nodded in agreement. "There are Indians, but we've got men here at the fort to protect us."

Elizabeth returned Harriet an icy stare.

CHAPTER NOTES

According to the William B. Pace journal, Robert Harris' group of returning Battalion boys met Perrigrine Sessions on 15 October 1847. Sessions was camped on the site of present Bountiful city. His mother, Patty Sessions, the famous midwife, recorded in her journal that Battalion soldiers traveled through the Sessions camp on their way to Salt Lake.

25

"I HATE IT HERE," ELIZABETH SAID over and over. She stomped out of her little adobe hut looking for a pail of water.

The hut had a hardened dirt floor and a dirt roof. Its only door consisted of cloth greased with fat. The entire fort and each house or hut had been built with the help of the Mormon Battalion soldiers who had returned from Pueblo. The fort compound was alive with people getting ready for the winter.

"Don't pay any attention to her," Harriet said to Robert over a breakfast of bread and the last potatoes the two women had. The food had been cooked outside on a sagebrush fire. Harriet spread jam on the bread made of serviceberries mixed with pulverized grasshoppers, a gift from the Utah Indians. "She's been up and down for months. She loved the valley when we first got here. She started hating it the minute she heard about Daniel staying in California. By this time next week she'll be loving the valley again."

"Has she been like this ever since …?"

"Ever since we lost Moroni," Harriet said. "I don't know who suffered more, her or Moroni."

Harriet went on to say that the typical Winter Quarters diet consisted of cornbread, salt, bacon, and a little milk. As a result of such a diet day after day with no vegetables, many children—and adults, too—suffered from black scurvy. "Poor little Moroni—black streaks began to appear up his nails; his pain was excruciating, especially in the ends of the fingers and toes. We ran out of raw potatoes. Poultices from potatoes can be used to combat scurvy, but we had none. I think little Moroni welcomed death so great was his pain."

Robert winced in pain himself as he listened. Winter Quarters had been called "Misery Bottoms," and it wasn't hard to understand why. When Elizabeth returned he told her how terrible he felt over Moroni's death. She became unhinged again for a few minutes. That, combined with the news about Daniel, made her almost unbearable and her depression was obvious. Gone were her personality traits such as a spirit of the wind and her life-giving miracle of fresh air, and gone was her perpetual ability to be happy. She reminded him of California racehorses that had spurted out in front and then finished far behind the winner. Gone was her chatterbox mentality. Instead, she was quick-tempered about her unpleasant living circumstances—out of a wagon box—and there was no patience tendered to either him or Harriet. He felt sorry for Harriet, who would have to endure her alone until Daniel's return next year. Robert wished Daniel had come to the Salt Lake Valley with him. Daniel was probably the only person on earth who had the ability to snap her out of this mood she was in. She needed a husband. She needed another child.

"There's not much water left," Elizabeth said when she came back into the adobe hut. "We have to haul it from the creek. Be nice to have a man here to do such chores."

"I'll fill up all the pails," Robert said. "Sorry I can't stay longer."

When Robert asked about life in Winter Quarters, Elizabeth criticized the experience with sharp words, telling about the lack of food and Indians stealing livestock. Death and sickness had been rampant, with Moroni being one of only hundreds of deaths. There had been successive waves of ague, typhoid fever, dysentery, pneumonia, and scurvy that had descended on the Mormon camps not only in Winter Quarters but elsewhere in Iowa. Harriet talked in more positive terms. Streets had been laid out on a grid pattern. There had been a welfare store, shops, woodworking huts, blacksmiths' forges, and much else. The women taught the children, babysat, spun yarn, worked in boarding houses, wove baskets and flour sacks, and made and sold wine from elderberries. Children in dugout schools learned spelling from Noah Webster's *1783 Spelling Book,* were taught singing and elocution, and took part in mock trials arranged by their teachers. Winter Quarters had been a grim experience, but it was not all misery. All ages enjoyed the parties when cakes, pies, and sweetmeats of hominy and maple syrup were produced.

Similar responses came when the conversation drifted to the trip from Winter Quarters to the Salt Lake Valley. Elizabeth talked about the burden of putting on sodden shoes every morning to continue the seemingly never-ending trek across the plains and mountains, shivering all night without a fire, nursing sick children, trying to find edible roots on the prairie, and coaxing other pioneers' whimpering children from their beds to milk cows. She also complained about the people who almost gave up, acting like they wanted to return to Nauvoo. Robert could tell that she had possessed a desperate motive to reach the Salt Lake Valley in order to meet up with Daniel.

Harriet, on the other hand, made the pioneer trip seem almost glamorous. In her view, the enforcement of trail discipline had been a blessing in disguise. It had been a discipline to which the Oregon and California immigrants would never have submitted. Her company had moved like a village on wheels, with a remarkable cohesiveness. Elizabeth talked of dissension, pedantic fussiness of company leaders, and too many long "nooning" stops. Harriet seemed to appreciate the asset of Fremont's maps and Lansford Hasting's *Guide*. Elizabeth called them woefully inadequate. Harriet talked of friendly Indians, even trading with some of them. Elizabeth talked of all the frightening experiences, beginning with the Pawnees at Loup Fork, the gutted remains of a government station near a Pawnee village caused by a Sioux raid, Indians stealing horses, and the burning of the prairie by the Indians to harass both the Mormons and the emigrants on their way to Oregon. Harriet talked about the refreshing water of the Sweetwater River and the impressive sight of

Independence Rock. Elizabeth told of holding her nose to avoid the stink of shallow alkaline lakes and gagging on brackish water when she put it to her lips. She also complained of how the bitter, dry winds had not only split her lips but split her furniture, too.

Elizabeth complained that nearly all the United Brethren converts had been left behind. Harriet countered by saying that John Benbow had been in Brigham Young's Pioneer Company as a captain over fifty, and that several English converts were planning on the trip next summer. Elizabeth made the charge that the only reason Benbow had made it was because he received preferential treatment by Wilford Woodruff, to which Harriet scoffed. Benbow had always shown strong leadership qualities, and that's why he was chosen.

Robert asked many of the same questions the Battalion boys had asked about the route, and then the women began asking him questions about California and his experiences in the Battalion. He concluded by saying that the war against Mexico had been a complete victory; all of California and New Mexico had been sheared off the Republic of Mexico and absorbed into the American dream of manifest destiny. Technically, the land Brigham Young had divided among the Saints still belonged to Mexico, but Robert reckoned it soon would be ceded to the United States.

Breakfast was finished and Robert took a morning stroll through the fort with Elizabeth and Harriet.

"Is California really the paradise Samuel Brannan says it is?" Harriet asked.

For Elizabeth's sake, Robert fibbed. "I'd say not. You've heard about the Donner Party haven't you? You might face a tough winter here, but you won't have forty feet of snow on top of you."

Elizabeth's sour mood continued, however. "Brannan must have had some kind of influence over Brigham Young. Brigham wouldn't have caused Daniel and the others to stay in California otherwise."

"I've met Sam Brannan," Robert said. "He didn't impress me or Daniel at all. My guess is that Daniel will work for Captain Sutter and not go to San Francisco where Brannan lives."

"I *don't* like this one bit," Elizabeth said. "Daniel's stuck in California and I'm stuck here without my husband." Next she started complaining about the swarms of mice that had infested every adobe hut in the fort, the threat of wild animals such as cougars and bears, and the millions of black crickets that had covered the ground in late summer. She said the Indians conducted cricket hunts, running them into traps twelve feet square made of sagebrush and greasewood, and killing them with fire. The Indians rubbed off their wings and legs and ate them by the thousands.

Robert tried a new tactic to brighten up Elizabeth. "You'll never guess who ended up in the American army to fight the Mexicans."

"I guess it *wasn't* Brigham Young, but it should have been. He's the one who took my *husband* away to serve in the army."

Robert went pale for a second or two. The way he remembered it, Elizabeth had encouraged Daniel's enlistment. "Henry Eagles," he said.

"Henry was in Fort Leavenworth before we were."

Elizabeth shrugged her shoulders in pretended disinterest but Harriet took on a curiosity.

"How'd he get there?" Harriet asked.

Robert told the story of the day Henry brought a wagonload of flour to the Battalion while the soldiers were still in Missouri, and the encounter with Colonel Price.

"Where is he now?" Harriet responded when Robert had finished the story. He had traced Henry from Fort Leavenworth to Santa Fe.

"He's probably out of the army, just like us," Robert explained. "He was either still in Santa Fe or there was the possibility he could have been used for the invasion of Mexico."

"I hope he doesn't show up *here*," Elizabeth said with a scowl. "He'd just be one more big hungry mouth to feed. He probably has a *Mexican* wife by now, knowing him."

Robert hadn't asked, but he knew the obvious. Katherine and Annie hadn't made it to the valley either. And neither had Levi Robert's family. In all, he figured there were at least thirty Battalion boys who were going to have to travel in his group back to Winter Quarters. Sixteen others, under the leadership of Captain P. C. Merrill, had already left the valley. He also knew without asking that there was not enough food in the valley to give much of anything to him or any of the other Battalion members who would have to leave by tomorrow.

Robert continued to tell his soldier stories: crossing the prairies and deserts to Santa Fe, learning how to kill and butcher buffalo, describing Toothless the sutler and former mountain man, drinking buffalo tea water, the battle of the bulls in Arizona, taking Tucson, soldiering in California, the relentless efforts to get him to re-enlist for another year, and his trip to the Salt Lake Valley. He also told them about Daniel's tormented decision to stay in California, and that Daniel likely was working at Sutter's Fort by now.

"I suppose there're Indians in California," Elizabeth said with a mournful look.

"There're Indians everywhere in America," Robert said.

"I don't trust the Indians here," Elizabeth said. "Brother Brigham says he wants to teach them agriculture, but it'll never work. They're too lazy and have backward ways. I just hope they leave us alone."

Harriet told Robert that no Indians lived in the Salt Lake Valley, which is one of the reasons Brigham Young chose the area. It was a land nobody wanted, not even the Indians. There were, however, three main groups of Indians not too far away—the Goshiutes to the northwest, Paiutes to the south, and Utes to the east. She said they frequently brought children they had stolen from other Indian tribes to the pioneers, offering them for sale. If the whites could not pay for the children, the Indians threatened to torture and kill the children.

Robert described his experiences with the Diggers along the Humboldt.

Elizabeth said the valley Indians had strange habits. They plucked out their beards and eyebrows, were afraid of witches, and believed in making medicine on paper to kill people. She said she had never seen an Indian with a baldhead, not even on the plains, and very few had any decayed teeth.

"Are you certain you have to leave tomorrow?" Harriet asked, obviously tired of talking about Indians.

Elizabeth gave him a mournful look.

"The sooner the better," he answered. "Even with horses and mules, it's going to take us well into December."

"We have nothing to give you," Elizabeth said. "And neither does anyone else."

Robert almost choked. His sister had rarely spoken so sharply to him. He could think of only a childhood spat or two, and the time she was struggling with polygamy. If it weren't for the fact that he now knew that everyone had already been rebaptized by the bishops here in the valley, he would baptize her himself and hold her under for an extra hour or two.

Harriet cleared her throat. "I'd be happy to share our flour."

"Don't give him too much," Elizabeth said sharply.

"You'll be able to buy flour at Fort Bridger in a few days," Harriet said almost helplessly.

"How far?" Robert asked, feeling hungry before he started.

"A hundred and fifteen miles."

"You'll have to sleep on the floor," Elizabeth said. "Or outside."

Robert laughed. "I haven't had a bed for more than a year. I'm so used to sleeping on the hard ground that I wouldn't get a minute's sleep if you offered me the softest feather bed in the valley."

The next morning, Robert's sister was in a better mood. She fixed her sad green eyes on him and said, "I'm sorry I was such a grouch yesterday."

Robert took a deep breath, a sigh of mystified relief. He couldn't imagine how someone like Elizabeth could take a hundred and eighty degree turn in her personality so fast, but he was grateful. "That's okay," he said, taking her by the hand. He was momentarily spellbound by the depth of her watery gaze. "I understand your frustration."

"I should keep my chin up more," she said. "I've always preached it to others, but sometimes I don't practice it myself."

Robert felt a pang of truth in her statement. He answered her by saying, "I want you to know how bad I feel about Moroni. I've never lost a child. It would be devastating."

Elizabeth gave Robert a squeeze of the hand. "It means Daniel and I have got to start over. I guess that's part of my frustration. Now I've got to wait another year, but I'll do it. I'll put on my happy face."

He framed his sister in a fervent stare. His voice cracked. "It's time to go," he said. "I've got to meet the Battalion boys soon. I hate to go; I'm tired of traveling. This is a nice valley."

Last evening there had been a reunion of sorts. Captain Pace had gathered together his group, including Robert, with several of the Battalion men who had made it to the Salt Lake Valley from Pueblo. They discussed the results of the war with Mexico, Kearny's return to the states with Fremont, and other experiences.

"There's a saying going around," Elizabeth said, her voice sounding a little louder and more relaxed. "The valley is a place where we Mormons can wive, thrive, work, and worship."

Elizabeth had finally said something that made Robert laugh. "Wive and thrive?"

Elizabeth laughed too. And then she turned serious again. "But Daniel has to be here to wive and thrive, doesn't he?"

"Yes, he does," Robert admitted. "I'd like to go back to California and get him, but my heart tells me to go to Hannah. Besides, Daniel will be here next summer—probably a wealthy man by then."

Elizabeth chuckled and winked at her brother. "I don't care if he returns wealthy or not. I just hope he gets here in time for us to plant some crops and start our farm life over."

Last evening the two women had told Robert how the pioneers had planted thirty-five acres of buckwheat, corn, oats, and other grains within the first eight days, and that the crops grew nicely despite the late start. Another eight acres of garden seed had been planted, too. Some pioneer companies hadn't arrived in the valley until late September and early October, far too late to plant anything. Food was projected to be woefully inadequate with everyone now praying for a mild winter. The pioneers were looking forward to the next growing season with enthusiasm, however.

Robert's chin twitched as he remembered the conversation. He became emotional again. "It'll be nice if our two families could share a farm again. Daniel will bring some livestock home from California with him next year. This place has promise. I'll bet Elder Woodruff and the others didn't want to go back."

Elizabeth nodded a quick agreement. "Heber C. Kimball's exact words were, 'I wish to God we had not got to return. Elder Kimball and Elder Woodruff didn't have their families here either; they were left behind in Winter Quarters, too."

Robert's voice hardened in frustration. A cold logic overcame him. "But they didn't march in the Mormon Battalion. Got to go."

"I'll pray for you," Elizabeth said as she gave Robert a last hug.

"I will, every night and morning," Robert promised.

"Pray for good weather for us," Elizabeth added. "The winters here in the mountains are supposed to be cold, colder than Nauvoo."

"And you pray for me," Robert countered. "Pray that I don't freeze to death between here and Winter Quarters."

CHAPTER NOTES

According to author Norma Baldwin Ricketts, in her book, *Mormon Battalion, U.S. Army of the West* (Utah State University Press, Logan, Utah, 1996), there were twenty-nine men who left Salt Lake Valley on 18 October 1847. These men had to goal to reach their families at Winter Quarters. Their names, as listed by Ricketts, are: Reddick N. Allred, Elisah Averett, Jeduthan Averett, Robert Bliss, Edward Bunker, Augustus Dodge, John Martin Ewell, Levi Hancock, Robert Harris, Abraham Hunsaker, William Hyde, Charles Jameson, Hyrum Judd, Andrew Lytle, William Maxwell, Levi H. McCullough, James Myler, George W. Oman.

James Pace, David Pettegrew, David P. Rainey, Alonzo P. Raymond, Levi Roberts, George W. Taggart, James L. Thompson, Luther T. Tuttle, Daniel Tyler, and Joseph White.

The author of this book is of the opinion that the following men may have made the trip from the Salt Lake Valley to Winter Quarters that fall also: Russell Brownell, George Catlin, Lorenzo Clark, Abraham Day, Simon Dike, Thomas Dunn, Elijah Elmer, Frederick Farney, David Garner, Edward Martin, P. C. Merrill, John Morris, Ira Miles, John Spidell, and Anciel Twitchell.

26

November 2, 1847

Fort Bridger

"AIN'T GOT NO FLOUR, AND I AIN'T GOT much else neither."

Jim Bridger's cold words shocked Robert; he had expected Fort Bridger to be well-stocked with provisions—at least the basics of flour, salt, bacon, and dried beef or buffalo. Bridger sipped on a hot cup of coffee from a creaky wooden chair inside the fort's provision store and did not seem too concerned with the plight of his guests.

Robert immediately felt a burn of regret that the Battalion boys had not kept more of the provisions they had purchased at Fort Hall. Instead, they had shared them with the Saints in the Salt Lake Valley. The returning soldiers had planned on buying foodstuffs at not only Fort Bridger, but Fort Laramie, too.

And they planned on killing wild game, including buffalo, at every opportunity. They had arrived at Fort Bridger in a blinding snowstorm. Snow was still falling. The situation seemed critical to Robert.

Robert shook off fiendish images in his mind, images of starving to death on the prairie between here and Winter Quarters. If the men had to eat their mules and horses, their travels would be slowed down so much they would freeze to death instead of starve.

"But what'll we eat between here and the Missouri?" Captain Pace asked Bridger, the crusty old former mountain man. Bridger was a leathery old wilderness veteran who had roamed the Rockies ever since he answered a fur company's help-wanted ad in 1822. Bridger had built his fort on the Black's Fork of the Green River four years ago to settle down, more or less, and was successful in making a dollar or two by providing emigrants with fresh supplies.

"Ain't my worry," Bridger said with steely eyes. "I've got some bacon, just a few pounds that I'll sell, but that's about all. But what I have won't last you long. I count more than two dozen of you." Bridger's eyes were placed a little too close together, too, giving Robert the feeling that Bridger trusted no one, not the Mormons, not the Indians, and not the emigrants that had passed through in droves. Bridger was dressed in buckskins. A winter coat made of buffalo skin was hung on a wooden knob. So were fur-lined leggings and fur caps, all of which Robert began to covet.

"What about oxen?" Levi Roberts asked. He, like Robert, had heard that

Bridger bought broken down oxen from emigrants, restored their health with rest and good pasture, and then resold them. The Donner Party, including Edwin Bryant and Governor Boggs, had done a brisk business with Bridger and so had most of the Mormon companies that had passed through during the year. Perrigrine Sessions had spoken of several trapper and Indian lodges that had surrounded the fort, but he had mentioned the dwindling supply of things such as flour, pork, powder, lead, blankets, butcher knives, hats, ready-made clothes, sugar and the like. The dwindling supply had totally dwindled down to nothing.

"Ain't no oxen either," Bridger said. "What wasn't sold to the emigrants was sold to the Injuns for food. Had an apron-faced ox as late as a week ago, but the Injuns ate her, too."

Robert turned away in disgust. Fort Bridger was a shabby concern anyway, built of poles daubed with mud. The poles were set in the ground, making a wall around the fort about eight feet in height. There were two miserable-looking log cabins inside the compound (one of which he was standing in) bearing but a faint resemblance to habitable houses. Under a layer of snow, the houses had dirt roofs. On the way in Robert had counted nine Indian lodges about a half-mile from the post.

Another soldier asked Bridger for anything that could be used for clothing or blankets. Luther Tuttle bought an old buckskin shirt from an elderly Indian woman, but other efforts even to buy goods from the Indians who were still hanging around the Fort were fruitless.

"See fer yerself," Bridger said. "I'm plumb outta buffalo robes, buckskins, elk skins, shirts, and pants. What leopard sweat I have left is fer my own use during the winter. You Mormons ain't partial to whiskey anyway."

Bridger's Indian wife sat silent with her arms folded. She was a stolid, fleshy, round-headed woman, not oppressed with lines of beauty. Her hair was intensely black and straight, and cut so that it hung in a thick mass upon her broad shoulders. She sat by a churn filled with buttermilk, but she didn't offer any to her Mormon visitors. Harriet, though, had told Robert that Jim Bridger and his wife had been friendly and courteous during her stop here. With nothing to sell, their attitude had changed, Robert concluded.

All Robert had to his name were the clothes on his back and the blanket he had been issued at Fort Leavenworth. He didn't even have a tent. He had left his old worn-out tent in Los Angeles. "But our people in the Salt Lake Valley said you had everything, food, robes, clothing … "

Bridger laughed. "Brigham Young is as chuckle-headed as a prairie dog. I told him that I'd give a thousand dollars fer the first bushel of corn grown there. The offer still stands. It freezes every night of the year in the Salt Lake Valley."

Robert didn't know for certain if that were true or not, but it had certainly frozen every night since Fort Hall. The weather from the Salt Lake Valley had been cold and uncomfortable and the Battalion boys had arrived at Fort Bridger in a blinding snowstorm.

"Hate to tell you this, but they planted crops and got a harvest this year,"

Captain Pace told Bridger.

Bridger was unimpressed. He referred to cabins that might have been built in the Salt Lake Valley as badger holes. "For a thousand dollars I'll take you to a valley where you can grow real crops."

Levi Hancock blew his top. "If God has damned a valley, wherever it is, then we want nothing to do with that place. God will bless the Salt Lake Valley, you can bet on it." Levi turned to face the Battalion boys. "We need to decide whether to continue toward Winter Quarters or return to Salt Lake."

Bridger had parting words. "Don't you Mormon boys go chousing up the buffalo, neither. I have enough trouble with the Injuns. It ain't the few coffee-cooler Injuns you see hangin' around the Fort. It's them wild hostiles you never see 'til it's too late."

"We've been through plenty of Indian country and survived," Robert countered.

"Well, you mind yer hair, and mind yer knobheels, too," Bridger said. "Injuns'll eat them knobheels, no matter if yer ridin' 'em or not. They'll eat the same as a mountain man, so you might have to feast on a fox, a wolf, marmot, wolverine, porcupine, or even a muskrat or a mouse."

The Battalion boys were camped not too far away in the river bottoms, in a clump of cottonwoods. The wind had filled their tents with snow. For several hours around a large campfire the men debated whether or not to return to Salt Lake. The snow had almost quit, but there were several inches on the ground. Robert had broken through several inches of ice in the river to water the animals.

"Lack of provisions is not our only problem," Andrew Lytle said.

"You're right," said David Pettegrew. "The weather's going to get worse."

"Our horses and mules are going to fail us," said Levi Roberts. He had never heard of the term "knobheel" for a mule until Bridger used it. "They've already ganted down. The grass is sparse anyway this time of year. Now the ground is covered with snow."

"It's four hundred miles to Fort Laramie, our next chance for provisions," said Captain Pace. "That'll take us two weeks."

"How will we make it without flour and without meat?" Edward Bunker asked.

"Jim Bridger warned us not to shoot any buffalo 'cause it'll rile up the Indians," said James Thompson.

Robert jumped to his feet and took hold of his musket. "I say we move out toward Fort Laramie in the morning. I'll shoot anything that moves—buffalo, elk, deer, or even a mouse. I'm gonna make it home by Christmas."

There were a few moments of silence as the men considered Robert's words.

"If I had Wilford Woodruff's fishing pole I'd catch you a mess of fish, but I don't." Robert was talking loosely. Not only was the river covered with ice, but even some of the fast-running creeks were also.

"Maybe we'll get a miracle," Lytle said.

"What kind of miracle?" Robert asked.

"Maybe the government will send a runner with my money."

Robert was confused. "What money? Army pay or something?"

"Naw," said Lytle. "My redress money. Back in 1839 a lot of us petitioned the government in Missouri for what we lost there, when the Missourians drove us out. I wrote up my damages: fifty dollars for moving into the state, a hundred and seventy-five for loss of property, and another twenty-five for moving out."

Robert and all the other men laughed. It was a fine time to make a joke and it loosened everyone up. Robert remembered Lytle as a member of the Nauvoo police. Apostates Robert D. Foster and Chauncey Higbee once had Lytle arrested on false imprisonment charges, which were dismissed. Lytle hated the old apostates just as much as Robert, and they talked about it often.

The men began discussing the options again. Some expressed the opinion that the Saints should have been more generous with their flour in Salt Lake. Some feared the Indians and didn't like Robert's brash idea to shoot buffalo, thinking it was unwise to go against Jim Bridger's warnings. Others thought that if they pressed on to Winter Quarters they would have to eat most of the mules.

Robert cast a quick glance at the mule Robert Pixton had given him. Starvation or not, he had pledged his word. Sister Pixton had to get that mule.

When Robert had his fill of bickering between the Battalion boys, and the decision made to continue on to Fort Laramie, he and a few other men returned to the warm interior of one of the fort's cabins to listen to more of Jim Bridger's lip flapping. Bridger had a remarkable sense of humor and he tried to shock his guests with his tall tales. Bridger tried a few, like petrified birds singing petrified songs, but he soon realized the Battalion boys were not tenderfeet easterners like most of the people who had passed through his fort. Since the men were Mormons, Bridger delighted in bragging about the fact that he had been the first man to see the Great Salt Lake, and admitted that he first thought it was a body of water linked to the Pacific Ocean. He had trapped the Provo River, the Weber River, the Bear River, the Port Neuf River, Cache Valley, and just about every other place Robert had heard about during his travels. Bridger told stories of how he and other mountain men had started out with nothing but their rifles and steel traps, had gone for months without seeing another living soul, and had lived upon the animals they shot or trapped. Robert figured if the mountain men could survive the Wild West, then he could too.

27

November 10, 1847

Fort Laramie

FORT LARAMIE WAS SITUATED ON a wind-swept snow-covered plain where the North Platte and Laramie Rivers met. It had come into view nearly a half-hour earlier, situated on a small bluff above the rivers. Its walls and bastions were made of sun-dried adobe brick. Robert could see a small herd of horses and mules, but none of them as poor as the horses and mules the Battalion boys were riding. Indian teepees were all around. Jim Bridger had told the Battalion boys that at times as many as six thousand Sioux Indians camped here, especially when they were organizing war parties to attack the Snakes and the Crows. There were far fewer than that now, less than four or five hundred in Robert's estimate. He could only see the faces of the Sioux women, but with their light copper color they were far more beautiful than the Digger women. The men were armed with bows and arrow, tomahawks, and knives; Robert also saw that a few men carried muskets.

"Cross your fingers, boys," Captain Pace said. "Let's hope there's some flour here."

Robert crossed his fingers and his heart, too. His stomach was sticking to his backbone. A few days out of Fort Bridger the Battalion boys had shot a buffalo while camped at the Sweetwater River, but other than that they had just about run out of food. He had wished Henry would pull up with a wagonload of provisions from Fort Leavenworth, but laughed off the thought. If there were no provisions at Fort Laramie, there would be certain starvation before the men reached Winter Quarters.

Just forty miles earlier a genuine snowstorm had struck, followed by extreme cold weather. Nine mules froze to death, generally demoralizing both the remaining mules and all the men. The storm had driven the buffalo to the hills, out of reach of Robert's musket. His jaded horse, A. J., couldn't have chased a buffalo anyway.

Luckily, the men came across an old blind bull that had been left behind by the herd. William Maxwell, who had been a private in Company D, helped Robert kill and skin it.

"I've got a good name for this old blind buffalo," Robert had said last night as they tried in every way to make use of the meat—roasting, frying, and boiling.

"What's that?" Maxwell asked, his curiosity piqued.

"Noah," Robert replied. "This here buffalo's been around a long time. He was probably was an original on Noah's ark."

The men all laughed, but it didn't make the meat tender. But the laughter seemed to warm things up. The ground by then was covered with eight inches of snow.

Jim Bridger had told the Battalion boys that fur trappers established Fort Laramie back in 1834. The trappers must have been paranoid of Indians because the entrance to the fort was a hole in the wall just large enough for a person to crawl through. Once in, however, Robert had the impression that he was in a small town. The Stars and Stripes were flying over an adobe building three stories high. The fort looked prosperous, as though it had done a brisk business with a wide variety of customers—Indians, emigrants, and all the Mormons who had come through during the year. Despite the winter weather, the blacksmith shop was fired up, carpenters were busy with repairs, and the store was open. Small knots of Indians, many of them drunk, were meandering through the fort. Some were stretched upon the frozen ground in helpless impotency or staggering from place to place with all the revolting evidences of intoxication.

Robert looked around before he sought the warmth of the store. The exterior walls of the fort were about fifteen feet high. The fort was divided by a partition; on one side there were storerooms, offices, and apartments. The other half was used as a corral, encompassed by high clay walls, where horse and mules of the fort were crowded for safekeeping away from the ever-searching eyes of unfriendly Indians. The main entrance had two gates, with an arched passage intervening. The gates were rarely open, however, as a matter of precaution.

"Are you men Mormons?"

The query came from James Bordeaux, manager of the fort. He was of medium height but had a huge barrel chest and thick hands.

"Yes, sir," Captain Pace answered for the group. "We are. On our way back to the Missouri to find our families."

"Scouts told me two days ago you were coming," Bordeaux said. "You're more than welcome here. We've had nothing but good experiences with the Mormon travelers."

Robert thought of the Pioneer Company headed by Brigham Young and Wilford Woodruff, following companies such as the one Elizabeth and Harriet had traveled with, and the return company also headed by Brigham and Wilford.

Bordeaux quickly gave orders for other men employed by the American Fur Company, who were wintering out here at Fort Laramie, to feed the mules and horses of the Battalion boys. "Tell you what I'm gonna do," Bordeaux said with a happy face. "I'm gonna feed your mules and treat you boys to a free supper and a free breakfast."

Robert's mouth watered. During the past week he had tried grouse, duck, and even crow meat. The crow meat was the worst. It cooked as black as the feathers and tasted as bad as it cooked. He now knew what it meant to "eat crow."

"Thank you sir," Captain Pace said in behalf of the men.

"Oh, I suspect I'll get even with you," Bordeaux laughed. "You'll find prices for provisions here high but fair. That's because we're about out of flour and everything else, too. If I sold you what you want, the trappers and their families here would string me up."

Bordeaux invited the Battalion boys to his sitting room while supper was being prepared. The room looked more like a barroom than anything else, ornamented with several portraits and drawings. A long desk, a settee, and some chairs constituted the furniture. The most interesting part of the pre-meal visit was Bordeaux's story of ex-Missouri Governor Lilburn Boggs. Boggs had passed through Fort Laramie the previous year and had tried to prejudice everyone in the fort against the Mormons, telling them to watch their horses because the Mormons would steal them.

"He's the one to talk," Bordeaux said with a note of disgust. "Everyone in the Boggs company behaved like the scoundrels they were. All the Mormons I've ever met have behaved like ladies and gentlemen, and I appreciate that."

He said that Boggs and those with him were no better than the Indians in holding their liquor. They were gloriously drunk the entire time they were in the fort, yelling and screeching, firing, shouting, swearing, and drinking everything in sight that would further intoxicate them. Bordeaux described their swollen eyes, bloody noses from fighting, and their chasing the Indian wives of the trappers.

"I felt like hauling them out into the plains, one at a time in their drunken stupor, and leaving them to the Crow Indians."

Robert's meal was the best he'd eaten since leaving Sutter's Fort. It consisted of fine cuts of a buffalo, fresh bread, boiled turnips, and boiled potatoes. Bordeaux continued his complimentary oratory toward the Mormons.

"Bordeaux wasn't kidding when he said the prices here were high," Levi Roberts said when he began examining the sacks of flour and other provisions.

"I suppose it's because everything has to be hauled in from places like Independence," Robert said.

"And a two-year drought," said a clerk.

Despite the fact that the fort was built next to the river, a full hundred yards wide, there was no irrigation system for the fields the Indians and trappers used for cultivation. Crops were at the mercy of rainstorms. Robert thought of the Salt Lake Valley and how quickly the Saints there had diverted creeks coming out of the mountains into irrigation ditches.

Robert figured the flour they were able to purchase would last no more than a week. The clerk sold them some hard bread and dried buffalo meat, but that's about all. Captain Lytle bought a pound of crackers for twenty-five cents—expensive and he would have bought more but the clerk held up a hand. The remainder had to be saved for winter storage for the permanent residents.

"Look for an Indian trader on the south side of the Platte River," the clerk said. "If you're lucky, he'll have some flour left."

"How's the buffalo hunting out here this time of year?" Robert asked the clerk.

"Not too good right now because the Indians hunt them hard," came the answer. "If you don't want any trouble with Indians, leave the buffalo be. You'll not only rile them up against you, but against us, too."

Robert scoffed inwardly. The thirty-two returning Battalion boys had at least five weeks travel, five hundred miles, across a snow-covered plain before they reached Winter Quarters. And they had only enough dried buffalo to last them two days and enough flour for maybe three or four days.

If I see a buffalo anywhere between here and the Bluffs, you can bet your buckskins I'm shooting it, Robert thought. *Death at the hand of the Indians can't be any worse than death by starvation.* He had shot the old bull, Noah, and eaten it. He figured there ought to be a few more blind buffalo on the plains between here and Winter Quarters. He'd shoot them too.

28

Late November 1847

Somewhere along the Platte River

ROBERT'S SPIRITS HAD SLIPPED TO an all-time low. It had snowed more than a foot during the night. His body was so cold he could hardly move. Winter Quarters was still three hundred and fifty miles east. Worse still was the fact that some of the men wanted to eat Sister Pixton's mule.

"Sorry, boys," Robert said grimly as he wondered what else they might eat. "I gave my word to Brother Pixton. This here skinny mule has got to be delivered to his wife."

"You can't present the mule to Sister Pixton if we all die on the trail," one of the men said.

"We'd just as well eat the mule as let the Indians get it, and us, too," another said.

"It's the only extra mule we have," said a third.

"Well, kill your mule and you can ride Sister Pixton's, but we can't kill this mule."

Robert and the other Battalion boys traveling in Captain Pace's lead group had been out of meat within three days of leaving Fort Laramie. They had found the Indian trader on the south side of the Platte River, but the trader had only a hundred pounds of flour to sell and he had charged twenty-five dollars—ten times the going price. Evenly split, a hundred pounds came out to no more than three pounds per man for the entire trip. That would be enough to only make gravy for a few days.

"If we could find another buffalo, we could save a mule," Robert's crestfallen comrade said.

The men had shot a bull and a calf shortly after finding the Platte River trader, but that meat was now gone. Shooting the bull and calf had been a hair-raising adventure. Robert and a few others had formed a hunting party, leaving the other men at their camp next to the Platte River. The hunt was successful, but while Robert skinned and butchered the two animals, the men saw smoke and discovered that there were Indians on the other side of the river.

"What'll we do now?" Levi asked Robert.

"Just act like we have as much right to these buffalo as they do," Robert suggested. "Let's pack it up and head back to camp. The sooner we start roasting this meat over an open fire, the better we'll feel."

"They warned us in Fort Laramie not to shoot a buffalo," George Oman said. "Maybe we ought to leave the meat for the Indians and move on out of here."

"If the Indians really wanted to chase us, we wouldn't get far on these worn-out mules," Reddick Allred said.

That had been several days ago. Now, that buffalo meat was gone. Robert agreed that a mule had to be sacrificed, but he repeated that they couldn't touch Sister Pixton's mule. All the men needed strength to help the mules and horses break a trail through deep snow.

The mule the men selected put up little resistance. It was a mule owned by David. P. Rainey, who had been a corporal in Company B. The mule had decided on its own that it could go no farther, so Rainey offered it. Robert drove a knife into its throat and the mule quickly, and weakly, collapsed to the ground.

"Maybe the smell of blood will draw the wolves in," Rainey said. "If they come, we'll shoot one or two and eat them."

Robert scoffed as he skinned the mule. "I don't know what would be worse, wolf meat or the meat off this poor mule."

"Can't be any worse than Noah's meat," Captain Pace said of the old buffalo they had eaten.

In a few minutes the Battalion boys were slicing off pieces of the mule, roasting it on the fire, and eating it as it cooked.

"This is the worst smelling meat ever," Robert said as he cooked his portion. The stench was immense.

"I wish I had some of that good California beef right now," Captain Pace said.

"And some of Hannah's biscuits," Robert said wistfully. He turned sick as he chewed on the meat.

29

Early December 1847

Loup Fork River

THE LOUP FORK RIVER WAS TURNING out to be the worst obstacle Robert had ever faced in his life. It looked to be a good four hundred yards wide but split into two streams by a large sandbar in the middle. A fear came over him; the river looked cold and deep enough to drown a horse. He figured Winter Quarters was no more than a hundred miles away as the crow flies, but it might as well be a thousand by the looks of that river. When the Battalion boys came to the river at dusk last evening, everyone agreed that a better crossing had to be found. They made camp around a large fire and rolled up in their blankets without anything to eat.

"The Pawnee Station ought be nor more than a few miles from here,"

Robert told the other men. His words smoked in the frigid air. Elizabeth and Harriet had spoken of the old mission there, and Perrigrine Sessions had too. Sessions had described how all the wagons had to be unloaded and pulled across by ropes.

"There ought to be a boat at the mission," Captain Pace said wistfully. "If they can see our signal, they could send it over to us."

"I hope so," Robert said. "I don't think any of our horses or mules can swim across, with or without a pack."

"It'll save our lives if we can get to that mission," said Hyrum Judd. "Surely they'll have some provisions to sell."

Judd was right, Robert mused. Elizabeth and Harriet had made some purchases at the Pawnee Mission, and saw fields of corn, beans, squash, and sunflowers.

"They'd at least have some squash to sell," Robert said mournfully.

The next morning, the Battalion boys urged their worn-out mules and horses down the west side of the river in a driving snowstorm. At mid-day, with ten inches of new snow on the ground, the snow stopped and the mission came into view.

Captain Pace shielded his eyes from the sun as he looked across the river. "The mission's been burned out. And worse, there's no boat on this side."

Robert dismounted and sank to his knees. The mission had turned out to be a hoax, a disappointing mind game. He guessed that rival Indians had burned the mission, perhaps the Osages. He couldn't remember if it had been the Catholics or the Presbyterians that had established the mission. He couldn't see any Indians there, but the men had seen some fresh tracks of Indian horses. The Pawnees and the Osages were around somewhere.

"What'll we do now?" Robert asked the captain. He was getting discouraged. For breakfast, the men had shared two prairie chickens they had shot. Two chickens divided by sixteen men equaled about three good bites.

"We've got to cross somehow, sometime," Pace said with an air of determination.

"We'd just as well do it now," Levi said. "Our horses and mules ain't gonna get any stronger. There's nothin' for them to eat."

"Who's gonna be first?" Pace asked.

"You're our leader," Robert said. "Nudge your horse into the water and see if he'll swim across."

Pace rode a bay gelding he had purchased from Isaac Williams in Los Angeles. Like most of the other horses the Battalion boys were riding, it had matured from a green bronco into a seasoned trail horse. Seasoned but weakened, the bay looked like he had lost three hundred pounds since California. The horse had always been leery of the water and on this cold winter day he was no different.

Pace seemed to set his jaw. "Three or four of you come with me," he said as he kicked into the bay's ribs.

Robert could see Hannah in his mind. She was on the other side of the river, no more than a five-day ride away. He rose from the frozen ground,

untied his saddlebags, threw them into a heap on the ground, and remount-
ed. "Hang onto Sister Pixton's mule for me," he said to Levi Roberts. "Here
goes nothing."

Two other men mounted, too, and urged their horses into the water.

"Come on, A. J.," Robert said to his horse. "Get me across."

The four horses entered the water almost simultaneously. A. J. pawed at
the water and then jumped in. The cold water shocked Robert's system and he
soon found himself floating, barely hanging onto the saddle. A. J.'s ears
twitched forward and then backward again, listening to anything Robert was
saying. The horse snorted frantically.

"Swim harder," Robert said in a panic. "A. J., the current's got us. Swim,
boy, swim!"

The men and horses were no more than fifty yards from the shore when
Captain Pace gave the command to turn around. "We'll never make it," he
said. His horse was already foundering.

"Back we go, A. J.," Robert said.

Suddenly, A. J. quit. His eyes rolled in his head. Robert and his horse
were being carried downstream at a rapid rate of speed.

Levi Roberts and the other men on the bank trotted along, yelling
encouragement.

"Get back, get back," Levi was yelling.

A. J. rolled over, a victim of drowning. Robert swam with all his strength,
tugging at the saddle. Horsemeat was just as good as mule meat, especially

when the men were starving. Slowly but surely, Robert and the horse carcass inched toward the bank. Levi and the men pulled them to shore. A. J.'s blue tongue was hanging out of its mouth.

Robert closed his eyes in frustration. He imagined his whole body was as blue as A. J.'s tongue. The experience reminded him of the time Henry hit him on the back of the head and tossed him overboard in the cold Atlantic. Only this time there was no Captain Wood and a mixture of brandy and cayenne to rub onto his body for instant warmth.

Pace's horse was not dead, but in cold shock. "Get a fire going men," he ordered. "And be quick about it. We're near froze to death."

A. J. was not the only dead horse. One of the others had also drowned.

"At least we'll have something to eat," Robert said in a dejected tone as he stared at his horse.

Levi patted Robert on the back. "Sorry, pal."

Robert stepped toward the fire t the men had started. "I'll let you do the butchering this time while I warm up. My knife is in my saddlebag."

As he huddled near the fire, trying to warm his frozen limbs, he caught the sight of four or five mounted Indian warriors on a bluff overlooking the river.

CHAPTER NOTES

The Loup Fork River crossing is near today's Genoa, Nebraska. The Robert Pace group reached the crossing in early December.

30

ALTHOUGH A. J.'S MEAT KEPT THE MEN alive, it did nothing to overcome their discouragement. With no boat, there was no way to cross the river.

"Our best hope is for the river to freeze over," Captain Pace told the men a day after the two horses had drowned.

"Or we'd best be building a raft," Levi said. "But I don't know what we'd use for augers and ropes."

Robert had seen the Indians again. Getting across the river soon was high priority.

The next day the weather had turned so bitter cold that the men began to see floating ice. The Indians were getting braver, and growing in numbers.

"I think they're Pawnees, not Osage," Captain Pace said.

"They don't look friendly," Robert said as the Pawnees reappeared on the bluff. This time he counted more than a dozen.

"Keep your powder dry," Pace admonished.

After traveling four thousand miles round trip through the American deserts and wilderness, Robert began to imagine how disappointing it would be to get shot by an Indian arrow this close to home, or by one of the muskets he had seen the Pawnees carry. Hannah was only a few days away. He wondered about the wives of the Pawnees. And he wondered about their children. He reasoned if it came right down to it, he would much rather shoot a Pawnee warrior and let the Indian's wife, parents, and children grieve than get shot himself and leave Hannah without a husband and his seven children without a father. If the Pawnees attacked, there would no choice. The Battalion boys would have to fight. There was nowhere to run. The Indians would end up with what few horses and mules were left, and the muskets that the army had issued them in Fort Leavenworth. Then the Indians would attack Captain Lytle's men and kill them too.

There wasn't anything for Robert to do but watch and pray, and try to overcome his fears. He prayed that the Indian's wouldn't attack. He prayed for Lytle's men to show up, which would improve their chances against the Pawnee warriors. He prayed that the raft they were building out of cottonwood trees would get finished.

The ice on the river had begun to build up. Robert counted that as both a hindrance and a blessing. An increased ice buildup would make it impossible for the raft to make it across the river enough times to get all the men and their animals on the other side. But if the Loup Fork iced over completely, the men and animals could walk across. But so could the Indians.

Robert had bundled up with every stitch of clothing he had, which wasn't much. The weather was cold enough to make ice in the fast-flowing river, and cold enough to freeze a man's blood.

"Keep your muskets loaded and one finger on the trigger," Captain Pace said to the men as the Indians seemed to grow in number and aggressiveness.

"My finger's about frozen off," Robert murmured. He had draped his wool blanket over his shoulders.

Levi cupped a hand over his ear. "I think I hear something."

The sound was coming from the west, among the cottonwoods. Robert threw off his wool blanket and looked for protection.

"It's probably more Indians," Captain Pace warned. He had his musket aimed too.

The sounds were unmistakable: horses, perhaps a dozen or more. The Indians on the bluff had disappeared. Robert figured they might be moving against the Battalion boys from the opposite direction.

Robert lay in the snow behind a fallen cottonwood and aimed his musket.

"Don't shoot," Captain Pace suddenly said. "It's Captain Lytle."

Robert breathed a sigh of relief as Lytle's group appeared from among the cottonwoods, following the same trail he had followed to this spot.

"We could sure use some hot bread and some beefsteaks," Captain Lytle joked as he led his men to the Pace group.

"Well, if you brought the flour and the beef, we'd sure accommodate you," Pace said with a smile.

The conversation made Robert's mouth water. There had been no flour for several days and the horsemeat they had been living on was gone too. Breakfast had been boiled saddlebags, once of the worst meals yet. Sister Pixton's mule was still alive, but he knew the men would like to eat it. He let his eyes sweep the bluff where the Indians had been. They were no longer there. Robert assumed they had been scared off. The Battalion boys now numbered around two dozen, a formidable force.

"Will that raft get us across the river?" Lytle asked Pace.

"It might when we get it finished," Pace said tersely.

The two groups talked about the river, the ice, and the Indians as they mingled. And survival. All the men were on the brink of starvation. Lytle's men had even dug out the brains in a mule's skull left by the Pace Group.

Just out of Fort Laramie, the Indians had captured one of Lytle's men, Reddick Allred. It happened one night when the men were camped a few miles above the Sioux Indians. A Sioux brave coaxed Allred into trading a mule for a pony. But the next day the Indians seized the pony out from under Allred, claiming it was stolen. So they took Allred prisoner. Only because one of the other Battalion boys had seen the incident did Allred get rescued. Allred lost the pony, but got his mule back.

As Robert listened to the story, he wondered if the Pawnees would appear again. There were probably enough Pawnees in the area to take all the men captive.

"There's got to be some food in that burned-out camp across the river," said one of Lytle's men, Abraham Hunsaker.

The ice buildup continued through the night and by the next morning it appeared that a crossing was possible. A huge bonfire was burning, with the men huddled around it, discussing the options. A few were working on the raft. No one had caught sight of any more Indians.

"Why are you loading those coals in that frying pan?" Robert asked Hunsaker.

"I think I can make it across the ice on my hands and knees," Hunsaker replied.

"You might ought to wait another day," Captain Lytle warned his man. "That ice might be too thin, especially in the middle."

"I can't stand the thoughts there might be some corn I could parch over there," Hunsaker said as he stared across the frozen river. "I'm so hungry I could eat my shirt."

Robert remembered how cold the Loup Fork had been. The freezing water almost killed him. "Don't ask me to go with you."

Hunsaker bit his lip and started for the riverbank. He used two long sticks as skis and pushed his hot frying pan ahead of him, inching along on his hands and knees.

"I believe he's gonna make it," Levi Roberts said when Hunsaker was no more than a dot on the other side. Just as he said the words, the dot disappeared into the water. A few seconds later, the dot reappeared and crawled onto the shore.

"Looks like he's there," Levi said.

Robert lit up like a lantern. Perhaps there was hope.

"If he can't get a fire going, he'll freeze to death over there," said Captain Lytle.

Hunsaker returned the next afternoon, and to the surprise of everyone, he brought food.

"Where'd you get that corn?" Captain Lytle asked.

"From a corn field by the burned-out mission," Hunsaker said. The ears were old; it was now December and the Indians had harvested most of the corn in August.

The men warmed the corn in their Dutch ovens as Hunsaker told his story. Yesterday he had gone completely under the water just before he reached shore, frying pan and all. His feet barely touched the bottom. He had to fight his way out, inch by inch, pushing chunks of ice out of the way. He felt half frozen to death by the time he reached shore. The old rotted stump of a tree was the first thing he saw, as if Providence had placed it there. He quickly gathered slivers from the stump and laid them over the soaked coals in his frying pan, which showed no signs of life. He blew until his breath was almost exhausted, and then he rested and blew again. Finally he saw a faint glow among the coals. He nursed it into a small flame and soon he had a roaring fire going. He dried his clothes and warmed himself.

Shortly afterward he found the Indian corn field. He didn't see any Indians so he scavenged the field by kicking up the collapsed cornstalks with his feet; all the corn was buried beneath the snow. He found a few withered ears of corn. He carried them to an abandoned earthen Indian lodge, renewed his fire in the old fire pit there, parched the corn, and ate until he was full. He slept in the lodge without a blanket and the following morning gathered more corn.

"That's when I saw the Indians," Hunsaker said.

"How many?" one man asked.

"Three, and they looked warlike. I thought to myself, *this is the end.*"

"What'd you do?"

"Tried to look fearless. I guess it worked, or they felt sorry for me. At any rate, they grunted a few times in disgust, turned, and rode their ponies away." Hunsaker went on to say that they could have killed him easily because he was unarmed. "The frying pan wasn't much of a weapon."

Robert scanned the horizon again. He could see no Indians. To his eyes, Hunsaker looked like a walking skeleton. He suspected he looked much the same and so he dove into the corn. Perrigrine Sessions had told him that the Pawnees worshipped corn. No wonder, Robert thought, as the food began to revive him. He felt a strong urge to cross the river and continue his quest to find Hannah and his family. He jumped up and took a few steps toward Coop, Sister Pixton's mule.

"Where you going?" Levi asked.

"I'm wondering if I could get Coop across the ice," Robert said. "All I need is a long pole."

Robert soon had a pole to his liking and he led the mule to the edge of the river. "Better go upstream a ways to start," he told Coop.

"You're crazy," Levi said to Robert. Levi's curiosity was up, so he followed.

"That's what I thought about Abraham Hunsaker, but he made it to the other side and back."

Robert led Coop upstream until he found a slow-moving and large piece of ice. It looked thick and sturdy, half clinging to the bank for the moment. Coop was nervous and half balky, but Robert urged him onto the ice. Robert used the pole to push his ice barge away from the bank into the icy corridor. "If I make it, then you come too," he said to Levi. "And then the others will follow."

The pole was twice as long as Robert was tall. He pushed it into the water until it found the bottom. Using all his strength and leverage, he managed to move his ice barge a few yards. And then he did it again, and again. When he was more than half way across Robert looked back and saw that the other Battalion boys had abandoned the raft idea and were urging their horses and mules onto the ice. A few minutes later, Robert and Coop were safely on the other side.

Hannah suddenly seemed a whole lot closer. But Robert had no idea what the men would live on during their final days on the trail.

CHAPTER NOTES
The story about Robert Harris crossing the Loup Fork River by means of a long pole comes from the Edward Bunker journal. The journal is quoted on pages 377-378 of the book, *Army of Israel, Mormon Battalion Narratives* (Utah State University Press, Logan, Utah, 2000), edited by David L. Bigler and Will Bagley. The crossing of the river occurred in mid-December 1847.

31

December 16, 1847

On the banks of the Elk Horn River

"HAPPY BIRTHDAY, ROBERT," LEVI Roberts said from a bed of snow. The night after the Battalion boys crossed the Loup Fork they had slept in abandoned Indian huts. Now they were sleeping in the open again, on the banks of the Elk Horn River, rolled up in their blankets.

"Thanks, but where's my birthday cake?" Robert asked as he pulled his wool blanket over his shoulders. Levi was right. It was December sixteenth, Robert's thirty-seventh birthday. He figured he was within thirty miles of Winter Quarters. With luck, he would see Hannah and the children by tomorrow night, the day before Daniel Browett's birthday.

"Sorry, but I ran out of flour about two months ago," Levi remarked. "Be nice to have some fresh cow's cream and sugar for the icing, wouldn't it?"

Robert smacked his lips. "Sure would."

Captain Pace brought the men back to reality. "What if we send two men ahead on the best mules and have a rescue team come back and get us?" he asked. "It's either that or eat our last mules."

Robert looked at Coop, Sister Pixton's mule. He was skin and bones but at least he was still alive. "Sorry, but we can't eat this here mule."

"We've got to eat or die," Captain Pace retaliated.

"We can't give up now," said Edward Bunker. "We've traveled nearly five thousand miles. I don't want to die this close to home."

Robert was so weak he could hardly talk. "Not Coop. We can't eat Sister Pixton's mule." Slowly, he rose to his knees. "Let's try praying again."

"Good idea," Bunker said.

As Robert rose to his knees, newly fallen snow fell off his blanket. His body was so cold he could hardly feeling anything. He had been praying constantly that he could return to Hannah's arms. He was still alive, had come this far, and trusted in the Lord. One by one, the men took turns as voice, pleading for the Lord to spare them somehow.

Suddenly, the woods where the Battalion boys were camped came alive.

"What?" said one of the men, his jaw dropping in disbelief.

"Wild turkeys, and lots of them too," said Robert.

He had hunted them in Illinois and recognized them instantly. Against the dismal winter background the turkeys looked beautiful, even iridescent, with varying colors of red, green, copper, bronze, and gold. The gobblers were more colorful and the hens a drab brownish color.

"The Lord sent them," said one of the men.

"There's droves of 'em," said another.

Robert didn't try to count. There were hundreds.

"Do you think we can get them all?" someone queried.

"We don't need them all, just a few," another answered. "This is a miracle that will save our lives."

Robert was glad he didn't have a mirror. He hadn't shaved and bathed since just before he'd reached Salt Lake. His fighting weight in England had been a hundred and ninety pounds. He figured he weighed no more than a hundred and forty pounds now, maybe less. The weather was still freezing cold. He was bundled up in every article of clothing that he owned; perhaps at first Hannah would not notice how much weight he had lost. At least he had a gut full of turkey meat as he straddled Coop for the last few miles into Winter Quarters. He could still smell the meat sizzling over an open fire.

"There might be a welcoming committee," Levi Roberts said.

That comment brought a smile to Robert's face. The men had never caught P. C. Merrill's group, so Hannah probably knew by now that he would arrive in Winter Quarters at any time. Robert began to visualize Hannah's face, her auburn-brown hair, and her silky skin. He tried to picture in his mind what each of his children would look like now that a year and a half had passed. Joseph would turn twelve in March; Robert could see his dishwater blond hair and blue eyes. He would be good help on his farm and ranch back in the Salt Lake Valley. Lizzy would be nine on April first, William had just turned seven, Thomas was nearly six, Enoch three and a half, and Sarah Ann a year and a half. Then there was his youngest, the boy he had never seen, the youngster Hannah had named after him—Robert Harris III. The baby was born in February, seven months after his departure. He didn't know if the baby resembled him or his mother, had brown eyes or blue eyes, and had a lot of hair or no hair. Robert had never been absent during the birth of one of his children.

"I can't wait to see that baby," he said to Levi as they trudged through the snow toward Winter Quarters.

Levi had a wife and five children waiting for him. "I'll bet you can't," he said. "I just hope all mine are healthy."

"Me, too," agreed Robert, thinking not only of Levi's but his too. He thought of the other Battalion wives, too, whom he would have to console once he arrived. Richard Slater had stayed in California although he had a wife and five children waiting in Winter Quarters. Just like Hannah, Sister Slater had been left behind. So had Eliza Cox, John's wife, and their five children. Robert Pixton had two children and a wife waiting in Winter Quarters. Robert had a gift for her—a mule named Coop

32

December 18, 1847

Winter Quarters

FROM THE TOP OF A HILL, ROBERT made out the dim outline of the settlement known as Winter Quarters. In faltering daylight, his heart did a dance. Somewhere among the distant collection of sod huts and small cottonwood log homes was his wife, Hannah, the baby he'd never seen, and his six other children.

"Come on, Coop, that there's your new home," he said to the mule as he dug his heels into its skinny ribs.

Coop's frosty ears suddenly and unexpectedly lurched forward. The mule's attention seemed to sharpen. The reason: Three men on horses were riding toward Robert and his companions. Captain Pace and Captain Lytle rode straight for them.

"Who goes there?" one of the riders asked with a raised hand.

"We're the Battalion boys, coming home," Captain Pace answered.

A smile graced the man's face. "We've been expecting you. Some of the other soldiers arrived here just a few days ago. We're just guards posted to watch the town."

"That'd be P. C. Merrill's men," Pace quipped.

"Pass on by," one of them said. "We know you're anxious."

"A couple of hours ago, before it got too cold, there were a few of your wives standing at the edge of town waiting for you," the third man said.

"One of them Hannah Harris?" Robert asked.

"Yes, sir," the man said.

Robert's heart did a tumble. His pulse quickened too. "Where will I find her?" he asked.

The man pointed to the north. "On Woodruff Street, up that way. About half-way down in the middle block, on your left hand side as you go to the river."

Robert kicked Coop in the ribs again as the three men were besieged with more questions about where other wives and families were located. One by one, the men of the Pace-Lytle group went their separate ways. Robert barely heard one of the three guards ask a question of the Battalion boys. "Encounter any Indian problems out there that we should know about?"

"At the Loup Fork River," Captain Pace answered. "That's the last we saw of troublesome Indians. They would've killed us, but our two groups came together about that time, and that saved us."

"Good luck finding your wives."

Coop could smell the hay. A very large corral held several hundred cattle on the outskirts of Winter Quarters. Coop brayed and made a beeline toward them.

"Coop, I know you ain't ate for two days, other than a few nibbles of frozen grass, but please take me to Hannah right now," Robert pleaded as he guided the mule north. "I'm hungry, too. The turkey's long passed through me."

Homes were spread out below Robert in neat rows. Streets looked wide enough to turn a wagon around without trespassing on private property. The Missouri River came into view, meandering close to the settlement on the north, but flowing away as it proceeded south. Due to the cold, most everyone was inside his home. A couple of men were returning from the livestock pens with buckets of fresh milk, less than half full.

Robert kicked the bony mule with both feet. There were a few grunts of protest, but Coop ambled north on Second Main Street. Robert counted the streets as he went by, barely able to read their names: Spencer Street, Carlos, Samuel, Hyrum, Joseph, Smith, Russell, and finally Woodruff. He passed half a dozen walkers who were swinging their arms despite being bundled up; they looked preoccupied. He turned east, toward the river. The bitter cold caused nostrils to stick together as he sniffed the air: there was an odor of pungent smoke coming from every hut and cabin. He wondered which cabin was occupied by Brigham Young. He resisted the urge to find him and give him a piece of his mind. First things first. Hannah and the children.

"Okay, Coop—where's Hannah?"

Coop's long ears didn't move. Robert jumped off the mule and walked toward the first door on the north side of Woodruff. Again, it was a small, sparse cabin with smoke bellowing out its chimney and a dim light radiating from its window. He banged on the door.

A man's voice answered. "Who's there?"

"One of the Battalion boys. Where's Hannah Harris?"

"Two doors down."

Robert left Coop and ran. He could hear the man's voice muttering another response: "She stood outside all day long, hoping she'd see you."

Robert expected to see a log cabin, but he didn't. It was a sod hut, and a poor one at that, its faint outline seen by a combination of a little light still coming from the western sky and a full moon rising from the east. It, too, had smoke coming from a chimney, not a stone one, but one made of sod. There were sounds coming from the hut—children's voices. His skin tingled.

"Do you think father will be here by tomorrow?" a child's voice asked from inside. No mistake about it, the voice belonged to Lizzy—Elizabeth—his oldest daughter, now nine.

The sound of Hannah's voice nearly brought Robert to his knees. "Dea

Lord, I hope so."

For the first time in weeks, Robert thought of his appearance. He pulled at his long beard with lean nervous fingers. His old felt hat was tied over his ears with rawhide. Every stitch of clothing he owned was clinging to his body—canvas cotton pants frozen stiff as a board, two flannel shirts, a buffalo skin, and a pair of worn-out leather boots made in California. He hoped Hannah wouldn't be frightened. There was a possibility she wouldn't even recognize him. There was one advantage about coming home in mid-December. At least he wasn't hot and sweaty like he'd been in Fort Leavenworth and along the Santa Fe Trail. But he was certain he smelled as bad as the worst mountain man who had ever trekked across the plains. At the last second he decided not to take a chance with his appearance. Surely, Hannah would recognize his voice.

With a pounding heart he stood at the doorway. "Hannah! It's me, Robert!"

For two or three seconds the voices inside the cabin went stone silent.

"I'm coming in!" Robert yelled.

Robert pulled the wooden door open, letting a gust of cold air into the home. Two sights quickly struck Robert as he entered the small hut. The first was his family—light from a lantern revealed the figures of a woman with six children huddled around her. The second was the sparseness of the home and the abject poverty it projected. His eyes settled on twelve round eyes staring back at him—fourteen counting Hannah. Hannah appeared impossibly thin with lean, sallow cheeks. Joseph was thin, too, but stood nearly as tall as his mother. Sarah Ann, two and a half, stood with her finger on her lip, and her mouth falling wide open. As Robert took a step toward them, Sarah Ann began to cry. So did Enoch, the four-year-old. Robert peeled off his hat and his buffalo robe, hoping to mitigate the frightful sight the children saw.

"It's me," he said, feeling a springtime quickening in his veins. His eyes glanced upward for just a second. His head barely cleared the ceiling of the small cabin. The blocks of sod had deteriorated and looked as though they could fall apart with the bark of a dog or a pop from the fire.

Although temporarily awestruck, Hannah's shock evaporated. "Robert! Robert!" She tore herself away from her children and ran to his arms. Tears streamed down her cheeks. "Robert! I can't believe it's you!"

Hannah was wildly appealing despite her bony ramshackle frame, her sunken brown eyes, and her auburn hair now sprinkled with streaks of gray. With a growing pang, Robert accepted Hannah's tight embrace as tears filled his eyes. He threw his arms around her and hugged her like the day they were married in the little redbrick Methodist church in Apperley, England, nearly thirteen years earlier.

"I don't know if you want to kiss me," Robert said through misty eyes. "I'm fairly rank."

Hannah pulled back to look at him. "I'll take my chances." She planted a warm kiss that filtered through his thick brown beard to his half-frozen lips.

Robert opened one eye to scan his six children, who seemed stricken half with fear and half with puzzlement.

"Mother," Joseph said. "Are you certain that strange looking man is my father?"

"I'm certain," Hannah said, still clinging to Robert. "My, what's happened to you? You feel like you've lost half your weight."

"Papa?" Lizzy ventured, taking one unsure step toward her father. William, Thomas, Enoch, and Sarah Ann remained frozen in their tracks.

To Robert's eyes, each child looked like an angel. Thin and peaked, but angels nevertheless. Robert could feel his insides taking a happy grip on the reality of the fact he was reunited with his family at last.

Hannah left Robert's embrace to encourage her children. "Come over here and give your father a hug."

Six-year-old Thomas was still hesitant. A roguish smile appeared on his face and then disappeared. He shattered the happy reunion with these words: "Aren't you going to tell him about the baby, Mother?"

A sudden pain gripped Robert's chest. He tried to suppress the terrible feelings that came to him and he cringed at the thought something terrible had happened. His searching eyes fell on Hannah and she began to sob. "Tell me," Robert said as his eyes narrowed, keenly aware he was about to receive bad news.

Hannah shook her head, still sobbing. Her head fell to her chest. There was a long and silent pause. Robert drew her to him. "What?" he said. "Tell me."

"Our baby died," Lizzy said, almost without batting an eye.

Robert took a series of short, sharp breaths. Grief stabbed at his heart. There were several seconds of silence in the little cabin. "When?" he asked morbidly.

"End of July," Lizzy said.

"The thirtieth," Joseph added.

One by one, the children slowly made their way into Robert's arms. The talk of death somehow cemented them together. In the faint lantern glow, a family of eight clung together like a mother hen gathering her chicks. Robert thought back. The day the son he'd never seen died, he had been passing over the Sierra Mountains in California, searching for Walker Pass and a shortcut to the Great Basin. He'd been killing and drying beef then, because the cattle they'd purchased from California ranches were slowly being lost in the mountains.

"I'm sorry," Hannah whimpered. "I'm sorry."

"It's okay," Robert answered. "I'm sorry, too. We've got each other. We've got six beautiful children." He wrapped his once-powerful but now-scrawny arms around them and drew them tighter. Poor living conditions and a lack of fresh fruits and vegetables had contributed to the deaths of both his baby son and Daniel's son, Moroni. Whatever it took, he vowed to himself he would keep the rest of his family alive and healthy during the deadly winter the Saints now faced in Winter Quarters.

"Papa, it really is you," Lizzy said.

"Yes, it is," Robert said to his oldest daughter, drawing her to his chest. "Yes, it is. I'm home."

"Katherine will be glad to see you, and so will Annie," Hannah said the next morning as she snipped at Robert's beard with her dull scissors. A pan of hot water waited for the shaving ritual.

Robert slumped in his chair. "Wish I had good news for her," he said as he flinched in obvious pain from Hannah's well-aimed snips.

Poverty, besides making Hannah thin and shapeless, had hollowed her cheeks and her eyes, and exaggerated her full mouth. She wore a ragged blue wool dress. She asked, "How long you had that strap and razor?"

"Ever since Fort Leavenworth," Robert answered.

"I half expect Henry to ride into Winter Quarters just like you did," Hannah said, knowing that such an event was quite unlikely. She was saying it mostly for Katherine's sake, and Annie's.

During the night Robert had told Hannah all he knew about Henry, that the last time he had seen her brother was at Santa Fe. He guessed he had gone south with Colonel Doniphan to fight in some battles against Mexico south of the border. He also told Hannah about many of his Battalion experiences, the battle of the bulls, and Daniel's painful decision to stay in California. He didn't look forward to seeing Katherine and Annie. There was no good news about Henry to report.

"There're so many people anxious to see you I don't know where to start,"

Hannah said as she quit snipping and pushed Robert in front of a mirror. "Thomas Bloxham has a surprise for you."

"What kind of surprise?" Robert asked.

"It wouldn't be a surprise if I told you," Hannah stated with an emphatic nod of the head. "And Sister Pixton will be one happy lady when she gets that mule."

Robert appeared to want to glance out the window, but there was none. The only opening had no glass. A blanket was stretched over it to keep the heat in and the cold out. Coop was in a pen with Victoria, the milk cow. Joseph had already milked the cow, but she hadn't given much. Hannah had insisted that Robert drink half of it himself and he almost did until feelings of guilt came over him. Six children needed milk, too.

Hannah said, "See if that old razor can get the rest of that straggly beard off." At least her husband smelled better. She had made him take a bath before bed, but it had taken a long time to heat enough water from melted snow to fill the old tub she had brought from Nauvoo.

Robert had almost finished shaving when he heard the sound of footsteps in the snow outside. A knock came to the door.

"It's me, Katherine," a voice said. "I've heard Robert's home. Is he in there? Is he decent?" The sun in her hair as she stood in the doorway made an aureole around her pallid face.

Hannah laughed. "Come on in; he's dressed, but he's still sporting an indecent beard."

Katherine entered the sod hut with uncertain steps, peering at Robert.

Robert put down his razor, wiped his face, and gave Katherine and Annie an awkward but warm embrace. The atmosphere was thick with curiosity as Robert and Katherine and the girl regarded each other. Flashes of the past went through Robert's mind: their mutual experiences on the ship across the Atlantic, the time in Nauvoo when he threw Henry over the fence for abusing Katherine, and the job Katherine had working as a deputized clerk for Sheriff Minor Deming during the trial of the murderers of Joseph Smith.

"Is my Papa coming home, like you did?" Annie asked her uncle.

Robert looked at Annie with a bundle of special warmth. "He might not be too far behind me." He hoped he wasn't giving the six-year-old child any false hopes. Despite all of Henry's faults as a member of the human race, it was apparent that Annie loved her father.

"We read your letters," Katherine said as she stared at Robert. "Did you see Henry at all after you left Santa Fe?"

Robert's weary tension dissolved a little. "Sorry, no," Robert answered. "I have a suspicion that he might have gone into Mexico with Colonel Doniphan, but I don't know for certain."

"Is Mexico dangerous?" Annie asked.

"From what I've heard, the American army won all the battles there," Robert explained. "We won the war."

"Then why isn't Papa home?" Annie asked innocently.

"Just never give up hope," Robert answered as he resumed his shaving.

For the next several minutes Robert explained to Katherine and Annie how he had met Henry in Missouri when Henry and Colonel Price had delivered flour to the Battalion, their days together in Fort Leavenworth, and meeting him again in Santa Fe. Robert didn't tell them about Henry's disappointing behavior, or the admonition he gave Henry before they parted ways.

"Before I go, could I talk to you alone?" Katherine asked Robert.

Robert cast a quick glance at Hannah. She gave a helpless shrug as though she hadn't the faintest idea what Katherine might want to say to Robert in private. "Sure," Robert said.

Bundled in a coat that he'd left behind, Robert strolled along Woodruff Street with Katherine. "Sorry I couldn't give you better news about Henry," he said.

"I didn't expect any good news, really," she remarked in a solemn tone. "I've given up on him. That's sad to say for Annie's sake, not for mine."

Robert thought of how poorly Henry had treated Katherine over the years, even beating her a few times.

"I hope you won't think my request too strange," Katherine said.

"Request?"

"I've written a letter to Brigham Young and Wilford Woodruff."

Robert scratched his head. "What kind of letter?"

"I don't believe Henry is ever coming back. I hope he doesn't. I'm asking Brother Brigham for a divorce from Henry."

Robert exhaled. "No, I don't think that request is strange at all. I'm sorry it's come to this."

Katherine bit her lip for a second. Her wide mouth was wryly curved. "In the same letter I've asked that you be allowed to take me for a wife."

Robert choked and turned brick red. He stopped walking. "Katherine, you can't be serious."

"Annie and I need someone to take care of us. Plural marriage is totally out in the open here in Winter Quarters. They say that no more than thirty men had plural wives in Nauvoo. It's got to be more than triple that now." She said all this very fast, her eyes wide and shining, her manner peculiarly excited.

"But Katherine …"

Katherine's countenance suddenly changed. Tears began streaming down both sides of her dish nose. "Say no more. You don't want me."

Robert let his air out. Never in his life did he feel more helpless. "I didn't say that."

"You didn't need to. I can tell."

"Katherine, I believe Henry will come back."

"I wouldn't want him if he did. He's been mean to me."

"Give him a chance."

"A chance to beat me again?"

"He might be a changed man."

"I've said that over and over to myself for eleven years. He hasn't changed a speck."

"Have you said anything to Hannah?"

"Of course not."

Robert turned around in the street. The cold December air seemed a few degrees colder. The sun appeared a little dimmer. "I don't know what to say or do."

"Pray about it. I have."

Robert shrugged his shoulders. "Katherine, this is not how I envisioned my first day home would be."

33

ROBERT WAS RELIEVED WHEN THOMAS Bloxham came walking up the street with his five children. It got Robert out of an awkward situation.

"Robert! There you are!" Thomas said in a loud voice. "We heard you're home."

The two men hugged and back slapped one another, both in tears. As they did, Robert caught a brief glimpse of Katherine fading away in the background. He let her go without saying anything more to her.

"I miss your sister," Thomas said with an emphatic nod of the head. "She was a wonderful wife. I didn't realize how much I loved her." Dianah had been Robert's oldest sister. She had been one of the first members of the United Brethren congregation to be baptized by Wilford Woodruff during his mission to England in 1840. Elizabeth—Robert's other sister—and Daniel had been baptized shortly thereafter, but Robert resisted and was not baptized until a few months later.

"I'd like to see her burial spot," Robert said with a note of sadness.

"I'll take you there," Thomas said teary-eyed. "It's by a creek a few miles away, where we were camped when she died. I've thought about moving her to the Winter Quarters cemetery, but it really is a beautiful spot where she's laid to rest."

"What's this surprise you have for me?"

Thomas drew a deep breath and looked Robert squarely in the eye. "I'd like you to baptize me."

Robert felt as though he could be tipped over with a feather. "Baptize you?"

"Don't look so puzzled," Thomas said with a little laugh.

"I'd be happy to. When did all this come about?" Robert asked. He stole a quick glance at the Missouri River down the hill in the distance. He could see himself chopping a large hole in the ice, and forming a makeshift baptismal font.

"Dianah's death caused me to do some serious thinking. I want our family to be a forever family. Brother Thomas Kington taught me the gospel. He wanted to baptize me two months ago, but I told him I was waiting for you to do it. He said that was fine with him."

Robert smiled at his brother-in-law. "I'll do it today, if that's what you want."

Katherine was square on Robert's mind throughout the remainder of the day and all through the night. He'd found out during the day that it was true that plural marriage was more out in the open in Winter Quarters. He couldn't blame poor Katherine for writing her letter to Brigham Young and Wilford Woodruff. No doubt she sincerely believed the doctrine of plural marriage as much as she believed in the doctrine of family salvation, baptism for the dead, anointings, sealings, and all other principles and practices identified with the priesthood and the temple. She had heard Joseph Smith preach that marriages ought to be performed not only for this lifetime, but "time and all eternity." It was true that Katherine had given up on Henry. He wasn't celestial material. But Katherine and Annie were.

"Do you think Henry will come back to Katherine and Annie?" Robert said to Hannah after their evening prayers in their tiny cabin that night.

"I'd throw rocks at him if he did 'cause he's been away so long," Hannah said, repeating what she'd said of Henry the day her wagon had pulled into Garden Grove a year and a half ago. "And then I'd hogtie him and keep him here, for Annie's sake."

"You didn't answer my question."

"I don't know."

"Do you think he'll ever get baptized?" Robert asked.

"Don't know. Go to sleep. I've lost enough sleep over Henry to last a lifetime."

Robert felt like balking the next morning as Hannah dressed the children for the Sunday meeting. The weather had moderated a bit and Brigham Young had called for a central meeting at the bowery located next to the Council House in the center of town. Word had been received that Brigham wanted everyone to meet the Battalion boys and welcome them home. Normally, religious services were held every Sunday morning and evening in each of the small wards—twenty-one of them—that divided Winter Quarters. A bishop and two counselors directed them; services included ward business, the sacrament, preaching, and the performance of various ordinances such as the blessing of infants.

"I'm so worn out from talking to so many people yesterday I've a good mind to stay home," Robert said. Hannah had her scissors out again. This time she was working on Robert's hair.

"Nonsense," Hannah retaliated as she aimed the scissors. "I'm showing you off at the meeting."

Robert used a lame excuse. "But my old clothes drown me," he complained. He didn't tell Hannah that his real excuse was that he didn't want to face Katherine again.

Hannah stopped snipping and reached for the pile of clothing that Robert had worn from California to Winter Quarters. Piece-by-piece, starting with the canvas trousers, she tossed them into the hot coals of the prairie sod hearth. They erupted in flames, bringing extra warmth into the tiny cabin.

"There," she said. "Now you don't have a choice. You're going to church in the clothes you wore before you enlisted."

Robert saluted as though he were still in the army. "Yes, sir—I mean yes, ma'am."

The six Harris children stood around Robert and Hannah. Their father was still an object of curiosity. Hannah had made Robert wait until the middle of the night, when she was absolutely certain that all six of them were asleep, before the couple enjoyed their few moments of intimacy. Each child was dressed in his Sunday best, clothing that had been carried in their wagon from Nauvoo across Iowa. Except for the cold, Hannah's children always preferred the large gatherings in the bowery to small meetings in the Council House or in the bishop's house.

"Is this the best Brigham could do for you?" Robert asked his wife as his eyes scanned the interior of her sparse cabin.

"We're lucky to have this, and don't you dare say anything to Brother Brigham or anyone else," Hannah warned. "We could be living in a dugout on the bluff. President Young has done a marvelous job keeping the Church together in the wilderness. If ever I've had a hero, it's Brigham Young."

Robert had left Council Bluffs in July of last year, eighteen months ago. Hannah and the children had lived out of a tent and her wagon box until mid-October. George Bundy, Job Smith, and a few other men had erected this small and crude cabin made of cottonwood logs and willows. It had one room only and measured twelve by eighteen feet. The wood had been rafted down the Missouri. Chinking had been woefully inadequate during the first winter, with the wind howling through large cracks. The cracks were sealed now with makeshift clay and straw caulking. The shanty had a dirt floor, frozen solid around the edges but warm near the hearth. For the first two months Hannah had done her cooking out-of-doors. George Bundy and the others erected her sod chimney shortly before Christmas. Until spring the mud roof worked fine. When torrents of rain hit, leaks in the roof became larger and larger. Water ran live rivulets into the shanty and down the streets. Clothing, furnishings, and even the children had been drenched several times. The problem was solved when Brother Bundy stretched both Hannah's tent and wagon cover over the roof and later got help to erect a more permanent roof using shake shingles.

Hannah could tell Robert wanted to say something about his resolve to chew out Brigham Young so she quickly changed the subject.

"After the meeting I'll show you where we buried the baby," she said, holding back tears.

The strategy worked. Robert calmed down. "I'd like that," he said.

"There are still a lot of people waiting to see you," she added, and then named off people like Daniel's sister, Rebecca Browett Hyde; Rebecca's husband, Orson Hyde; and Rebecca's mother, Martha Browett. She also mentioned his boyhood friends Joseph Hill and Edward Phillips, along with his cousin, John Gailey, and John Hyrum Green.

"It'll be good to see them again," Robert said as he wet his razor in a basin of hot water and began shaving for the second straight day, facing Hannah's mirror.

"I'm sorry," Hannah said as she gathered the remains of Robert's long whiskers and threw them in the fire.

"Sorry for what?" he asked.

Hannah fell apart momentarily. "About the baby," she wept. "I so wanted him to live. He was such a special baby. I named him after you."

For the first time, Robert asked the hated question. "What happened to him?"

"I don't think I was that healthy when he was born," she began. "There wasn't enough to eat, especially things like potatoes and turnips. He struggled as a baby. When spring came, both of us did a little better. But I got the ague during the wet spring and summer, and so did most everyone else."

In the recesses of her mind, Hannah remembered how life had been the past year and a half in the place now nicknamed "Misery Bottoms." That first winter had been cold and wet. The following spring the sky had brought unparalleled rains, with overflowing water from cesspools contaminating the wells. During the summer the Missouri River diminished to half, threading feebly southward through the center of the valley. The mud of its channel made a wide tile pavement between the choking crowd of seeds and sedgy grasses, and growth of marsh meadow flowers. She remembered the ooze at water's edge, which stank in the hot sun like a naked mussel shoal. There were yellow pools of what children called frog's spawn. Great clouds of mosquitoes rose from every area of the river. And she remembered the venom-crazy snakes, too—lucky that she had not lost another child to snakebite.

Robert drew a deep breath. He thought he was the one who had suffered.

Hannah continued. "Elizabeth was gone, but there's nothing she could have done. She was out of quinine anyway. I shook until my bones were pulverized. I wept. I prayed. But I couldn't make milk. The baby began to suffer with black canker."

Robert suddenly remembered the day Thomas Bloxham had coaxed him not to enlist in the army, to stay home and protect his children against diseases like black canker.

Thomas had said, "Try to picture your two-year-old, little Sarah Ann. From New Mexico Territory you won't be able to see the lesions that'll pop out on her skin, her uncontrolled drooling, her painful barking cough, how her neck will swell from pussed-up tonsils, the terrible fever she'll have, how her little heart will almost quit beating from the strain of it all, and how her muscles will stop working. I've seen black canker come on kids, and it ain't good."

Sarah Ann was alive and healthy. But black canker had killed Hannah's baby.

Joseph did his best to explain. "Mother was just a skeleton last summer, Pa. We're lucky she didn't die."

Hannah remembered how thankful she felt when she could supplement her family's diet later in the year with chokecherries, melons, strawberries, grapes—and with vegetables obtained not only from their own gardens but from Missouri farmers. But it had been too late to save the baby. She had managed to hide the baby's mournful condition from her children by wrapping the child's rotting legs in blankets. More than five hundred people had died in Winter Quarters during Robert's absence, and more in the other settlements such as Miller's Hollow.

Robert stopped shaving and drew Hannah to his chest. "I just don't understand why they didn't take better care of you Battalion wives, and our families."

Hannah snorted. "Don't start that again. The people here did the best they could."

CHAPTER NOTES

Two sources conflict on the exact date that Robert Harris arrived in Winter Quarters. Ricketts, in *The Mormon Battalion, U.S. Army of the West,* has the Pace and Lytle groups arriving on Saturday, December 18. Bigler and Bagley, in *Army of Israel, Mormon Battalion Narratives,* have the Pace and Lytle groups arriving on Friday, December 17. For the purposes of this novel, I have chosen to have them arrive on December 17.

34

ROBERT WAS MAKING A BEELINE TOWARD Brigham Young when Hannah jerked on his arm. "There's Sister Pixton. Tell her about the mule."

Robert had been focusing on Brigham Young. Despite the large crowd and Hannah's protests, Robert vowed to pull on the Church leader's arm after the services and give him a piece of his mind.

"Later," Robert said, dragging his resisting wife toward the Mormon leader. Brigham was surrounded with well wishers, congratulating him on his talk, asking questions, and shaking his hand. He had made warm welcoming remarks about the Battalion boys who had returned from California. Brigham was dressed in a black wool suit with a heavy overcoat. The December sun was bright, but not warm. There was no breeze and a few blackbirds could be heard in the distance.

Brigham had just covered his reddish-brown hair with a top hat when Robert finally planted his feet directly in front of him. "You're one of the Battalion boys," Brigham said, extending his hand in a friendly gesture.

Robert accepted the handshake. He hoped the Church leader wouldn't bring up the letter from Katherine just now. "I have a question for you, Brother Brigham."

"I get questions all the time, brother. Fire away."

"My wife won't admit it, but I don't think she got much of the money I sent her from Fort Leavenworth and from Santa Fe. Why is that?"

Brigham tried to force a laugh. "I've been asked that more than once, Brother…"

"Harris, Robert Harris."

"Alright, Brother Harris."

"Seems to me you remembered my name just fine when you wanted me to enlist in the Battalion a year and a half ago."

"Robert, you're embarrassing me," Hannah said.

Robert set his jaw and let his eyes lock on his Church leader. He ignored his wife.

Brigham looked puzzled, as though he were not used to having a member of the Church talk so directly to him. He forged his answer. "I suppose you could say we treated the money like tithing. We tried to use it for the good of all the people."

Robert's blue eyes flared with anger. "My baby died while I was away. My wife couldn't buy the kind of food she needed to keep herself and the baby healthy. It's a wonder all my children didn't die."

A sad look came upon Brigham's face. "Brother Harris, we did the best we could under trying circumstances to meet our obligations to the dependents of the Battalion. There were too many things beyond our control, such as the weather and wholesale prices out here on the frontier."

"Has it ever occurred to you that perhaps my child would be alive today if you had kept your promise to take the families of the Battalion west with you? You promised when we left that you'd get our families out there even if you had to leave your own family behind."

Hannah turned away, clearly embarrassed. Looking down, she said, "Robert, I've already told you. The baby was sick, in no condition to travel. I made the decision myself to stay here in Winter Quarters."

Brigham cleared his throat and spoke with emotion. "Brother Harris, I did leave my family behind."

Robert stammered for a moment as he tried to think of what to say next. A woman wormed her way toward Brigham and spoke in a loud, unforgiving voice.

"Brother Brigham," the woman said, "I've not had the courage to speak out until now, but listening to Brother Harris gives me that courage."

Brigham's eyes flitted to the woman. "Sister Scott?"

"Yes, Margaret Scott," she answered. "My brother was Corporal James Scott. He died in Pueblo."

Robert grimaced in remembrance. James Scott had been a corporal in Company E. The young soldier and his sister had not come to Nauvoo until the spring of 1846, just before Robert had left the Illinois city as part of the exodus.

"And what can I do for you?"

The young woman began to cry. "I just want to know what course the Church will pursue to ensure the memory of those who have fallen."

Brigham drew his arms around the woman and began consoling her. Robert turned his gaze to dozens of members of the Church waiting to either comment on what the Church leader had said in his remarks, compliment him on his leadership, or chew on him as Robert had done. Levi Roberts and his wife were there, and so were Captain Pace and his wife, along with several of the sixteen men who had traveled with the Battalion boys from the Salt Lake Valley. There were other Battalion boys as well, the ones who had traveled with P. C. Merrill. For those who had borne the cost of war, questions and concerns were unavoidable. Robert yielded to Hannah's tugs.

"You've said enough," Hannah said as she pulled him away.

Although unloading on Brigham had made him feel a little better at the time, Robert now felt a sense that perhaps he shouldn't have said what he did. He put himself in Brigham's shoes. There was no way to keep everyone happy. He thought of the behavior of some of the Mormon soldiers, such as Private Davis, who had a fondness of drinking and ended up in the guardhouse in Fort Leavenworth for a short spell. If every member of the Battalion had kept his covenants at all times and had done exactly as Brigham had instructed, there would have been far less trials and tribulations. And that was true for the entire membership of the Church, Robert concluded. He began to think of Daniel and the Battalion boys who remained in California. He said a prayer in his heart that they would behave themselves.

Hannah was still tugging on Robert's coat. "Go talk to Sister Pixton."

Robert let his gaze fix on Elizabeth Cooper Pixton, and her daughter, Charlotte. Her husband, Robert Pixton, had been converted to the Church on a Mormon immigrant vessel late in 1841. Sister Pixton immigrated in 1843. During the exodus, Brother Pixton had driven some teams across Iowa for Brigham Young.

"She still has only one child?" Robert asked Hannah as he walked toward Sister Pixton. He knew that the Pixtons had lost two young children previously, a newborn baby immediately after her husband left for America, and another newborn in December of 1844.

"Just like us, she lost another baby while you Battalion boys were away," Hannah explained. "They named him John Helaman Pixton. He's buried in the Winter Quarters cemetery, not far from our baby. She's never complained."

Robert let out a big breath. "What you're really saying is that she never looked up Brigham Young after a Church meeting and gave him a piece of her mind."

Hannah let a winning smile grace her face. "That's correct."

A flush of red came over Robert as Hannah's words soaked in. Sister

Pixton had spotted Robert and was only a few steps away.

"I've already heard the bad news about my husband," Sister Pixton said as she reached out and touched Robert's hand.

"It was a hard decision to make, whether to stay in California or come home," Robert began. He assumed from the comment that she had already spoken to Captain Pace or one of the other Battalion boys, or heard it from one of P. C. Merrill's men. "It was tough on my brother-in-law, Daniel, and it was tough on Brother Pixton."

"Well, as much as I'd love having him here with me, I suppose he had to be part of the half that stayed," Sister Pixton said. "We have only one daughter." She pulled Charlotte to her side. "You have six children. It was only right for you to come home. Hannah needs you."

Robert now felt worse. Sister Pixton's faith and support of Brigham Young amazed him.

"Tell her about the mule, Robert," Hannah said.

For a moment Robert wondered if one of the other Battalion boys had already spilled the beans. Sister Pixton just stood there with a curious look, so Robert said, "Your husband sent a gift to you. A mule. It's in the corral."

Sister Pixton turned her eyes south where the large community corral was located, and the haystacks. The men of Winter Quarters had worked hard last summer and fall to cut and stack thousands of tons of hay there. She began to cry.

"He's a skinny thing," Robert added. "Not much left of him. But if we can keep him alive until spring, he'll be a fine mule."

After a few seconds Sister Pixton wiped away her tears and said, "From the stories I've heard, I'm surprised you didn't have to eat the mule to survive out there."

"There were those who wanted to."

The Winter Quarters cemetery in the northwest corner of the city was a forlorn place, with a few inches of snow covering the frozen turf. A frozen-over Turkey Creek bordered the city on the north, and Forest Lawn Creek bordered it on the south. There were dozens and dozens of graves in the cemetery. Hannah had told Robert more than three hundred people had died here since he left, half of them children under age five. There were two new graves; the burials had taken place yesterday. Moroni Browett was buried here, not far from his own son's grave.

"Let me tell you something," Robert said as his family huddled around him. The children were bundled in winter clothing. The cold winter day had produced red cheeks and runny noses. Joseph, Lizzy, William, Thomas, Enoch, and Sarah Ann squinted their eyes against the brightness of the midday sun.

Robert stammered a bit.

"What, Father?" asked Enoch, the four-year-old.

Robert regained his composure. He stared at the grave of his son, Robert Harris III. The baby had died at the age of seven months. "Our family should number nine souls," Robert began. "But there are only eight of us. We lost a child due to a lack of proper food and poor conditions. This will not happen again. I promise. Somehow, some way, we will survive this place. I will take you to the Salt Lake Valley as soon as I can. It's a healthier climate there. We'll start over. I'll build you a new home. We'll have a new farm. Daniel will bring some horses and mules home with him from California, and money, too. We'll share in all that. Daniel and I will be partners again."

"Where's California, Papa?" Lizzy asked.

"Way out west, Lizzy," Robert said, stretching his arm in that direction. "A thousand miles from here."

"Is that where the Salt Lake Valley is?" William asked.

"No, the Salt Lake Valley is west, but closer than California."

"When will Uncle Daniel be home?" Thomas asked.

"By late summer or fall," Robert answered.

"Uncle Daniel won't come home to Winter Quarters," Joseph, the oldest, said to Thomas. "He'll go home to Aunt Elizabeth, in the Salt Lake Valley."

"And to Aunt Harriet," Lizzy corrected.

"Will we be there to meet Uncle Daniel when he arrives in the Salt Lake Valley?" Joseph asked.

"That's our goal," Robert said. "It's the Salt Lake Valley, or bust."

"But we don't have a wagon, or any oxen," Lizzy said.

There came a sudden hush over the children. Hannah, who held little Sarah Ann by the hand, looked away.

"What do you mean we don't have a wagon or any oxen?" Robert asked. He stepped in front of Hannah. "Do you have something to tell me?"

Tears streamed down Hannah's reddened face. "I sold the oxen so we could buy food. And I gave our wagon away last spring. Someone needed it more than we did. Our wagon is in the Salt Lake Valley. We'll have to get another one."

For a moment Robert wanted to explode. Hannah, the woman who had complained about George Miller taking their wagon in the winter of 1845-46, had given away the wagon Robert and Daniel had built to replace that one. Robert fought to regain his composure. He let his eyes scan Winter Quarters, laid out before him, a city laid out a mile long, northwest to southeast. He could see a water-driven mill at its north end, west of Brigham Young's home—the Council House. Among all the sod and log homes there were three blacksmith shops and two schools. Horses, mules, and cattle were penned up in the corrals nibbling on hay. Brigham Young and the Twelve had already made the decision to abandon the city in the spring, but for now, this was home.

Robert began to get a grip on reality. Reality was a hard thing, but it was reality nevertheless. "Well, I guess I'll have to build a new one, or buy one," Robert said. He began to wonder where he might gain employment, and what he could get paid. He had used all his Battalion money to survive the trek home.

"I'm sorry," Hannah said, still sobbing. "I'd like to leave this dreadful place and get to the Salt Lake Valley and be with Daniel and Elizabeth and Harriet, but I've made it difficult for us."

"Nonsense," Robert countered. "You did what you had to do. I'm here now. I'll get to work and we'll land back on our feet."

CHAPTER NOTES

There is a story among some of the descendents of Robert Harris, undocumented, that Robert indeed did seek out Brigham Young and gave him a piece of his mind relative to the fact that Robert's family had not been brought out to the Salt Lake Valley in 1847. The author uses that story in this chapter to illustrate the fact that there was indeed some controversy over those things. The reader should not gain the impression that Mormon Battalion members did not support their Church leader. They did, as evidenced by their enlistment, their endurance, and their faithfulness.

Several sources document the deaths at Winter Quarters. One, *Old Council Bluffs,* published by the LDS Institute of Religion (7 August 2000), containing the writings of Gail Holmes, states there were 360 deaths in Winter Quarters. There were probably more than that, she states, but because of the cost of burial, many bodies may have been buried outside the cemetery.

PART THREE

California
Gold

35

Late January 1848

Coloma, California

ONE THING ABOUT CALIFORNIA THAT thirty-three-year-old Henry Bigler didn't like was all the rain that came in January. The winter rains had begun in earnest two weeks ago, on the ninth, followed by cloudbursts. The rain came so heavily that the American River reached flood stage and threatened to wash away the three-foot-high dam. Not only that, but it demonstrated that the mill had been set too low and the race would not carry off the water.

"I hope Captain Sutter doesn't show up just now," said Bigler to Marshall. From Sutter's perch at the fort, Sutter always assumed nothing could go wrong. The river flow was subject to the reality of substantial seasonal fluctuations, with unpredictable flooding episodes that could easily tear apart any structure situated within the stream's natural levees.

"Me, too," said Marshall. "He wouldn't understand."

The mill site was well upstream of Sutter's Fort, well outside the boundaries of the captain's Mexican land grants. But at this point neither the military government nor any other official body showed any desire to regulate land use and ownership. Neither Sutter nor Marshall had given any thought that the sawmill was located on Indian land, near a Nissenan Indian village.

Bigler and the rest of the crew worked nearly around the clock until the thirteenth when the weather finally changed. Thursday morning dawned clear as a bell. The water level fell and the nearly completed dam was safe.

After that, Bigler and the crew turned their attention to another problem: The tail race needed to be deepened, a fact that half delighted Bigler. That's when he got to use his blasting skills.

In Bigler's opinion, Marshall had a good crew at the site. The crew consisted of several Battalion boys besides himself. William Barger and James S. Brown had the job of felling timber and dragging it to the mill yard with oxen, aided by native Indian workers. Alexander Stephens hewed the logs to fit the mill's design. William Johnstun, assisted by non-Battalion men—Charles Bennett and William Scott—assembled the structural framework. Bigler's job was to blast rock out of the mill race so that Indian laborers could clear it out. Bigler also hunted game to help feed the crew. Three other men helped on miscellaneous tasks: Israel Evans, Azariah Smith, and Ephraim Pearson, Jr.

To Bigler, the country here looked wild and lonesome. He was surrounded by high mountains covered with a heavy growth of timber, infested with wolves, grizzly bears, and Indians. He was glad he brought his musket—most of the other men had left theirs at the fort. The only modern convenience was a nice double log cabin about a quarter mile from the mill, occupied not only by the men but also by Wimmer's family.

The Indians, at Wimmer's command, dug up and threw out mud and rocks during the day. Then every night Marshall ordered the floodgate opened to allow the water from the river to run through the excavated channel; that way loose sand and gravel were carried off by the swift current. Afterward, Marshall would inspect the channel and tell Wimmer where to put the Indians to work.

It was on January twenty-third when Marshall made his customary inspection. Wimmer and the Indians were working near the lower end of the tailrace. Bigler was busy with his drill, making preparations to put in another blast of powder. As he was packing in the powder, Bigler stopped to observe Marshall. Marshall seemed to be captivated by something in the tailrace, perhaps the granite. Over the roar of running water, Bigler could barely make out Marshall's words.

"Go fetch me a tin plate," Marshall told one of the Indians. Marshall wore a broad Mexican *sombrero*, a serape, soiled white linen trousers, over which he had donned oily buckskin leggings. It had rained again during the night, but only a little. The grass on the hillsides was still wet, and water dripped from tree branches.

A new cabin had been built by the white workers and that's where the Indian went, making a trail in the mud, asking for a tin plate from young James S. Brown, who had just turned nineteen.

"What does he want with a tin plate?" Brown asked the Indian.

The Indian just shook his head and waited patiently for the plate. Brown followed the Indian back to Marshall's location. Bigler strolled toward the other men and watched with interest as Marshall scooped some material into the plate.

"This is a curious rock," Marshall said to Brown. "I'm afraid it'll give us trouble."

Brown gave the rock an intense stare, making his close-set eyes seem to pop out of his narrow forehead. "What do you mean?" he asked.

Marshall was washing the sand and gravel around and around in the plate. Not satisfied, he chipped off some of the granite with a pick and washed that in the plate too.

"What are you looking for?" Bigler asked.

"Quartz," said the superintendent of the sawmill project. "The white flint-like rock that's so plentiful around here. Sometimes there's gold in it."

Bigler was unimpressed. He had studied geology as a schoolboy. Quartz was as common as bad breath, and he didn't see any gold in the pan or in the tailrace either. Bigler went back to work and in a short time had made a successful blast. The Indians began digging again.

Marshall didn't give up, certain he had seen something. Just before the men quit work for the day, Marshall came up to Bigler and the others. He held some small specs of mineral in his hands. This time, to Bigler's eyes, it really did look like gold.

"I think I've found us a gold mine, boys," Marshall said.

Brown was the first to scoff. "If there wuz gold here, the Spaniards would have found it years ago."

"Or the Indians," Bigler said. Bigler suspected Marshall of being a little drunk. Sobriety was scarce on northern California's interior frontier.

"We'd never have that kind of luck," said Azariah Smith.

Bigler began to laugh at the notion. He'd known Marshall as a man who took a notion to wild imaginations anyway.

Marshall was unperturbed. "I want you boys to turn a good head of water from the river into the raceway tonight. Throw in a little sawdust, rotten leaves, and some dirt. Make it all tight. I'll see what shows up early in the morning."

Two mills hands went to the head of the fore bay early the next morning and closed the gate, exactly as Marshall had instructed. During breakfast the men talked about Marshall's "gold," and had another good laugh. Afterward everyone went to work. Bigler went down to the ditch to do some more drilling before putting in a blast of powder near the place where the waterwheel was to be set. It was a cold morning. Bigler shivered as he worked.

After a while, around seven-thirty, Marshall appeared and walked directly to the millrace, inviting no one. Bigler began to wonder what the sweeping waters might have left revealed during the night. Bigler could see Marshall bend over, put his hands into the icy water, and bring them up again. The mill superintendent appeared to study his hands for a while, and then dip them into the water again. Marshall picked at his findings with his fingers, reflected a while, and then repeated the process. He knocked in the crown of his old slouch hat a little, and placed pieces of something in it.

After Bigler made his blast, he saw Marshall approaching the mill yard. He was carrying his old white hat in the curve of his arm and he had a big smile on his weathered face. He was pleased about something. Bigler followed Marshall to the carpenter bench.

"Boys, I believe I've found us a gold mine," Marshall said to the carpenter, William Scott.

Bigler shook his head in derision, remembering the good laugh the men had at breakfast. Scott and the others laughed, too.

Alexander Stephens stopped his hewing of a timber. "What's in the hat?"

"Gold!" Marshall answered with a confident air.

"Oh, no, it can't be," exclaimed carpenter Scott.

Marshall had assigned two of the youngest and strongest men to saw timbers by hand. James S. Brown and James Barger had worked up a good sweat sawing another board. "Stop for a minute," Brown said to his companion. He walked towards Marshall and Bigler and the others. "Did you say gold?"

Marshall had placed his hat with the gold on the carpenter's bench. In the dented crown Bigler could see a number of small pieces of some yellow substance. They varied in size from tiny particles to as large as a kernel of wheat. Some were rounded, some resembled little cubes. One by one, Bigler and the others picked up a piece and bit into it.

Brown became the first believer. "It's gold, boys! It's gold!"

Alexander Stephens, Azariah Smith, and William Johnston came running. So did the Wimmers. Smith drew a five-dollar gold piece from his pocket, part of his army pay, and placed it next to Marshall's gold. "I don't know, it doesn't look as bright as the real thing."

At that remark Brown took one of the larger pieces and placed it on the bench. He grabbed Scott's hammer and pounded away. The small gold nugget did not shatter; rather it flattened. "Well, it passed that test," Brown said.

"Still don't believe me?" Marshall asked.

"Let's give it the manzanita wood test," Bigler suggested. The Mexicans used manzanita wood for smelting gold and silver ore, something the Battalion boys had learned while marching through New Mexico. Stands of small manzanita trees grew in California, too, about ten or twelve feet high, and they produced a reddish berry.

Brown carried some of the small nuggets into the men's cabin, placed them on the tip of a shovel, buried them in the hot coals, blew on the coals, then extracted the nuggets. The nuggets had not changed their appearance.

"It's gold for certain," Brown admitted.

"Where'd you get these nuggets?" Smith asked.

"Follow me," Marshall said.

Soon everyone was looking in the mill race and in the pockets and crevices of the river, just beneath water level. James Barger was the first to find a nugget. Bigler's eyes were attracted to something, too. He took out his jack-knife and pried a small nugget out of the stream.

"Well, I'll be ... all you have to do is look," Bigler said.

36

Late January 1848

Winter Quarters

"I'VE GOT TO HAVE A JOB OF SOME KIND," Robert said to Hosea Stout, the head of the Winter Quarters police force.

"I'd like to have you, but I'm limited to just a few men," Stout replied as he leaned on the top rail of the corral. "If someone quits, I already have a waiting list."

Robert had already learned that the police force here had been organized in the fall of 1846 initially to protect cattle from the Indians and other intruders. Its duties had been expanded to prevent crimes and sedition, provide security for Church leaders, spy out against possible attacks from the federal government, and be a watchdog on camp obedience. They had a mandate to report any moral or religious indiscretions to authorities such as Brigham Young and Orson Hyde.

"Well, put me on the list," Robert said. "I'm in a desperate situation." In his mind, returning Battalion boys ought to be put on top of every employment list automatically. They had sacrificed a year of their life for the good of the Church.

"It's a long list," Stout said. "Just about everyone's in a desperate situation. You probably wouldn't like the work anyway."

"Why do you say that?"

"You'd think that baptized members of the Church would be a hundred percent obedient, and not get into trouble or cause us problems," Stout replied.

Robert laughed. It seemed to him that the devil worked harder on members of the Church than anyone else. Some baptized members not only reverted to worldly sins, but became apostates. He was thinking of men like William and Wilson Law, and the Higbees and the Fosters back in Nauvoo.

"What kind of problems?" Robert asked.

"You've been on the police force in Nauvoo, so you probably understand," Stout said. "Among thousands of people, there are always small handfuls that cause us all our problems. We not only deal with cattle theft from the Indians, but things like one man stealing a cow from his neighbor. Desperate people do desperate things. We've had to break up a whiskey ring, counterfeiting at Garden Grove, gambling, and even a plot to murder members of the

Twelve."

Robert thought of all the plots to murder Joseph and Hyrum Smith. The plotters had finally succeeded.

"Then we get political pressure, too," Stout admitted. "We get a few complaints that we act as a morality squad, and going beyond the mark. But we just try to do our job."

Robert had heard enough. The police played a valuable role in protecting the camps, keeping people honest, and in upholding the law. But it was obvious Stout didn't need him. "Any suggestions for me? Where can I get work? I've got a large family to feed. Our bread pantry is empty."

Stout shrugged his shoulders in a helpless gesture. "Lots of men here are in the same fix. Look around."

Robert had already investigated several options. There was a little sod hut where people made baskets and washboards out of willows for trade in Missouri in exchange for grain and other necessities. Some men had fur-hauling contracts with Peter Sarpy and Indian agents. Others had contracts to furnish heavy timbers, studs, rafters, and framing materials for building, but the cold weather had slowed that activity to a standstill. Turkey Creek had frozen over, so there was no activity at the water-powered mill on the city's northern edge, where the Saints had created flour and cornmeal. The city was going to be abandoned in the late spring, so there was no fence building going on, or construction of new sod huts or cottonwood log homes.

There were a few options left. The store operated by Newell Whitney, and Robert's old profession—butchering cattle. A third option, going to Missouri to labor as hired hands for farmers, wasn't available until spring. He'd heard of a few men working as lard cutters in a St. Joseph pork-packing house for a dollar and a quarter a day. But that was in St. Joseph, too far away. He had been away from Hannah for a long time. He had no intention of separating again, even for a few weeks.

Robert's meeting with Newell Whitney got off on the wrong foot and seemed to stay there.

"We hire very few people," Whitney said. "All we have are clerks and teamsters. We're stocked up for the winter and we have plenty of men on contract to purchase things from St. Louis. Besides that, Brother Brigham says I'm to close the store in March anyway. I guess you've heard we've got to move across the river and get off Indian lands."

"I'd appreciate it if you'd find a way to use me until March," Robert pleaded. "After all, I've been in the Battalion and just returned. I sent my clothing money and part of my monthly pay back to help fund this store, so please consider that."

According to Hannah and the other Battalion wives, Whitney's store had gouged its customers since the day it opened about a year ago. The store had been made possible only after Hannah and the other wives turned over a large amount of cash to the Church. Robert could remember with remarkable clarity the time Orson Hyde, John Taylor, Parley Pratt, and Jesse Little came to

Fort Leavenworth for the Battalion money. They acted like they had expected a combined total of more than twenty thousand dollars—forty-two dollars per soldier times nearly five hundred men—but Pratt had returned to the Mormon camp with only a little over five thousand dollars.

"Sorry, I don't have a position right now," Whitney repeated.

Robert drew a deep breath, entering a territory he hadn't planned on. But he couldn't help himself. "My wife said you and the others arm-twisted her and other Battalion wives until you got most of the money we sent back," he charged.

The color went out of Bishop Whitney's face. He stammered a bit and then began to explain. "Brother Brigham considered the Battalion money a manifestation of divine providence at just the right time. It was a lifesaver for all the Saints at Winter Quarters."

"Let me get this right," Robert said. "Hannah gave you my forty-two dollars; you bought goods from St. Louis, and sold them to her at a profit."

"Brother Harris, you need to understand that we had to pay high prices in St. Louis, plus we had the cost of shipping," Whitney explained.

"Nauvoo merchants had to pay shipping, too," Robert charged. "Hannah says the prices you charged here in Winter Quarters were a lot higher than stores charged in Nauvoo."

Hannah had told him that Whitney had charged two dollars for two pounds of molasses, for example, but she was used to paying seventy-five cents for the same amount in Nauvoo. Sugar, saleratus, and rice were higher too.

About the only thing cheaper in Winter Quarters was flour.

"It's the freight charges," Whitney said. "Believe me."

"Then give me a freight contract," Robert said. If Henry Eagles could be a teamster, then so could he.

Whitney threw his hands apart in frustration. "Sorry."

By far the richest resource of the Mormons at Winter Quarters had been the massive herds of livestock owned by members of the Church. Robert figured the stock had numbered around thirty thousand cattle at one time. Although that number had been reduced during his absence due to a constant slaughter for food and constant loss to Indian theft, there were still thousands of cattle in and around the city.

"I hate being a butcher, but I guess I've got no choice," he told Hannah after he returned and told her of his experience with Hosea Stout and Newell Whitney.

"It's a worthy occupation," Hannah said with a smile. "Do what you have to do."

Robert grimaced as he fondled the knife he had carried with him during his time in the Battalion. "Maybe they've got too many butchers, too."

Hannah bit her lip. "Lots of men slaughtered their own beef while you were gone. But you may as well go to the stockyards and ask around."

The stockyards south of town were where the "old beeves" were kept for slaughtering. In the summer cattle grazed on Indian lands, but now they were kept in the large corrals and fed the tons of hay that had been put up.

"Who's on the beef slaughter committee?" Robert asked Hannah.

She named a few men Robert didn't know.

"Well, I'm off to find them. I hate blood and offal, but I'll do it to support my family."

37

Late February 1848

Gristmill Site, California

DANIEL DIDN'T FIND OUT ABOUT THE GOLD discovery until near-ly a month later. News came at the end of February in the form of a letter from Henry Bigler, directed to the men working at the gristmill.

"How we gonna keep a thing like this a secret?" Wilford Hudson asked after the men had gathered around under a tree to read the letter. Hudson had been a private in Company A.

Bigler's letter had been addressed to Israel Evans, who had been a mess-mate to Bigler during their time in the Battalion. So had Jesse Martin and Ephraim Green, who kept staring at the letter like it was gold itself. The other gristmill workers—all Battalion boys—were Robert Pixton, Sidney Willes,

Levi Fifield, Samuel Rogers, Jonathan Holmes, Daniel Dennett, James Douglas, Joseph Dobson, and David Moss.

"We have to," Hudson said as he pointed to the letter. "Says right here that Marshall and Captain Sutter want to keep it that way until they find out how extensive the gold might be."

It was a mild day, in the seventies, a fact that Daniel thought unique. Two years ago he had been in Nauvoo where the February weather was freezing cold and a foot or two of snow on the ground. He liked the warmth here, but it was not home. He wished he were still in Nauvoo, in his little white frame farmhouse near the area they called The Mound.

"What if gold runs the entire course of the American River, and all the creeks too?" Jonathan Holmes asked no one in particular.

That comment caused Daniel to dream for a few seconds. He could see himself picking up a few small nuggets. But he could also see the framework of the mill, more than half constructed over the raceway. He had a passion to get it finished for Sutter. Captain Sutter had supplied everything needed; there were ox teams, plows, scrapers, spades, shovels, and picks.

"We've been working along the river for weeks and I ain't seen no gold," Willes said.

Daniel shook himself back to reality. As he thought about it, he hadn't seen any gold either. If there were gold in the bottom of the millrace, or out where the dam was located, wouldn't he have seen it? Didn't it glitter in the water? Didn't gold have a "pick me up" sign written all over every tiny nugget?

"This thing about gold at Coloma might not amount to much of anything at all," Daniel said. "What we ought to do is keep our nose to the grindstone. We'll soon have enough boards from the sawmill project, and that means we can get this gristmill finished. We've hired on to build it and I aim to see it through."

Hudson stood ramrod straight for a few seconds and jutted out his jaw. "I'm going up there and see for myself."

"Me too," said Sidney Willes suddenly. He began to fidget, standing on one leg and then another, as though he wanted to leave within the hour. Levi Fifield said he was going too. The three of them said they would hunt for venison, too, so the trip would have value even if the gold thing turned out to be a fluke.

Daniel thought about this for a few seconds. No doubt about it, without boards the work had lagged. The race was done, but Daniel needed lumber. Hand-hewing logs and hand-sawing boards was hard work. Daniel knew it was useless to try to keep all the men away from Coloma. A look of resignation came over him.

"Well, don't be gone too long," Daniel said. "While you're at Coloma at least find out when the sawmill will be done, and when we'll get boards."

The story that Willes and Hudson told when they returned several days later gave Daniel a bad case of gold fever.

"I just used my butcher knife and picked up six dollars worth of gold in a couple of hours," Hudson told Daniel in excited breaths. A light rain was falling. The men ignored it and stood out in the open, next to the millrace.

Daniel felt his own pangs—irked, mainly, that these two men had a glimpse of the gold, whereas he had hung around the sawmill supervising the slow work of hand-sawing more timbers and boards. He didn't let on that he was irked, so he pursed his lips and said, "Wow. Right at the sawmill?"

A sly smile came over Hudson's face. "Oh, we found a few small nuggets there all right, but there's a better place to look for gold, and it's not too far from here."

Daniel's eyes brightened further and he felt like a rich man already. He looked down the river, in the direction the men had returned from the sawmill site. "Exactly where?"

"Less than a day's ride," said Willes. "We found a small creek running into the American River through a ravine. When we examined the bedrock, sand, and gravel, we found gold. I'd bet there's more gold there than at the sawmill."

Fifield, the third man who made the trip, was far less optimistic. As more gristmill workers gathered around them, he said, "Don't get your hopes up, Brother Browett. To be honest, I don't know if there's enough gold in the river to worry about." He pulled out a white handkerchief and opened it. It was littered with a little gold dust. Fifield said it was worth only about fifty cents. "Not much to show for my efforts for half a day."

Daniel was now confused. Was the discovery of gold on the American

River a major thing, or was it just a false alarm? He'd heard of more stories coming from the sawmill site, but didn't know what to make of those either.

"I've been at the fort a time or two while you've been gone," Daniel said to the three men. "Rumors are floating through there like blow flies on a cow."

"Such as?" Fifield asked.

"While you were gone the Swiss teamster came to Sutter's Fort and tried to pay for some brandy and other provisions at the store owned by Sam Brannan and C. C. Smith," Daniel explained.

"You mean the man named Wittmer?" Fifield queried.

"That's the man," Daniel said.

"Did Smith take the gold?"

"No, he refused," Daniel said. "So Wittmer went straight to Sutter. Sutter verified the claim, so now the word's out. I'd be willing to bet that Smith has informed Brannan, and if so, Brannan will blab it all over San Francisco."

Hudson grimaced at the explanation. "How did Sutter know?" he asked.

As Daniel knew the story, Marshall had arrived dripping wet at Sutter's Fort on a rainy afternoon. Marshall told Sutter he wanted to meet with him secretly. In the privacy of Sutter's office Marshall pulled a rag from his pocket and dumped two ounces of gold on his desk. After consulting what the *Encyclopedia Americana* said about gold and after tests in the apothecary shop, Sutter declared Marshall's specimens to be of the finest quality, at least twenty-three-carat gold. With a promise that Sutter would visit Coloma, Marshall departed in the rain without taking anything to eat, so complete was his excitement.

"I suppose Sutter will be on his way to Coloma soon then," Hudson said.

"Right away," Daniel predicted.

Almost at once, before the gristmill workers had accomplished much more, Daniel had cause to regret that he had ever agreed to let Hudson and Willes ride off up the American River. Now they began to talk about quitting their work and hunting for gold full time. That frightened Daniel. He didn't want any of the men to do anything that would upset Captain Sutter because Sutter hadn't paid them a cent yet and probably wouldn't until just before the Battalion boys left for the Salt Lake Valley.

"But I need you to work here until the gristmill is finished," Daniel said to them the day then announced their intentions. "It'll only take a few more days. Then we'll all hunt for gold."

Neither Hudson nor Willes said much at first. They just stood there holding the reins on their horses as Robert Pixton cooked breakfast, such as it was, while the other men waited for Daniel's reaction.

"We can't get the boards we need anyway, so what's the use?" Willes countered.

Daniel threw his hands apart in exasperation. "But we should get them soon," he said.

Willes and Hudson weren't quitting, they said. They were merely going to spend their time looking for gold until boards could be obtained to finish the gristmill. In a way, Daniel could see the logic. But if Willes and Hudson left, how long would it be until the rest of the helpers at the gristmill left also?

"When will you be back?" Daniel asked as they left on their horses. The men took their tents, too, and camping equipment.

"Get us some boards. We'll be back when you get some boards," Willes said.

Daniel reached out and caught Hudson's horse by the bridle. "Don't get too distracted. We need to get all the Battalion boys together in a few weeks and talk about the trip to the Salt Lake Valley."

"Get it organized," Willes said. "We'll attend. Maybe by then we'll have enough gold so that we can buy up a lot of livestock to take home."

Daniel immediately began to take the challenge to get the Battalion boys together for a meeting, as though it were a mandate. Most ex-Battalion solders still planned to work only until spring for Captain Sutter, and spring was about here. As the men had gotten together over the months, most of the talk had been of reuniting with their families. Daniel's heart did a jump. Elizabeth and Harriet were only a few months away.

"Brother Browett, you've got a lot to do," Hudson said as he left. "Finish the gristmill, talk to Sutter, and organize a meeting."

"I know," Daniel responded.

"You ought to do one other thing," Hudson added.

"What's that?"

"Go see Coloma for yourself. And the ravine we're talking about."

"I suppose so," Daniel concluded.

Daniel got something of a surprise when he rode into Sutter's Fort several days later to visit with Captain John Sutter. He found himself invited on a trip to Coloma with not only Sutter, but the editor of the *California Star*—Edward Kemble. Now here he was, headed toward the site of the sawmill, meandering through the bogs that lined the American River in places. Two big hawks were skimming the trees above them.

When Sutter's mule stumbled in the thick mud, Sutter didn't panic; rather he talked to his mule. "God bless me, Katy. Now den, child. De oder foot. Atta girl. Now de oder foot."

The brown mule calmly walked through the bog without lurching, and without dumping Sutter into the mud. It was a good thing, Daniel concluded. Sutter had dressed up for the occasion. He wore a broad-brimmed planter's hat and carried a silver-headed cane across the pommel.

Daniel had met Kemble a year earlier while still serving in the Battalion while occupying Los Angeles. Kemble had served in the California Battalion under Fremont. The purpose of the trip, in fact, was to escort Kemble to the site of the gold discovery and let him do a story about it—whether the rumors were true or not. Kemble had arrived in California on the *Brooklyn*, with Samuel Brannan. Kemble was still not a member of the Church.

The winter rains had not quit in the Sacramento Valley and along the Sierras. Today, however, warm rays of sunshine peeked through a layer of intermittent clouds. The improving weather enlivened Daniel and had enlivened his men at the gristmill site, too. They were all in good health now, and working hard. The gristmill was nearly finished thanks to boards sent to them from Coloma.

"Quite the gentleman," Edward Kemble said of the Swiss owner of the fort. Daniel and Kemble rode their horses behind Sutter. Sandy, Daniel's horse, had avoided the swampy area.

"I agree," Daniel admitted as he wondered how a young man of only nineteen could already be the editor of the newspaper in San Francisco. That morning Sutter had treated Kemble, Daniel, and a handful of other men a hearty meal of beef and frijoles before they started out on their trip.

Daniel's constant meetings with Sutter had continued to produce positive results on behalf of the Battalion boys. Together they had caught up on the books. Together they were working out a satisfactory payment schedule for each of the Battalion boys who had worked for Sutter.

Once they were past the gristmill and hit the emptiness of the little valleys that lined the river, Daniel began to worry about Indians. He was not alone in his worrying. Kemble had heard so much about scalping and torture and mutilation of bodies that he often tugged at his own hair as if to reassure himself that it wouldn't come off easily. Sutter, who almost slept in the saddle so relaxed was his ride, was astonished that neither Kemble nor Daniel had ever seen a scalped person or a mutilated body. Sutter had seen both during his early years as a Santa Fe trader, right after he immigrated from Switzerland. He also had seen such things as a mountain man for a couple of years, and as a California settler in the Sacramento Valley.

The talk of wild Indians made Daniel shudder. "I thought you tamed all the Indians around here," he said to Sutter.

Sutter laughed. "Ve can't tame dem all," he said. "De's some bad ones out dere."

"I suppose the Indians in these parts ain't entirely civilized," Kemble stated. "But I've seen white men meaner than Indians, with less excuse."

"I wish we'd talk about something else," Daniel said. "Talk about gold." For certain, Daniel felt, he was going to have bad dreams of Indians tonight. He could see a big Indian knifing him just before he woke up.

When the group reached Coloma, Kemble asked where they might look for gold. Marshall, in a crusty mood, just waved at the river. "You'll find it anywhere you've a mind to dig for it down there," he said.

To Daniel's surprise, Marshall's crew appeared to be living out-of-doors. Blankets, cooking utensils, and boxes of food were scattered in seeming disarray. The crew had chickens. Two or three of them were scratching around Daniel's feet. Daniel wondered where the hens hid their eggs. He could sure use some eggs for dinner, or even breakfast.

Marshall pulled Daniel aside, pointed to Kemble, and asked, "What's that damn newspaperman doing here?"

Daniel shrugged his shoulders in a helpless gesture. He had nothing to do with Kemble's assignment. Kemble had come of his own accord, or on assignment from his boss—Samuel Brannan. "Just his job, I suppose," Daniel replied as he let his blue eyes scan the sawmill site. Both the stony bar on which the sawmill had been erected and the millrace were inundated with high water, victims of the spring rains and snow runoff from the mountains. "What's it going to take to get your mill running again?"

Kemble and the others were trying their hand at finding gold. Sutter nervously paced between the gold seekers and the sawmill. Daniel couldn't see any mill hands, including Henry Bigler. He assumed they were either idle or farther up or down the river looking for gold.

Marshall's tone was still icy. "What are you worried about?" he asked. "Didn't you get enough boards to finish the gristmill?"

Daniel felt like patting Marshall on the back. "Yes, I did, and thank you," he replied. "But I'm just thinking about Captain Sutter. I think he'd rather make money by exporting lumber than he would by finding gold."

"Get these spring rains over with fer one," Marshall replied indignantly. "Get my men to quit lookin' fer gold fer another. And make certain I don't get any more visitors, especially newspapermen."

Daniel sighed and his stomach growled. He looked forward to the evening meal. He felt Marshall's remarks slightly insulting, but he let them pass. Marshall had a reputation for being eccentric anyway.

Marshall suddenly wheeled and pointed to a tree-covered hill. "There comes another distraction."

Daniel could make out the forms of three men on horseback. They came so quietly it greatly unnerved him. He thought how easy it would be for Indians such as these to sneak up on a man in the night, or even in the day for that matter.

"Danged Indians," Marshall said. "They must've heard Sutter's here already. There'll be a passel of 'em here pretty soon, all wantin' gifts and hand-outs."

Daniel shuddered and felt a flush of fear.

There was more than a passel of Indians. It seemed to Daniel they had crawled out of the woods for hours and now they were huddled around a roaring campfire, talking through interpreters to Captain Sutter. They were supposed to be all tame ones, but some of them were armed like they were wild. One had a quiver full of the finest arrows Daniel had ever seen, and probably the deadliest too. They looked like they were poisoned six inches up, obsidian tipped, and could pierce a man's body almost through and leave him lifeless in an instant. Another brave had an English half-axe that looked like it could bash a man's head in with one powerful thrust.

Daniel's attention was drawn to one older Indian whom the men referred to as El Capitan, or chief, who was now talking in Spanish. An interpreter translated his words into English for Captain Sutter. The chief was a man about forty-five, of large frame and big muscles; his countenance was heavy, dull, manifesting neither good humor nor intelligence. His long coarse hair, matted, fell down upon his shoulders in a neglected condition. A faded cotton handkerchief was tied around his head. He had obtained his clothing from white settlers, but he was accompanied by three men who were naked except for loin cloths.

Daniel didn't get eggs for dinner, but he did dine on pork and wild geese. He was still smacking his lips when he heard the interpreter say to Sutter, "El Capitan says you shouldn't hunt for gold." A wave of concern flooded Daniel.

"Why not?" Sutter asked as he fanned a wisp of smoke that floated by. He had donned a coat in the coolness of the evening. The loincloth Indians appeared unaffected by the cold.

"Very bad medicine," the interpreter answered. "The old chief says that he has always known there is gold in these mountains. His ancestors knew it, too. But the gold is the property of a demon that lives in a mountain lake. The shores of that lake are lined with gold. He warns all of us that the demon gobbles up anyone who searches for gold."

Daniel didn't laugh at all, but he could see that Sutter and the other men were suppressing the urge to laugh. Sutter said, "How do I know dat?"

The interpreter asked the question in Spanish. The Indian muttered some words. And then the interpreter answered, "He says a member of his own tribe has been gobbled up while hunting for gold."

Sutter told the interpreter to ask the other Indians what they thought. He did, and they replied that they believed the old chief.

A skittish chill went up and down Daniel's spine. Demons were real, in his opinion. Satan had been cast out into the earth with a host of perhaps millions or even billions of evil followers. There were certainly enough demons to inhabit the mountains of California and even the waters of the American River, right down to the nuggets of gold that were hidden among the cracks and crevices of its banks and even its bed. If a demon could gobble up an Indian, a demon could gobble up a white man, too. The demon would do it by putting it into the head of a man that gold was more important than anything in the world, including a man's family, home, principles, or even the gospel. Daniel felt a new urge to leave California. More than ever he wanted the comfort of a home wherever the Saints were located, a home with Elizabeth and Harriet. He missed Robert and all the rest of the Battalion boys who had left last September. He missed his mother, his sister, and leaders of the Church such as Brigham Young, Wilford Woodruff, and Orson Hyde.

Listening to one Indian after another depressed Daniel. Some of them had low, throaty voices. Others talked in a chant, in high-pitched tones. After a while Daniel left the campfire and wandered aimlessly around the sawmill site, but that depressed him, too. There was no moon and he couldn't see anything at all, so he began to fear what might be lurking about among the trees or along the river. Soon the gathering broke up, the Indians made their own camps and fires, and Daniel retreated to a campfire made by the newspaperman, Kemble.

"I sure didn't like those Indian stories, especially the one the old chief told about demons and gold," Daniel said. He could feel his mouth tighten as he talked.

"Aw, don't worry about it," Kemble said. "It was probably just some old fable."

"I don't know," Daniel replied.

"I'll bet it's just something told by the early mission padres around here to scare the Indians and keep them working."

Daniel thought about it for a few minutes and tried to accept the explanation as a good one. He was anxious to put the thoughts of demons out of his mind, so he asked Kemble another question. "Did you personally see any sign of gold in the river this afternoon?"

Kemble shook his head in the negative and began to chuckle.

Daniel had noted that Marshall remained on the hillside whittling on a piece of wood while Kemble and the others spent several hours wading from one location to another. One of Sutter's clerks, a man named Reading, had succeeded in washing a tiny bit of color into a borrowed Indian basket, one tightly woven with native grasses and ornamented with brightly colored feathers.

"I know what I'm going to write in the newspaper," Kemble said.

"What would that be?"

"Great country. Fine climate. Full flowing steams. Mighty timber. Large crops. Luxuriant clover. Fragrant flowers."

"But what about your report on the gold? Isn't that why you came?"

"The talk of gold here is humbug. Nothing but pure humbug."

CHAPTER NOTES

Sidney Willes and Wilford Hudson are credited with the late February discovery of Mormon Island, a sandbar in the American River halfway between Coloma and Sutter's Fort. It turned out to be the third major gold strike in California, one with very rich diggings. Willes and Hudson started working the area for gold on 7 March 1848, according to Captain Sutter's New Helvetia diary.

Newspaperman Edward Kemble visited Coloma in mid-April with Captain Sutter. The story of the Indian chief telling Sutter and Kemble about demons and gold is related in the book *James W. Marshall, The Discoverer of California Gold,* by Theressa Gay, pages 181-184.

38

April 1848

Gristmill Site

THE TALK OF DEMONS AND GOLD LINGERED in Daniel's mind for days. Late one afternoon as the boys at the gristmill were sitting around Robert Pixton's cook fire, waiting for their evening grub, Daniel looked up from his plate and saw eight or nine riders breaking through the trees. They were riding good horses and leading pack mules.

"Why, that there's Richard Slater," Daniel remarked to Pixton, who was stirring a pot of beans with a generous portion of beef. Slater had been one of Pixton and Daniel's messmates in the Battalion. He had found work at Sutter's Mill running the bowling alley. Most of the men with him had been working in San Francisco.

The most surprising thing was that Slater and the other men looked like they had packed for a long trip. This made Daniel uncomfortable. Had they quit their jobs in San Francisco early? Were they going to try the Truckee route over the Sierras in the spring, when the snows were as bad as when the Donner Party members met their fate? Were they headed out alone, without consultation with any of the other Battalion boys?

Daniel had received his first shipment of lumber from Marshall's sawmill earlier in the day so his mood had been good until now. The boards were good ones too, long and straight, although a little too green.

"Where are you boys headed?" Daniel asked as Slater dismounted and began eyeing the food in Pixton's Dutch ovens.

"Mind if I make a meal?" Slater asked.

"I suppose you're as welcome around here as gold," Daniel said. "That goes for all of you."

"Sam Brannan has hired us to deliver newspapers," Slater said as he helped himself to a plate of beans and beef.

Daniel now recognized the other men: William Hawk, Nathan Hawk, Sanford Jacobs, Daniel Rawson, and Silas Harris. Silas had always claimed he was something like a fifth or sixth cousin to Robert. They were into the beans and biscuits, too. Daniel suddenly realized that there wasn't much food left in the Dutch ovens.

"Delivering newspapers?" Daniel asked.

"Brannan asked for volunteers, so we volunteered," said Silas. "We're taking two thousand copies of the *California Star* all the way to Missouri. From there they'll be sent east, all the way to New York City."

Daniel stood up and tightened his pants. He was unable to decide who he was more aggravated at, the visitors eating all the food, or Samuel Brannan. "Another of Brannan's big ideas to promote California?" he asked.

Slater nodded and spoke through a mouthful of beans. "You've got that right."

"What does the newspaper say?" Daniel asked. "I'd like to see a copy."

Slater was only five-foot-eight and had been riding a tall black horse, perhaps sixteen hands. He had to stand on the tips of his toes to reach into his saddlebag. "Got one right here someplace," he responded. He rummaged through what looked like sacks of seeds and few young starts of fruit trees. But he found the newspaper; it contained a six-column article entitled, "The Prospects of California." Daniel glanced through it. It extolled California's climate, fertility, agricultural potential, fisheries, and strategic position for world trade. It also bragged about the great Sacramento Valley and predicted that a railroad would soon connect California to the United States. C. C. Smith, Brannan's store partner, ran an advertisement touting the arrival of a new assortment of summer clothing.

The rest of Daniel's crew were sitting like statues, awed by the fact that they had just lost their supper. This struck Daniel as funny, so he regained his good mood and began to chuckle a little. He concluded that the sudden appearance of wild Indians would not have affected the men so much.

"Do you know what I think?" Daniel asked.

Slater's brown eyes opened wide. "What?"

Daniel shook his head in a sad gesture. "Step-by-step Samuel Brannan is getting more into the world and less into the Church. I think he sees himself as the czar of all California, making money on people coming and going."

"Oh, you're absolutely right," Slater said. "He's a strange duck. Did you hear about the New Year's costume ball in San Francisco that the Brannans attended?"

"Yes," Daniel answered. "All that stuff reaches even our ears." Daniel had heard that Brannan dressed up as Satan, complete with a long tail that he had switched back and forth as he strutted through Robert Parker's new City Hotel. Dozens of guests had attended and Brannan's antics had not gone unnoticed.

Daniel scanned through the newspaper again. "I don't see anything about the gold discovery." Several of his crew had gathered behind him and were looking over his shoulder.

"Just look harder," Slater said. "It's there. Most of the stories were prepared in late February. They had a small space unused, so at the last moment Edward Kemble inserted an announcement that gold has been discovered here."

Daniel ground his teeth together. That was another thing that aggravated him lately. There had been a steady stream of people making their way to the gold mines from San Francisco, Monterey, Sonoma, San Jose, and other parts of California. They had come pushing and cursing with their picks and shovels, stealing Sutter's livestock, and helping themselves to the best spots on the American River.

Daniel finally found it. "I wonder what kind of impact this will have back East."

"Doesn't matter to me," Slater said. "I'm going back to my family in Winter Quarters, bringing them out to the Salt Lake Valley, and staying there." Slater had a son and four daughters waiting for him.

More than ever before, Daniel became sentimental about the upcoming trip to the Salt Lake Valley. His night dreams flashed through his mind for a few seconds, and his skin flushed hot with thoughts of being with Elizabeth and Harriet. "Lucky you," Daniel said. "I wish I were going with you as far as the valley."

"How long do you plan to stay with Sutter?" Slater asked.

"We're having a meeting at the fort on Sunday, right after our sacrament services," Daniel responded. "It's time to end our work here and make plans for our trip home."

"Oh, by the way," Slater said. "I forgot to mention something. Brannan rode with us as far as Sutter's Fort."

Daniel felt a flush of red. "Oh, no."

Slater talked apologetically. "He'll be at your Church meeting, and at your other meeting too, I suppose."

Daniel gnawed on his bottom lip. "I suppose he has a right, since he's the president of the Church in California. But I have a bad feeling every time his name is mentioned. I don't much want to be around him."

Slater dumped the last of the beans onto his plate. "You should have tried some of this," he said to Daniel. "Good fixins."

Daniel pretended to ignore the remark. "When are you leaving?"

Slater pointed up river. "We're going to try our hand at the gold for a few days before we skedaddle. It'll be a rough ride over the Sierras; there's a lot of snow up there this year."

Nathan Hawk, one of Slater's companions said, "I was there when Brannan walked the streets of San Francisco screaming that gold had been discovered out here. We can't help but try our luck at it."

Daniel shrugged his shoulders. He was tempted to warn them about the old Indian chief and his story of gold and demons but he didn't. "Can't hold that against you," he said to Nathan. Then he turned his attention to his stomach and back to Slater. "I suppose you packed food on those mules," Daniel said.

"We stocked up at the fort," Slater said. "And we bought a lot of horses."

"Good. Let's open up the packs and see what you have to eat. I'm starving."

Daniel supposed that at one time there was probably no more likable man than Samuel Brannan. All during the sacrament meeting at the fort, Daniel tried to assess his feelings for the man, even to the point of forgetting all the bad that he had heard and giving the Spirit a chance to talk to him just in case his prejudgments had been wrong.

Brannan was a Yankee, raised in New England, but never talked about his Irish heritage. Brannan was almost ten years younger than Daniel and, at a very young age, had been wiped out in real estate ventures during the Panic of 1837—three years before Daniel had joined the Church in England. Brannan was still in his teens that year. For several years after that he wandered the country as an itinerant printer. As a missionary, Brannan became one of the "Young Lions of Mormonism" in the city of New York, and became involved in publishing two of the Church's newspapers there. Beguiled by tales of the West, and envisioning a Mormon kingdom on its shores, Brannan led the first shipload of American emigrants to California two years ago. The Brooklyn arrived in San Francisco on the thirty-first of July, 1846—called Yerba Buena then—just weeks after the port was seized by the American navy in the war against Mexico.

By now Daniel was well aware of Brannan's conflicts with Battalion veterans who had been a substantial part of his flock in San Francisco, such as William Coray and James Ferguson. Coray was the first to accuse Brannan of appropriating Church funds for his own use. Ferguson, perhaps the most literate enlisted man in the Mormon Battalion, had constantly accused Brannan of unethical business practices. Because of his high living while others struggled—especially the needy such as the poor, the widows, and the orphans—Brannan had his conflicts with others, too. He had dispatched an outspoken

Mormon, William Glover, to the south on some kind of concocted trading expedition intended to raise money for the new settlement at Salt Lake. He had continuously schemed with Lansford Hastings, who had led immigrants to California, to monopolize California's newspaper business.

Brannan and C. C. Smith had established their store in the Baquero House in Sutter's Fort the previous October. It had quickly become a general frontier emporium that Daniel and the others called a "shirt-tail store." It contained a general assortment of hardware, clothing, and outfits for men wishing to cross the mountains with pack animals. With the talk of gold, Brannan seemed poised to leave all his problems in San Francisco behind. Daniel cringed at the thoughts that Brannan might have a stronger personal presence in the Sutter's Fort area and among the Mormon men still working for Sutter and those in the river trying their hand at gold. It seemed to Daniel that if anyone deserved the title of a demon, it was none other than one of his fellow Mormons—Samuel Brannan.

Daniel didn't mind Brannan presiding at the sacrament meeting, but when he took over the other meeting, dominating with his forceful personality, Daniel became agitated. Outwardly, a good spirit was manifested, but Daniel's gut was twisted inside. After all, the meeting was for the Battalion boys and the Battalion boys only. Daniel didn't mind visitors, and would have welcomed Captain Sutter himself, or even James Marshall, if they had something to contribute. As long as Brannan was his in-line priesthood leader, Daniel felt compelled to accommodate the controversial Mormon. In truth,

Brannan had a lot to offer. He had traveled over the Sierras several times and had acquired more than a passing knowledge about California, its wagon routes, and even the old mountain man and Indian trails.

As the meeting began, Robert Pixton approached Brannan and told him that the Battalion boys at the gristmill had seen Richard Slater and the men delivering the newspapers.

"I hope they didn't dilly-dally around too long," Brannan said tartly. "They should be over the Sierras by now."

Daniel saw Pixton stifle a laugh. Brannan apparently had no idea that Slater's group was panning for gold on the American River.

Brannan looked no different than the first time Daniel saw him last September. Daniel and the Battalion boys were on their way to the Salt Lake Valley, camped on the other side of the Sierras. Brannan rode into the camp all alone—alone because he couldn't get along with the men he had started out with from the Salt Lake Valley. Today Brannan had the same sharp features, a dark but well-trimmed beard, thick and wavy black hair, and was attired in eastern dandy clothing.

The meeting was held in the adobe fort compound in mild weather. There were no sounds coming from the blacksmith shop or from the distillery. Not because it was Sunday, but because Sutter's workers had left for the American River to try their hand at gold. Normally, even on Sunday, a launch would be in the process of being loaded with freight for the regular run between the fort and San Francisco Bay. Previously the tannery was doing extensive business; now the vats had been left filled and a quantity of half-finished leather was spoiled. There were no hunters coming in with bear furs and skins, and none going out, either. Two-thirds of Sutter's grain harvest was still in the fields. The Indians, too, had gone gold seeking. Now bands of robbers from the redwoods near San Francisco were rumored to threaten Sutter's holdings. And if that weren't bad enough, as gold seekers passed through the fort area they seemed to help themselves to Sutter's cattle, sheep, and crops at will.

Daniel quickly scanned the men in the meeting. Out of a hundred Battalion boys who had turned back to work in California, everyone was here except Slater's group and a few other men who were still in places like San Francisco.

Daniel called the meeting to order and quickly presented a litany of items that needed to be discussed. The first items had to do with numbers: How many men, how many wagons, how many animals would be making the trip to the Salt Lake Valley? The other items included the touchy subject of how to collect the Battalion boys' pay from Captain Sutter and the best time to leave.

It was here that Brannan took over the meeting. "I know you're thinking of following the Truckee route over the Sierras. But you'd better blaze a new road if you're taking wagons and provisions back to the Salt Lake Valley."

Daniel's immediate reaction was negative. It had been widely rumored that Brannan had advocated opening more roads into California to feather his own business nests. "California immigrants make it over the Truckee route so I reckon we can too," Daniel said.

Ezra Allen stood in support of Daniel. "I don't know if I want to find a brand new road. Blazing a road up in the Sierras means a lot of hard work with picks and shovels and axes."

Brannan's dark eyes glared at Ezra and Daniel. "Lots of snow up in them mountains this year, boys."

"Isn't there every year?" a young Henderson Cox asked. Unmarried at only nineteen, Cox had been a private in Company A.

"Yep. That's what doomed the Donner Party last year," Brannan said. "But it's much the same this year. The Truckee passes are clogged. Slater and his men can get through with just horses and pack mules, but not with wagons."

"But that'll be the case up and down the Sierras," said Jonathan Holmes, one of the gristmill workers.

Brannan was not to be deterred. "When are you leaving?"

"We haven't talked in detail about that yet," Daniel answered. "But I suppose we want to strike out by mid-June and be over the Sierras a month or so later."

Brannan pointed a bony finger at Daniel. "There are other factors you obviously haven't thought of," he continued. "Spring runoff on the Truckee River will be an obstacle. Do you know how many river crossings you have to make?"

Daniel hadn't counted them, but he remembered several during the trip last August and September. He shrugged his shoulders. "A dozen, maybe more."

"Twenty-seven," Brannan roared.

There was a long pause while Daniel and the other men processed this information.

One of the gristmill workers, Samuel Hollister Rogers, spoke. He had been a private in Company B and spent time in San Diego. "There's apt to be another way to get to the Humboldt River from here."

The remark agitated Daniel some, for he didn't want to yield to Brannan's suggestions just yet. And he hadn't gained a good feeling about him. But Brannan was gaining support.

"I sure don't want to try and get a wagon up over Roller Pass on the Donner route," said Robert Pixton.

"But what are the other choices?" Rogers asked.

Brannan dismissed Walker Pass, named after mountain man Joseph Walker, because it was too far south. Instead, Brannan proposed the route taken into California from the Great Basin in 1844 by John C. Fremont during his second expedition into the West. To his knowledge, Brannan said, no other white men had ever come this way on the route. At the time, Fremont was searching for the mythical "Buenaventura River," described by earlier geographers and shown variously on some old Spanish maps as flowing into the Gulf of Mexico and on others into San Francisco Bay.

Daniel had lost control and he knew it. To the other men, Brannan was making sense. Daniel fell into silence for a spell, weighing every word of the conversation, but revived himself when it was suggested that a search party be organized to scout the potential route.

"I think you men ought to organize an exploration party and see if you can find that old Fremont route," Brannan said. Fremont's scout on that expedition was Kit Carson.

The right hand of Jonathan Holmes immediately shot into the air. "I propose that Brother Browett lead that expedition," he said. Dozens of hands shot up, seconding the proposal.

Daniel didn't know whether to protest or not. He didn't like the fact that Brannan had made the suggestion and seemed to know a lot about this part of California, but the whole thing seemed to make sense nevertheless.

"We ought to leave within two or three weeks," said James Sly, a former private in Company B. "I volunteer to go with you, Brother Browett."

Within a minute or two, Daniel had several other volunteers: Ira Willes, Israel Evans, Jacob Truman, Ezra Allen, James Allred, Henderson Cox, and Robert Pixton. As the men had a short discussion on when to leave—they decided that it should be no later than the first of May—Brannan sat with his arms folded across his chest, looking puffed up.

"It's time to approach Captain Sutter about our pay," Sly said to the men.

Holmes reported that he had talked to Sutter a few times about it. "Sutter always uses the excuse that his books are not up-to-date."

Robert Pixton laughed. "That's because his bookkeeper has gone off to look for gold. Soon all of California will be up in the sawmill area looking for gold."

Holmes pointed to Daniel. "In my opinion, Sutter has more respect for Brother Browett than anyone I know. Daniel's going to lead our exploring expedition, so why not appoint Brother Browett to talk with Sutter?"

Ezra Allen stood again. "While you're at it, Brother Browett, I have another proposal. Why don't we buy two cannons from Captain Sutter? He's got more than he needs now that the war is over. The time might come when we'll need them to defend ourselves in the Salt Lake Valley."

"Good idea," said Henderson Cox. "The Missourians might track Brigham Young all the way to the Great Basin."

Brannan scoffed. "Just don't use them against immigrants coming to California, Missourians or not."

CHAPTER NOTES

There are several sources that document the meeting that was held by the Battalion boys at Sutter's Fort on 9 April 1848. Henry Bigler referred to the meeting in his diary, and so did men like Samuel Hollister Rogers. "Daniel Browett was appointed to inform Sutter of their decision to leave and to obtain wages, cattle, and other articles," states Norma Baldwin Ricketts in her book, *The Mormon Battalion, U. S. Army of the West,* page 202. Apparently he was appointed to lead the exploration party, too (see *Kingdom in the West,* Volume 7, *Gold Rush Saints,* page 162). Perhaps it was only natural for the former soldiers to turn to Browett for leadership. Most of them had served as privates in the Battalion. Daniel had served as a sergeant.

During the meeting, Brannan steered the Battalion boys into exploring what is today known as Carson Pass. Although it is named after Kit Carson, Carson did not discover it, or ever claim that he had. Fremont did not name it "Carson Pass," or give it any name at all. He simply recorded it in his report as "the pass." However, Fremont did name a river in the area "Carson River" after his hunter, scout, guide, and friend. And Kit Carson did leave his blaze on a tree at the top of the pass.

When Brannan went east to meet Brigham Young he had five companions. Two of them he sent south along the Sierras to explore the possibility of a better pass than the Donner. Those two men founded a small post that became today's Woodords, near Hope Valley. These two men may also have blazed what later became the Carson Route that was followed by the Battalion.

39

April 1848

Winter Quarters

"BROTHER HARRIS, THERE'S SOMEONE HERE to see you," another
of the butchers said.

Robert was in a grouchy mood. His apron dripped blood from cutting
throats, and the muscles in his arms ached from skinning one beef after another. A carcass hung from a pole, beleaguering him in a light but cold rain.
Katherine had not given up her pestering; she still wanted to be his plural wife.

"Who is it?" he asked without looking up from the black and white skin
that hung from the half-skinned carcass.

"He wouldn't say," the man said as he left to feed more cattle at the corrals. Spring was near. There would soon be fresh grass. The hay at the corrals

was all but gone. Some residents of Winter Quarters had already moved south to new settlements around Council Bluffs.

Robert pegged his knife into a wooden block and walked in the direction his visitor was supposed to be. Cattle, some brown, some red, some black, and some black and white, bawled to be fed. There was a swooshing sound of a huge metal mallet; another steer toppled to the ground. Thousands of hungry mouths were waiting to be fed in Winter Quarters.

There was something familiar about the black-bearded man that stood holding a bay horse. The man was heavily built. He took off a weathered felt hat; straight and unkempt black hair fell over his face. He smiled, revealing missing teeth.

"Henry!" Robert squealed. "Is that you?"

There was emotion in Henry's raspy voice. He spoke barely above a whisper. "Where're Annie and Katherine?"

Robert almost kissed Henry he was so happy. His voice cracked as he said, "Not far from here. *Where've* you been?"

"At war, just like you," Henry said. "Sorry for my voice. I rode all night in the rain. I guess I caught a bad cold."

Robert thrust out his right hand. "Welcome home, Henry."

Henry accepted the handshake. "Thanks. It's good to be back."

Robert felt like Henry meant it. Henry looked the same, sounded the same, but Robert was feeling something for the first time being around his wayward brother-in-law. "Hannah will be glad to see you."

"I'll be glad to see her, too," Henry said. "But I want to see Annie and Katherine first."

Robert pointed north and gave Henry directions. "Can we talk later?" he asked.

"I reckon there'll be plenty of time to talk," Henry answered.

Hannah didn't know quite how to assess her feelings the next day when she wrapped her arms around the brother she hadn't seen for nearly two years. She had brothers in England that she'd never see again. One brother, Elias, had come to Nauvoo but she would never see him again either. He had disappeared the day Joseph Smith was murdered. And she had a sister, Nancy, whom she'd never see again; she was at the bottom of the Atlantic Ocean. Hannah's father was dead, buried in England. Her mother almost boarded the *Echo* to come to America. But she turned back at the last minute. Ann Eagles was happily remarried, but Hannah would never see her again either.

"I didn't know if you'd ever come back," she said as tears came to her eyes. She couldn't tell if the tears were for the fact that Annie had her father back again, that Henry and Katherine had the potential to work things out, or that she was just happy to see her own blood brother.

Annie, now seven, was a picture of happiness. She'd always been pale and poor-looking to Hannah, especially over the winter, but today she had a nice pink to her skin. Her brown hair was braided up perfectly and she wore a bright blue dress. She nuzzled close to Henry and held onto his hand, acting as though she never wanted to let go.

"I've had a lot of time to think," Henry said. He had lost his dark beard. He rubbed his freshly shaved face with the other free hand. Katherine stood behind him with one hand on Annie's shoulder and the other on Henry's. For the first time ever, the three looked like a family to Hannah.

For some reason unknown to Hannah, Katherine appeared to avoid eye-to-eye contact with Robert.

"I'm all ears," Hannah said, still taking stock of her brother. "Tell me where you've been."

Henry drew a deep breath and began talking in his labored, whispering voice. He started with the time he left Katherine and Annie in the middle of the night in Nauvoo and how he ended up in St. Louis and then Independence. He told of meeting Bernard Bogart on the steamboat and how he ended up in the army as a teamster working for Colonel Sterling Price.

"At first I fit right in with all the Missourians," Henry said. "Colonel Price was my kind of man. He drank corn whiskey and not only hated Mormons, but he cursed them and did anything to cause them trouble."

Hannah sensed that Henry's life had changed somewhere. "If you fit in with them at first, does that mean later you didn't?" she asked, crossing her fingers in a gesture of hope. She framed her brother in a fervent stare as she waited for the answer.

"Oh, not for quite a while," Henry answered. "I liked Santa Fe, and I liked the lifestyle of the Missourians there—or at least I thought I did."

"You may have liked it, but I didn't think much of Santa Fe," Robert said.

"Something you told me there kept coming back to my mind, time and time again, when I got into Mexico with Colonel Doniphan," Henry said.

"My Papa won the war for the United States," said Annie, still beaming.

There were sounds of children playing outside. "We're talking adult talk, Annie. Will you please go out and play for a while?"

Annie looked a little disappointed but left nevertheless.

"What did Robert tell you?" Hannah asked, her curiosity brimming.

Henry's face turned a shade serious. "Strange how I can remember what you told me Robert. I can almost recite it word-for-word."

"We had a lot of conversations, but you've lost me," Robert said.

"I was about to leave with Doniphan to go into Mexico. Just about all the soldiers in Santa Fe, except for the Mormons, were Missourians. I didn't like Doniphan because he liked Mormons. You talked about the behavior of a soldier, how he should act, and how he should behave. Remember now?"

"Just a touch," Robert admitted.

"You said that soldiers usually commit atrocities in war that make heaven weep. You tried to get me to imagine what it would be like for someone to invade Council Bluffs and murder, rob, and rape our wives. You predicted that a year from now Mexican newspapers in Chihuahua and Mexico City were going to be filled with accounts of how the Missouri volunteers acted—let me see if I get this straight now—you called them bad smelling bandits, long-bearded drunkards, fornicators, adulterers…"

"I remember now," Robert said, shaking his head up and down.

"But that's not all," Henry said, looking deeply troubled now. "You predicted that the Missourians would defy the laws of nature, drink whiskey out of holy vessels in the Catholic churches, and sleep in the niches devoted to the sacred dead."

Hannah turned a bit sarcastic. "Why Henry, I've never known you to think those things would be off limits."

Robert sat in stunned amazement. "You mean those things actually happened?"

"And worse," Henry said. "Far worse. What I saw in Chihuahua was beyond description."

An iciness raked Hannah's flesh. "And that's what changed you?" she asked.

"I was in a couple of battles," Henry said. "I pretended I was brave but I have to admit now I was scared out of my wits. That's when I began to miss Annie and Katherine, and you and Robert, too. I even admitted to myself that I liked living around Mormons. But when I saw the Missourians acting worse than dogs during the occupation, that's when I wanted to come back. Doniphan did what he could, but he couldn't control them. They were worse than dogs."

Hannah asked the obvious question. "Does this mean you're going to the Salt Lake Valley with us someday?"

Henry nodded. "I've thought about taking Annie and Katherine and going somewhere else, but I don't know where. I didn't like St. Louis and I didn't like Independence. Now that I think about it, I didn't like Santa Fe."

Hannah kept pressing. "So what's your answer?"

Henry's voice was wrought with conviction. "If that's where you're going, and if that's where Annie and Katherine want to live, that's where I'll be," he answered.

"Does this mean you're going to be baptized someday?" Robert asked.

"I wouldn't go so far as to say that," Henry said. "Living with the Mormons is one thing; being one is another. Let's take it a step at a time."

Hannah felt that was a good answer for now.

Henry turned to front Robert. "By the way, where's Daniel?"

"Brigham Young asked half of the Battalion to stay in California to work until spring," Robert answered. "Spring's here, so I'd expect they'll be planning to leave there soon."

"I'm sorry for what happened to you in Nauvoo, the way you were driven out by Mormon haters, and that you lost your homes and farms," Henry said.

Robert smiled. "It's all over now. Daniel will be home soon. He's promised to share what he makes. He's gonna bring me some livestock too. We're gonna make a new start in the Salt Lake Valley."

"Are you going to the Salt Lake Valley this summer?" Henry asked.

Hannah accepted Robert's soft gaze. She answered for her husband. "We can't afford it this year. Maybe next."

40

May 1848

Sutter's Fort

DANIEL'S MEETING WITH CAPTAIN SUTTER went better than expected. The old Swiss gent apologized for being behind in his books and was in a fair mood.

"Nobody but ze Mormons have ze integrity," Sutter said as they sat down in an office in the fort.

Daniel felt apologetic but his loyalty went to his priesthood leader. Brigham had instructed the former soldiers to work only until spring; then they should buy supplies and return to the main body of the Church. "I'm sorry we can't stay and work longer," he said. "But we're anxious to get back to our families."

"Vell, I understand, I understand," Sutter said. "I vish ya all couldt stay forever, but I know it's impossible. Yah?"

Daniel knew what was going through Sutter's mind. The spring rains had hit California, which meant more snow in the mountains. Daniel half expected Sutter to ask him for another work contract that would bind all the Mormon workers through July. That's when the passes would finally allow wagons to go through. Sutter said that if Mormons had been available years ago he would be a rich man by now. Instead, he feared there was no way he could pay his obligations. With only a few exceptions, Mormons with contracts fulfilled them—Daniel with the gristmill, and Henry Bigler with the sawmill, for example. All the other men had quit unannounced for the gold mines. Men from outlying areas such as San Francisco had helped themselves to his cattle and sheep herds, not paying for anything. The distillery was idle. So was the tannery.

Sutter further apologized for not having cash to pay Daniel or any of the other Mormon workers. "I'm very sorry. You take horses and wagons instead, ya?"

Daniel said "yes"and began a process of working out how much Sutter would charge for wagons, horses, mules, and cattle. "This will take a few days. It will need the approval of each man." In fact, each man would have to come in on his own and work out his final pay with Sutter. They would not only need livestock, but plows, picks, shovels, iron, seeds, plant cuttings, and anything else useful to take back to the Salt Lake Valley.

"Ya, ya," Sutter commented. "Ve take all da time ya need, ya?"

Daniel smiled. "Ya, ya. We'll work it out. I have another request."

"Vhat's dat?"

"You've got a collection of cannons here at the fort, more than what you need."

"Ya, ya. De kome from de merchant ships. I buy dem for protection."

"How about selling me a couple of them?"

Sutter seemed to go into deep thinking. With the Mexican War over and the Russians gone, Daniel felt there was a good chance the Swiss gent would approve.

"Ya, ya. You kin have two of dem."

When Daniel said that he was leaving in a few days to explore a new route over the Sierras, Sutter issued a solemn warning. "De veather is very bad now. Rain, snow in ze mountains. How can ye scout ze new roadt?"

"It's got to be done," Daniel replied. He told Sutter he was trying to find the route used by John C. Fremont and Kit Carson in 1844. Sutter shook his head positively, recalling when Fremont and Carson arrived at his fort that year. All of Fremont's animals had survived the trip, but were in such poor shape that all of them had to be replaced. The horses and mules had transported many hundreds of pounds of instruments, notebooks, charts, and mineralogical and botanical specimens over the mountains.

"Yah, perhaps you tink it has to be done," Sutter said as he scratched his head in disbelief. "But ye vatch for Indians, too. Ze wild Indians live in ze mountains."

Sutter was right about the weather. Daniel rode Sandy up the backbone of a gradually ascending mountain in the Sierras in a blinding snowstorm. In the trees, visibility wasn't absolutely zero, but he couldn't see much at all out in the open. He had purchased a Russian-style fur hat which he had pulled down over his ears and neck.

"Where do you think this goes?" a half-frozen Ezra Allen asked from his hunched-over position in the saddle. The other men rode silent, inwardly wishing Daniel would turn back.

Daniel reached inside his wool overcoat and pulled a compass out of his vest. "We're headed almost due east," he said. "This mountain will have to peak out sooner or later, and then start its descent. But we'll never find the big lake in this weather. It's too far away."

Daniel was looking for Lake Bonpland, named by Fremont after the famed French explorer and botanist Alexander Bonpland. Daniel figured if Fremont could make it through with some sixty-seven horses, he could do the same thing with only nine horses.

"If Fremont and Kit Carson came this way, they did it in better weather than this," Henderson Cox added.

Daniel thought about that statement for a moment. As he understood the story from Brannan and Captain Sutter, Fremont was trying to cross the Sierras with sixty-seven horses and mules in the dead of winter—something that had never been accomplished previously. Because of the animals, they had to travel along ridge tops at the highest elevations because there the wind had removed most of the snow and deposited it into the bottoms and canyons below. That's precisely what Daniel and his men were doing—following the tops of the ridges.

Better weather or not, Fremont's men had suffered hardships on that trip in 1844. Two men in his party were driven insane; one wandered off never to be seen again.

Daniel and his eight men had begun making preparations for their exploratory into the mountains on the first of May. The men delayed their departure for a day because of rain but made twenty miles in a southeast direction the first afternoon. With rising waters, gold hunting would be far less productive at Coloma and at Mormon Island. Most of the men would be forced to lay off a few days anyway.

The next day Daniel and his men made another twenty-four miles before camping where Sutter's shingle-makers had been working. The following morning, with spits of snow flying through the air, they started up the main divide between the American and Cosumnes Rivers. That's when they saw their first wild Indians, but there were only two of them and they quickly disappeared. The men continued up the divide the next day, making another twenty miles, through a heavy forest of pine and fir. That night, three inches of snow fell, blanketing the ground.

Daniel pulled Sandy to a halt. The visibility on the ridges was getting worse. In the trees, where he was traveling now, there was too much snow. The horses were falling through the crust of the old winter snow, up to their bellies near a peak called Iron Mountain. "I guess this is where we turn around, boys," he said. "It has the prospects of being a good route, better than the Truckee."

"How do we know it'll get us to the Humboldt?" Ezra Allen asked.

"Well, we've been going the right direction," Daniel concluded. "We'll have to explore it another time."

"Let two of us go just a little farther," Israel Evans begged.

"Alright, take Brother Willes with you," Daniel said. "Your horses seem to have a lot of stamina left. We'll wait in the trees. Be back in two hours, no later."

"Yes, sir," Israel said as he turned his horse up Iron Mountain.

When Evans and Willes returned, they reported that they had reached the summit but could not see what was on the other side. "I don't know if it qualifies for a wagon route or not," Evans said.

"We'll be back another time," Daniel said.

For the return, Daniel led the men first to Coloma. It was chaos there, with new miners paying no attention to Marshall and Sutter's claims. The men left and then proceeded to the sandbar on the American River now known as Mormon Island. There they found Sidney Willes and Wilford Hudson digging on the bar for gold. There were a lot of other men there, too, perhaps a hundred and fifty. Some of them were Battalion boys, but most were not.

"Any luck?" Daniel asked as he jumped off his horse. If there were, he planned on staying here for a few days. He'd been in the saddle for a week, averaging twenty to thirty miles a day.

Sidney pointed to a flour sack on the ground. Mounds of gold nuggets glittered in the afternoon sunlight. "Twenty dollars a day on a poor day."

"How about a good day?" Daniel asked.

"I'll answer that," a voice from behind said.

Daniel whirled to see Samuel Brannan wading the American River towards the Mormon Bar and the Battalion boys from a camp along the bank. Mormon Island was not an island at all, but rather a bar. During high water times the river had made a partial channel around the bar, leaving deposits up to fourteen feet deep of gravel, boulders, and sand highly laced with gold. The hills above the river were covered with flowering dogwoods, olive-colored oaks, towering cedars, and yellow pine.

"A hundred dollars a day, sometimes two hundred dollars, or even more," Brannan roared. "And that's even after the thirty percent taken out."

"Thirty percent?"

Brannan seemed all puffed up again. "Ten percent each for Willes and Hudson, and ten percent for my collection fee."

"Collection fee?"

"Or you might think of it as tithing," Brannan said without a note of hesitation.

Daniel reeled at the thought. "Who thought that up?" he asked.

Willes and Hudson both pointed at Brannan. "He did," one said.

"Seems fair to me," said Robert Pixton who was watering his horse. "After all, those two men found Mormon Island."

Daniel didn't argue, but it seemed to him that the mountain demons the old Indian had talked about had struck Mormon Island. Even after talking to some of the Battalion boys that had lived in San Francisco, Daniel could not think of one thing Brannan had spent Church money on except himself. The collection fee was as bogus as goblins. If there was any tithing to be paid, Daniel resolved to pay it directly to Brigham Young.

Hudson spoke to Pixton and the other men in Daniel's group. "If you want a tract here, we'll organize you into companies of five men each. Each company has an area five yards square."

"Only five yards square?" Ezra Allen asked.

Daniel let his eyes scan the bar he was standing on. The deposits of rocks, sand, and dirt were an iron-rust color with a reddish tinge in places. Fine gold particles could be seen, pervading the whole deposit. Men with common milk pans were filling the pans with dirt, taking them to the river, washing the dirt away, and dumping the remaining contents onto another pan. Quicksilver was added, which gathered all the gold, and then the refuse was thrown away. Others were merely taking the pan contents and pouring it onto flour sacks. Gold, and a lot of it, settled on the cloth sacks.

"That's all you need," Willes answered.

Henderson Cox protested. "But at Coloma, where we just came from, they're allowing each miner eighteen feet of river frontage."

Brannan interjected himself again. "That's based on the old Hispanic system of mining claims. This is the Mormon system. Take it or leave it. I've got Natomas tied up too."

Daniel knew the term. Natomas was another gold strike location a short distance downstream. Here, two other Battalion veterans by the names of Benjamin Hawkins and Marcus Shepherd had discovered another extremely rich placer deposit. It was now widely known that both Mormon Island and Natomas were richer and more abundant with gold than the area around Coloma. Here on Mormon Island, Daniel could see men gleaning gold out of every scoop of dirt and sand. At Coloma, the miners were still trying to pry nuggets out of crevices with knives.

Willes seemed to summon his courage. "You don't need to leave it. Companies that have five yards square are making twenty, thirty, and forty dollars a day for each man. Help yourselves."

"You pay me the thirty percent toll, and then I'll see that Brother Willes and Brother Hudson are paid," Brannan said.

Daniel felt not only trapped but torn. Gold fever had been building up in him as well as any other man. His contract with Sutter had ended. Sutter had promised to pay him and all the other men with horses, mules, cattle, wagons, and provisions. He was blocked by weather and melting snows from leaving for the Salt Lake Valley just yet. There was a window of at least three or four weeks until a departure date could be set for certain. By then, by his own quick calculation, he could make several hundred dollars, perhaps even one or two thousand dollars—even with the toll taken out.

"What do you say, Daniel?" Pixton declared. "Let's form a company."

"I'll be in your company," said Henderson Cox.

"Me too," said Ezra Allen.

While the other men in Daniel's exploration party were deciding, Jonathan Holmes stopped digging from his five-square-yard plot and walked toward Daniel. "We ended up with six men in our company, Brother Browett. How would it be if I became your fifth man? I could show you how we find the gold."

Now Daniel was trapped. When he said "yes" he felt like he had been sucked into a dark hole, a hole that the gold demons controlled. But he agreed to the proposition nevertheless. He could see the number of livestock that he was going to take over the Sierras triple, and could feel the weight of a sack of gold around his neck. Elizabeth and Harriet would be surprised and he would have the immediate power to take them out of the poverty that surely impoverished the Saints in the Salt Lake Valley. Robert would be proud of him—as partners they could own one of the biggest farms and ranches in the valley. They could use the horsemanship skills they had learned from the vaqueros. They could own saddles decorated with silver. They could each build a large house that would rival those lived in by Church leaders such as Brigham Young and Wilford Woodruff. Daniel stared at the dozens of men working the black sand on Mormon Island. He watched them using their knives, picks, shovels, watertight willow baskets made by Indians, and even a few roughly made wooden rockers to sift through the rocks and sand for anything that glittered. Some were using quicksilver to separate the gold from the sand. Flour sacks were spread out on the grass where the gold was temporarily held until it was transferred to leather pouches.

"Let's make a camp and get started," Daniel said to his four new partners. He hated to admit it, but he had gold on the brain just like all the other men.

"Whoopee!" yelled eighteen-year-old Henderson Cox.

CHAPTER NOTES

Lake Bonpland is today known as Lake Tahoe. Daniel and his men were not following the exact trail of Fremont and Carson, but they were close. The route Daniel followed exists today as a fine secondary highway in California, variously known as Iron Mountain Road, the Mormon Immigrant Trail Road, and Alternate U.S. 50. It goes up from Jenkinson Lake Reservoir, past Iron Mountain, Leek Spring, and joins California Highway 88. The ridge is also the historic boundary of the Maidu Indians on the north and Miwock tribes to the south. Fremont and Carson were actually following a trans-Sierra trade route used by the several tribes including the Washos, and very likely by people long before the Washos, Maidus, and Miwocks. It remains today as a stock trail.

Mormon Island, located twenty-five miles above Sutter's Fort, was indeed discovered as a source of gold by Sidney Willes and Wilford Hudson, Battalion veterans, just as portrayed in this novel. For a period of time it yielded more gold than any other location in California. Today it is under the waters of a man-made lake.

41

June 1848

Mormon Island, California

THE MEN ON MORMON ISLAND weighed their gold with a homemade balance that imitated the scales of justice. The scales were made of two chips, a stick, and a string. On one chip Daniel would place a Spanish coin and on the other chip he would place gold. In this way he could estimate the value of a day's work. Even after the thirty percent toll he was averaging more than fifty dollars a day. The day he made a hundred dollars, gold fever hit him more than ever. Daniel hated to leave Mormon Island, but other duties beckoned. He and the other men too had to make ox bows, ox yokes, pick out cattle from Sutter's herd, buy horses and mules, buy pans and kettles, and hold more meetings. All this "fitting out" had to be done at Sutter's Fort, and the fort was a one-day ride down the river. A one-day ride was one day that gold couldn't be found, and one day fitting out was a day that gold couldn't be found, either. So at least once a week Daniel would leave and make a short trip to the fort, fit out some, and then return to the diggings. At a June eleventh meeting at the gristmill, the men decided that it was time to leave for the Salt Lake Valley. The snow in the mountains had thinned out, evidenced by the swollen rivers.

"Where will we start from?" Ezra Allen asked. He had spent most of his diggings money on horses and cattle, but the leather pouch that hung around his neck still bulged with gold dust.

Henry Bigler raised his hand. "We ought to rendezvous at a little valley that me and some of the boys found a few weeks ago."

"Where's that?" Henderson Cox asked.

"Other side of the old dry diggings about ten miles," Bigler answered. "We call it Pleasant Valley." The "old dry diggings" was a term used by three area ranchers to describe a new area where gold had been discovered, not far from Weber Creek.

Daniel agreed and felt a tinge of excitement. Elizabeth and Harriet were almost a reality now. "How far from here?"

"I'd estimate forty-five miles from here, but only twenty miles from Coloma," Bigler said.

"By the time everyone arrives, we're going to have big herds of cattle and horses and mules," Daniel said.

"Well, the first ones to get there ought to be the ones to build a temporary corral, then," Bigler said. "It might be me and the boys who have been at the sawmill site. We're ready to strike out."

"I'll meet you all there then," Daniel said. "I'll bring the cannons." Daniel had taken delivery from Sutter of the two cannons a month earlier. Both had been placed on runners and ready to haul in a wagon. They were small, decorated, parade cannons off a merchant ship—one a bronze four-pounder and the other an iron six-pounder. They both worked; both made a big boom when loaded with gunpowder and ignited.

Enough of a big boom to scare off Indians.

"Heard the news?" Ezra Allen asked Daniel as they began their journey from Sutter's Fort to Pleasant Valley.

"What news?" Daniel asked. Like all the other Battalion boys, he had his wagon loaded to the hilt with provisions. And he had his own herd of horses and livestock. Two mares, one a sorrel and one a bay, had cost twenty dollars each—far more expensive than horses had been in Los Angeles. Sutter, however, had let him have a cream colored mare for eight dollars and a young buckskin stallion for only two dollars. A yoke of oxen had cost him eighty dollars and the wagon a hundred and fifty. Daniel had also purchased a belt and a sheath for his knife for a dollar twenty-five, a new tent for six dollars, plus a stock of shoe leather to take back to Salt Lake City.

Sandy, the horse Daniel had purchased at Los Angeles and named after Dr. George Sanderson, trailed behind the wagon with the new horses

Henderson Cox was in charge of the herd.

"A messenger just came into the fort from San Francisco," Ezra said. "California's now part of the United States."

"How'd that happen?" Daniel asked, though he knew the United States had won the war with Mexico and something like this was expected.

"It's called the Treaty of Guadalupe Hidalgo," Ezra explained. "The treaty not only officially ends the war, but the United States paid fifteen million dollars to Mexico."

"For what?" Daniel asked as he pulled a face. He'd never heard of the winner of a war paying the loser for anything.

"For all of upper California, New Mexico, and Texas."

The statement made Daniel feel good about his surroundings. He let his gaze sweep across the Sacramento Valley, and down the river. California was a good place, a territory worth having. Instead of being in a foreign country, Daniel was in the United States. It wasn't home to him, and he didn't feel like it was, but it felt good. Pleasant Valley was within the boundaries of the United States, and so was the pass at Iron Mountain, the route along the Humboldt, and even the Salt Lake Valley.

"Do you feel sorry for the Mexicans?" Daniel asked Ezra.

"No, I don't feel sorry for the Mexicans, or the Spaniards, either," Ezra said. "They mistreated the Indians and raped the land."

"I mean in regards to the gold," Daniel said. "Seems like their whole purpose was to find gold in the Americas, just as they'd done in South America."

Ezra laughed. "I suppose you're right. They'll miss out on the gold in California, but I don't feel sorry for them. The United States is our country again, now that the treaty's been signed. The United States will get the gold, and that's good."

"I don't think you'd get that opinion from Mason right now," Daniel said. Richard C. Mason, governor of California, was faced with massive desertions. Practically everyone working for the government here—including the soldiers—had abandoned their posts for the gold rush.

Daniel had the sense too that John Sutter's dream of creating an empire in the Sacramento Valley was at risk. Masses of people were going to descend on the American River, not to give Sutter business, but to steal from it and destroy his holdings. There likely would be no great Sutter fiefdom. Both the sawmill and the gristmill had been shut down. The military governor of California, Richard D. Mason, was scheduled to celebrate the Fourth of July with Sutter, but Daniel figured not even a governor would be able to save Sutter.

"Are you certain we're doing the right thing?" Ezra Allen asked as the wagons and livestock rolled toward the rendezvous at Pleasant Valley. "There's apt to be more gold here in California that we could ever imagine."

Daniel felt the tug of the diggings at Mormon Island. Ezra was probably right. Who knew where the next discovery might be? Every river and every creek, if properly explored, might yield rich veins of the ore. More than once Satan had whispered into Daniel's ear, *Why not remain another year? Think of what you could do with the gold riches of another twelve months. You could do more to assist the poor Saints in the Salt Lake Valley, and the widow and orphan, too. Gold would make you famous and well-respected.*

"We're doing the right thing," Daniel answered as he drove his ox team away from Sutter's Fort. The last time Daniel saw Captain Sutter, the Swiss immigrant was in a tizzy. Now that the Mormons had quit him, he had no one working at all. Even the Indians had quit the fields and were searching for gold. So were fifty Kanakas, from the Sandwich Islands. Grog shops in tents were popping up all over. A swarm of miners from all over California had swept upon the entire American River and Sutter's Fort, mining gold. In his last few days on the river, it seemed to Daniel that everyone in California was mining gold. Miners stomped out Sutter's fields and stole from him. Someone even had stolen the four millstones at the gristmill, much to Daniel's dismay. He felt like his work of the past several months had gone to naught. Both the gristmill and the sawmill were idle. Only the embarcadero at the fort flourished, but in a bad way. The waterfront was overrun with more inbound miners, hell bent for the gold of the American River.

"I've had dreams about staying and dreams about going," Ezra admitted.

A few Indians followed Daniel's group, making motions they wanted to make trades.

"Me, too," Daniel said. He felt a sense of honor and duty tearing him away from California and toward the Salt Lake Valley.

At his last night in his shanty at the gristmill, Daniel related to Ezra a dream in which a personage appeared to him. *Look up the river,* the personage had said. Daniel did, and instead of seeing water he saw a hot, black substance like pitch rolling sluggishly down the bed of the river. The pitch moved slowly toward a multitude of men digging and washing gold. The personage said, *Look again!* He looked and saw the sludge rolling at a much more rapid pace but still the men kept at their gold labor. Only when the hot sludge measured hip deep on the miners did they seem willing to quit, but only if they could recover the gold then spread out on the rocks on their cloths and buckskins. *Look again!* said the personage. Now the black pitch resembled a solid mass more than twelve feet high, filling the river bank to bank, burning hot like molten lava. A few of the men, including Daniel, were able to make their escape. But the great multitude was carried away and lost to his view.

"I've had dreams just like that," Ezra said. "And I know what they mean."

"We need to return to the body of the Church in Salt Lake," Daniel said emphatically.

"If we don't," Ezra concluded, "the world will get us."

Daniel grunted his agreement but didn't tell Ezra of another dream he'd had, one that had been a recurring dream throughout his adult life. In this dream he was alone in a canoe and rowing gently across a river in the mist of a great darkness. The waters suddenly cast him about until he came to a fork in the river. At this point he had to choose which way to go. He kept choosing the right fork, and as he did so, the mist became a little lighter but the waters rougher. His goal was to reach the light he could occasionally see through the mist. When he could see the light, it was bright, inviting, and peaceful. But every time he paddled hard to reach it, he woke up.

I wonder what would happen if I ever reached that light, he wondered to himself as the wagon rolled toward Pleasant Valley.

Daniel heard a "pop" and the oxen jumped. He pulled the oxen to a stop and jumped to the ground.

"What's wrong?" Ezra asked.

"Broke the fore bolster," Daniel said as he stared at the always troublesome box bolster that sat atop the axletree and connected the wagon bed to the front running gears. A kingpin that ran through the bolster and the axletree allowed the wagon's front wheels to turn.

Ezra groaned out loud. "Oh, no. That'll take all day to fix."

"I know," Daniel said shaking his head slowly. "It's bad luck. I hope it's not an omen of things to come."

By now a few Indians had swarmed around Daniel, wanting to make trades—gold for things like dried fish and buckskin pantaloons.

"No trade," Daniel said as he continued to stare at the broken bolster, his mood getting cranky. He wondered how many times his wagon, and the wagons of all the other men, would break down between here and the Salt Lake Valley, especially over the treacherous terrain of the Sierras. He wanted to be one of the first to arrive at Pleasant Valley, not one of the last. Sutter had given him the responsibility to foreman the gristmill. The Battalion boys had asked him to negotiate with Sutter for wages and for the two cannons, and after the meeting with Samuel Brannan to lead the expedition of eight other men to explore a new route over the mountains. He felt the younger men needed him at Pleasant Valley, too. The wagon breakdown was a frustrating complication to him.

"No trade, go away."

Several things struck Daniel the moment he arrived at Pleasant Valley. There was the stark beauty of the valley in the mountains, the faces of Battalion veterans he hadn't seen for a while; the presence of only one woman—Melissa Coray, wife of William Coray; the agreeable summer weather; and the enthusiasm of the camp. But the foremost thing that struck Daniel was the wealth of wagons and livestock that had been accumulated. The Battalion boys had been blessed with piles of gold the past few months and it showed. By Daniel's count there were seventeen wagons and more than three hundred head of livestock, counting all the horses, mules, oxen, and cattle held in temporary corrals. This mass of humanity, animals, and provisions had to be transported from California to the Salt Lake Valley—eight hundred miles away.

"Good to see you again, Brother Browett," Henry Bigler said as Daniel deposited his livestock in the corrals. "Welcome to Pleasant Valley."

Daniel quickly scanned the expanse of green grass surrounded by tall yellow pines, foothill oaks, and the lower mountains of the Sierra Range. "Beautiful place," he said in a complimentary tone.

Bigler gave some orders to a half-dozen Mexican herdsmen, warning them not to let any animals stray. Bigler then asked Daniel, "Did you bring the cannons?"

"In one of the wagons," Daniel replied. Most of the Battalion boys had donated five to twenty-five dollars in gold each to make the purchase from Sutter. Total cost had been five hundred and twelve dollars.

"The Fourth of July is a couple of weeks away," said Bigler. "Can we fire them off to celebrate that day?"

"I bought a supply of gunpowder, too," Daniel said as he laughed. "I'm thinking of test firing them tonight to keep the Indians away."

Jonathan Holmes, who had worked with Daniel on the gristmill and who was one of the seven presidents of the Seventy for the Battalion boys, approached Daniel with a wide smile beaming from his face. "Welcome, Brother Browett. You're just in time. We're having a meeting tonight. We've waited for you because most of us feel that we want you to lead us to the Salt Lake Valley."

Daniel's face turned slightly red. "I think I'll nominate you instead."

The mass meeting, attended by forty-one Battalion veterans, five other men, and one woman, was held around a small campfire. Addison Pratt, a returned missionary, and John Eagar, who had been a passenger on the *Brooklyn*, were there too. No one needed the warmth of the fire—the early evening temperature was in the seventies. Daniel was elected president of the return company; he selected Holmes as one of his counselors and Samuel Rogers as the other.

Rogers had been a private in Company B.

A few days later, as Daniel stewed and worried while waiting for a few more of the Battalion boys to show up, he made it known to some of the men that he wanted to leave ahead of the others.

"I think I need to strike out ahead of everyone and finish the job I tried to do in early May," Daniel told everyone at another evening campfire. He felt he had let the men down then, bad weather or not.

"What do you mean…finish what job?" Holmes asked.

"Explore the route over that mountain," Daniel said as he pointed. Iron Mountain lay looming to the east, lit by a spectacular sunset.

Holmes pulled a face scored with doubt. "You know where you're taking us, don't you?"

"Partly yes, partly no," Daniel said. "It was storming the entire time. Plus we had to turn back before we reached the summit. I think it would be a good idea to find out what's on top."

Samuel Rogers had been listening. He was one of eight men who accompanied Daniel in that early May expedition up the long spine of Iron Mountain. He said, "We know that Captain Fremont came that route, so it's not going to drop us off into nothingness. I say we all go together."

Daniel politely waved Samuel off and found himself repeating what he had already said in part. "Fremont had horses and mules loaded up pretty heavy all right, but he didn't have wagons. We've got nearly thirty wagons to get over that summit. I don't feel right about not knowing what's on the other side of Iron Mountain, or even for that matter what's on top."

The country between the Battalion boys and the Humboldt was the wild, austere, uncharted Sierra wilderness. It was known by Indians, but the only whites known to have crossed this part of the country was the Fremont party of 1844, with Kit Carson employing one native Indian after another to get them through.

Robert Pixton had not gotten over his habit of making food for Daniel and John Cox, members of his old mess. He had been stewing a pot of beef. "I agree with Samuel," Pixton said. "Don't get in such a hurry."

"But it's the twenty-fourth of June today," Daniel complained. "If we keep laying around Pleasant Valley here, we won't get into the Salt Lake Valley until late fall." He had visions of finding a large plot of ground there to establish his ranch. And he had visions of watching Elizabeth and Harriet drop their jaws as he pulled in dressed like a *vaquero* and trailing a herd of cattle and horses.

"Have you already picked two men to go with you?" Samuel asked.

"Henderson Cox and Ezra Allen volunteered," Daniel answered. Henderson and Ezra had been with Daniel and Samuel on the previous trip up Iron Mountain.

"I still don't like it." Samuel said. "Three men on that mountain all alone? You're asking for trouble."

The warning had a noticeable effect on Daniel. He squirmed and twisted, thinking about Indians again. "We're all taking our muskets and pistols, too," he said. "We'll be careful."

CHAPTER NOTES

Here is what author Norma Baldwin Ricketts says about the cannon Daniel Browett purchased: "The ex-soldiers of the Battalion decided to buy two small decorated brass parade cannon from Captain John Sutter to take to the leaders of the Mormon Church. The cannon had been left behind in Moscow as the defeated Napoleon fled during the winter of 1812-13. Later the cannon were brought to Fort Ross in northern California, the Russian fur trade outpost. Sutter purchased the cannon from the Russians, along with other supplies, when the Russians closed Fort Ross" (*The Mormon Battalion, U. S. Army of the West,* page 301). However, author Will Bagley, in his book, *Gold Rush Saints, California Mormons and the Great Rush for Riches,* says "It appears that the cannons bought by Sutter by the Battalion veterans had come from merchant shipmasters, either purchased directly by Sutter or received in trade..."

Dozens of the Battalion boys, along with Saints who had been passengers on the *Brooklyn,* made contributions toward the purchase of the cannon. Even Sam Brannan donated $2.50.

Many iron cannon were brought to California and used to make nails, tools, and other items. Cap Cresup, a member of the Mormon Battalion organization now residing in California, finally discovered the two cannon purchased by Daniel Browett from Captain Sutter. All these years they had been in storage in the Church Museum of History and Art, but not properly identified. One was bronze and the other was iron.

42

WITH TWO MULES PACKED WITH CAMP gear and food, Daniel was ready to mount his horse Sandy for the trip up the spine of Iron Mountain.

"Brother Browett," Robert Pixton said over a mouthful of hot bread that he had baked for breakfast, "I need to ask you a personal question."

The remark startled Daniel. He couldn't figure out what kind of personal question anyone in the world needed to ask him, let alone his good friend Robert Pixton. "Sure, go ahead," he said.

Pixton just blurted it out. "Are you wearing your garments?"

Daniel went beet red in a hurry. "How did you know?"

"Sleeping in a tent and bathing in a creek is not too private, as you ought to know," Pixton said somewhat sheepishly.

"It was my last pair," Daniel said. "They were so badly worn out they wouldn't even stay on my body. I properly burned them in the fire."

"You ought to ask around," Pixton said in a huff. "Maybe someone has an extra pair. You need the protection of your garments."

"Don't have time right now," Daniel said as he swung into the saddle. He wore a new tan hickory shirt he'd bought at Sutter's Fort, along with new boots and new buckskin pantaloons. Whether or not it could be attributed to the temple garments he had worn under his clothing since his endowment in the Nauvoo Temple in February of 1846, he had never been injured in his travels across the Santa Fe Trail or even in California. No broken bones, no bad cuts, either. "We'll travel fast and be back in just a few days. I'll be able to tell you boys if we're headed for bad trouble or not."

"Well, don't let any Indians steal that new shirt off your back," John Cox said as Daniel spurred Sandy with a pair of huge Spanish spurs he'd also bought at the fort.

"That's a worthy goal," Daniel snapped without looking back.

"I remember the first time I met you, Ezra," Daniel said at a camp late that night. The three men had ridden all day long up the mountain. Sandy and the other two hobbled horses were nibbling on young and tender grass shoots that grew in a small meadow.

"I remember too," Ezra replied. "My wife was sick that day, and so was my baby."

Ezra, himself afflicted with chills and fever, had come to the Browett house seeking Elizabeth's help with her knowledge of herbal remedies. Ezra's wife, Sarah, recovered, but a baby son died.

"I wonder how your wife is doing way out there in Winter Quarters, and your children, too?" Daniel said in a tender tone.

"I hope well," Ezra said. He suddenly began to tear up. "I miss her. She still seems so far away." A few tears stained the red vest his was wearing.

Daniel remained silent, letting Ezra regain his composure. In some ways, Ezra resembled Daniel. Both were the same height—five foot ten, both were of medium build, and both had blue eyes. Daniel had blond hair, however, and Ezra's hair was brown. Each had a leather pouch tied around their neck, dangling under his shirt. The pouches contained gold dust. Daniel fingered his pouch for a few seconds and determined to hide it in his saddlebags for the remainder of the trip.

"I pray to God that Sarah will be in the Salt Lake Valley when I get there," Ezra finally said.

"I guess there's no guarantee, is there?" Henderson Cox said.

"No, unless someone takes her under their wing, I suppose I'll have to go all the way to Winter Quarters and get her and the kids." Tears still filled Ezra's eyes. He had two surviving children, a son and a daughter.

Ezra, born in New York in 1814, was due to turn thirty-four on the twenty-eighth of July, just a month away. He had married Sarah Fiske in 1837, joined the Church in 1841, and moved to Nauvoo in 1843 where he supported his family by working on the Nauvoo Temple almost full-time. He left

Nauvoo in late April and made it to Council Bluffs about the same time as Daniel.

"With this gold dust around my neck, and with all the money I've sent my wife, we should be able to make a good start in the Salt Lake Valley," Ezra commented. He had made good money at Mormon Island, digging with men such as Wilford Hudson and Levi Fifield.

Daniel nodded his agreement. Like all the other men, Ezra had sent much of his clothing allowance to his wife, plus a good portion of his earlier monthly salary. Not only that, but Ezra had a half dozen cows and steers back at Pleasant Valley, plus two extra horses. The worst thing Daniel ever saw Ezra Allen do was drink too much of a padre's wine while in Santa Fe. It had made Ezra and another soldier, Abner Blackburn, a little tipsy, but they got over it just fine.

For a while Daniel talked about his early life in England, his marriage to Elizabeth, his conversion at the hands of Wilford Woodruff, his trip to America aboard the *Echo*, and his life in Nauvoo. He recounted Elizabeth's frustrations at not being able to have a child, her blessing, and the eventual birth of Moroni. He also talked about his second wife, Harriet—her trials and tribulations over losing a husband to cholera, losing a potential husband in a well accident, and his eventual marriage to her after a "calling" from the Prophet Joseph Smith to enter into plural marriage.

"Listening to you two talk like that makes me wish I had a wife to go home to," Henderson Cox said.

"Oh, I think there'll be plenty of pretty young girls in the Salt Lake Valley when we get there," Daniel said with a chuckle. "You're not even nineteen yet, are you?"

"Not until November," Henderson said, blushing slightly.

Henderson was born near the Wabash River in Warren, Indiana, in 1829. His parents moved to Missouri in 1835, found out about Mormonism, and converted to the Church in January of 1838. Henderson was baptized that year too. After the expulsion of virtually all Mormons there, his parents moved to Quincy, Illinois the next year, and later to Nauvoo in 1843. Just as Daniel and Robert Harris had done, the Coxes left Nauvoo in May of 1846 and arrived in Council Bluffs just in time to find out about the Mormon Battalion. Henderson was only seventeen when he enlisted.

"Can you remember what your father and mother look like?" Ezra joked.

Henderson's brown eyes brightened several notches. "Sure can," he answered. "And I can remember what it's like to be hugged by them too. It feels good, and I miss it."

"What are you going to do with your gold?" Daniel asked. Henderson, too, had a pouch full of gold. Instead of tying it around his neck, he had placed it in his packs, like Daniel had done.

"Give it to my parents and buy something nice for all my brothers and sisters," he answered. Henderson came from one of the largest Mormon families Daniel knew of; Henderson was the next to the youngest of fifteen children, eleven living.

"And your cattle and horses?" Ezra asked. Just as the older men had done, Henderson had also prospered in the gold fields.

"Give them to father," Henderson said.

"Won't you need some of your gold and some of your cattle and horses to start a new life for yourself if you get married right away?" Daniel asked.

"Then father can give me back what he can afford," Henderson said without blinking an eye.

Indians, but only three of them, made their appearance on the third day of Daniel's scouting expedition. Henderson saw them first, among the chaparral and trees. They were riding horses, but poor ones at that.

"What'll we do?" Henderson asked, eyeing them with huge amounts of suspicion.

A chill went through Daniel. "We're so close to the summit I hate to turn back now. I wonder if there are others?" Sandy and the other horses were making their way through occasional snow now, left over by the hard winter. Ahead of him, closer to the summit, the snow would get even deeper—a fact that Daniel long ago had accepted in his mind.

Ezra was busy scanning the horizon. It was a calm day in the El Dorado; the skies were partly cloudy and a mild breeze sifted over the ridges. Except for the three Indians, there was nothing but thick stands of conifer, fir, and sub alpine trees, littered with chaparral and wildflowers. "Can't tell for certain. If there are more Indians out there, they're doing a good job keeping out of sight."

Henderson tried to calm his fears by asking more questions. "What kind of Indians are they?"

Daniel summoned his courage. He was Henderson and Ezra's leader so he tried to show it. "Either Miwok, Maidu, or Nisenan I'd suspect," Daniel said. "Maybe even Washo." During his year in California he'd tried not to go out of his way to learn a whole lot about Indians. What he knew, he'd learned from Captain Sutter. Ezra was another matter. Ezra had made it almost a hobby to know about Indians. "What do you think, Ezra?" he asked.

"I think we're between eight and nine thousand foot elevation," he answered, trying to make a joke.

"Does that mean that one variety of Indians or another can't breathe at this elevation?" Henderson asked.

Ezra laughed. "Fremont and Kit Carson met the Washo variety of Indians up here four years ago. By sign language, the Indians urged Fremont to turn back. They told Fremont that it was six sleeps to the nearest place where white men lived. The Washos urged Fremont to go back to the lake, the lake we're trying to find on the other side of the summit."

"Fremont kept going," Henderson said. "Brother Browett, does that mean we keep going, too?"

Daniel didn't answer because he didn't know. He felt compelled to go on, but his old fears told him to skedaddle down Iron Mountain and back to the Pleasant Valley camp to safety. Down there, he had seen Miwok lean-tos, made of bark. Up here, however, he hadn't seen any Indian shelters. The only evidence of Indian was the three that were following them now.

"I say keep going," Ezra said. "There're only three of them. They're poorly dressed, and their animals are poor too. They probably just want something to eat. They know our two mules are loaded with food."

"Yah," Henderson said. "Maybe they want all of it."

Ezra carried his musket across the pommel of his saddle. He held it in the air for a moment, then returned it to its original position. "I can't see from here, but I don't see any rifles with them Indians—only bows and arrows and knives. Maybe a hatchet."

Henderson had more questions. "Do you think we're close to the exact spot Fremont and Carson came through? If so, will that be good enough? Or do we have to keep going on?"

"Captain Sutter said that Kit Carson told him he carved his name in a tree up here somewhere," Daniel said. "Look for it."

"I'd rather keep my eye on them Indians," Henderson said.

"Maybe the Indians know where that lake is," Ezra suggested.

"There's a string of small lakes, and then a big one," Daniel said. "But the main thing is to determine whether or not wagons can make it over the pass, and down the other side—which is apt to be steep, according to what Fremont told Sutter." Daniel was still in a quandary, whether or not to turn back or gain sight at least of the first lake. There were only three Indians but his hands were shaking a little, a fact he was trying to hide.

"What's the verdict?" Ezra asked Daniel.

"I guess keep going," Daniel answered as his throat choked up a little. The snow was deeper, two and three feet in places, but the summit closer. They had found a drift or two that they estimated some fifteen feet deep.

Henderson was still full of questions. "How will the gold discovery affect the Indians around here?"

Daniel had his eye on the three Indians, who were riding silently about seventy yards away, but riding up the final hurdles of the Iron Mountain summit, just like Daniel and his two companions.

Ezra made the answer. Daniel figured it was good to make talk, rather than harbor up more fears as they rode in silence. "Nothing but bad, I suppose. Folks in these parts say there were more than three hundred thousand Indians in California when the Spanish founded the first mission. Now the population's been whittled down to half."

The statement caught Henderson's attention. "Wow—what caused that?"

"Simple," Ezra answered. "The Indians resisted Spanish rule. The missions weren't merely religious institutions. They were instruments designed to bring about a total change in culture in a brief period of time. When the Indians resisted, they paid—killed by the hundreds, killed by the thousands."

Daniel had heard such stories during his time in San Diego, Los Angeles, and in the El Dorado area around Sutter's Fort. Foreign visitors such as the French reported Indians in irons, others shackled in the stocks, and others whipped and flogged without mercy.

"Even worse was the white man's diseases that came upon the Indians here," said Ezra.

Daniel had heard that, too. Three major epidemics broke out during Spanish rule. In 1777 there had been a respiratory epidemic, in 1802 pneumonia and diphtheria epidemics, and a measles epidemic in 1806, leaving .thousands more dead. More recently, smallpox and scarlet fever devastated the native population.

"And starvation and poor nutrition, too," Ezra went on. "Thirty years ago the Spanish governor of California reported the deaths of more than forty thousand Indians. Indians had been used to a different diet, not the one imposed on them by the missions and the presidios."

Daniel was feeling sorry for the California Indians at this point. After all, they had nothing to eat but acorns, roots, grass seed, and the occasional taste of deer and elk meat. In such a nice area of the world, with a climate that produced all kinds of fruits and grains without much effort, he wondered how such a thing could happen. But it did. The three Indians following him didn't look well-fed, and neither did their horses.

"Ever hear the story of the Jose Maria Amador expedition ten or eleven years ago?" Ezra asked.

"Nope," Daniel admitted as he glanced at his packs. He had gold in them, gold that would get Robert and him off to a good start in the Salt Lake Valley. At all cost, he had to protect his gold.

"Me neither," Henderson echoed.

"It happened about the same time Captain Sutter established his New Helvetia. Indians around here were revolting against the large land grants given to Mexican citizens, and naturalized citizens, too," Ezra explained. "You can put Captain Sutter in that category, and John Bidwell, too."

"Let me guess," Henderson said. "The Mexicans sent Amador to make a statement to the Indians."

"You've got it right," Ezra said. "Amador came here and invited all the Indians—wild and Christian—to a feast of pinole and dried meat. As they were eating, the Mexican troops surrounded them and tied them up. They separated about a hundred Christian Indians and took them on a march. At every half mile or so they put six Indians on their knees to say their prayers and then shot them with their own arrows. Any who didn't die immediately were killed with spears. Another group of Mexican troops, under threat, baptized all the Indians back at the feast. Immediately afterward those Indians were all shot in the back."

"That's terrible," Henderson said.

"And it wasn't the first time things like that happened," Ezra said. "Just six years earlier a Father Mercado massacred twenty-one Pomo Indians in the Russian River Valley area of northern California during the malaria epidemic."

Daniel gasped. He glanced at the three Indians again, still keeping their distance among the trees and chaparral. He felt a sorrow that he'd never felt before. Not only had the Spaniard's religion been forced on California Indians, but hard labor too, along with disease, torture, and forced death. He felt an urge to make amends. There were only three Indians on the summit of Iron Mountain with him, but three was a start. A gesture of friendship surely couldn't hurt. He had two mules laden with cookware and food. Indians, as he understood it, were descendants of people who had migrated from Israel in the year 600 B. C. They were Lamanites all right, a fallen people. But they were his brothers, same as Ezra, Henderson, and the Battalion boys waiting back at Pleasant Valley.

"So how's this discovery of gold gonna affect the Indians?" Henderson asked.

"I've been thinking about just that for the last few weeks," Ezra said. "So I'll make some predictions. "Some lawmaker back in Washington, D. C.,—someone like Senator Benton of Missouri, will quickly get rid of an old Spanish law that gives the Indians fixed rights to the land around here, especially the land that has gold on it."

"Probably so," Henderson admitted.

Daniel thought about the Treaty of Guadalupe Hidalgo again. The Spaniards and Mexicans had brought plenty of evil to the native people of California—and there was probably more than enough evil to go around without them. Sometimes the Indians killed each other faster than the Spanish or Mexicans had killed them. The United States had its share of evil people, too, like the Missourians and those people Satan had riled up all over the land to oppose the restoration of the gospel and the establishment of the Church. Bad men, seeking for quick riches, were sure to descend upon California. The number of immigrants would rise to the tens of thousands by next summer. Places like Coloma, Mormon Island, and even San Francisco had the potential to double their populations every ten days if gold fever swept the country.

"The number of Indians in California will keep decreasing," Ezra predicted. "The Spaniards started it, the Mexicans continued it, and our country will be no different. This war of extermination will continue to be waged until the Indians become almost extinct."

Daniel continued to harbor his sorrow for the Indians until he topped out on the summit. He could see a string of small lakes below him, to the east, their waters silvery in color, lined by green trees. "Well, I feel better now. There're the lakes we tried to see on the first trip. Look at them—God did a mighty good job in the creation, didn't He?"

Daniel let his gaze rest on the lakes for a few seconds. They were nestled beneath a big mountain and over it a thunderstorm loomed. In his mind, based on what he'd learned from Captain Sutter about Fremont's trip over this pass, he made a wild guess about how far the big lake was from here—forty-five to fifty miles. Then he said, "I'd declare our trip a success now."

"Those lakes are still frozen over," Ezra commented.

Daniel looked again. Ezra was right. That's why they looked so silvery.

"How are we going to get wagons down there?" Henderson asked.

"Somehow build a road," Daniel answered. He had to admit the summit was rough country, not fit for a wagon. But the Truckee Pass was worse as he remembered it. "I suppose our wagons will break down up here, but we'll just have to fix them and keep going." In his mind he could see broken reaches, felloes, hounds, tongues, and axles.

"It'll keep Wilford busy all right," Ezra admitted. Of all the Battalion boys waiting at Pleasant Valley, Wilford Hudson was the best wheelwright among them. He was a skilled blacksmith, and he would have to be more than skilled to repair king and queen pins, bolts, and chain links at the top of this mountain in the rarified air.

Henderson let out all his air as he gazed at the rocky terrain. The wind at the summit had swept most of the snow away, exposing giant rocks. "We'll have to use every pick and every shovel we have."

The three men rode for another twenty minutes, rapidly descending into a pretty valley. Daniel pulled Sandy to a halt. In fading daylight he said, "Boys, I think we've seen enough. It's a bad summit all right, but with a little work we can get our wagons through here. I hate to admit it, but Sam Brannan was right. This is going to be a good route. When we get done, immigrants coming into California will have a better road to use."

"Are we going back now?" Henderson asked, excited at the prospect.

"Yep," Daniel answered. "This has got to be the worst of it. When we get our wagons and livestock up to here, all we have to do is go down this other side and then strike out in a northeastern direction. We'll find the Humboldt sure as I'm sittin' here on this horse."

"Suits me," Ezra said as he turned his horse around.

"Where we gonna camp?" Henderson asked. "I'm tired and I'm hungry."

Daniel began to follow his tracks and the tracks of the other horses and mules. "We passed a nice little spring about an hour's ride from here."

The Indians appeared again as the three Battalion scouts turned back, but they kept their distance. "Are we gonna feed them Indians tonight?" Henderson asked.

"Haven't made up my mind," Daniel said. "But I want you to keep your eyes out for two things."

"What two things?" Henderson asked.

"The Indians—of course," Daniel answered. "Look for signs of more Indians. Feeding three Indians, and worrying about only three, is one thing. But if they've got another bunch hanging back, that's another. We wouldn't have a chance if they turned out to be bad Indians."

"What's the other?" Henderson asked, sounding like he didn't want to dwell on the prospect that the Indians might be bad.

"Captain Sutter told me that Kit Carson blazed his name on a tree up here somewhere," Daniel said. "If you're a real good scout you'll find it."

With the Indians still skirting the three whites, Henderson found the tree in about twenty minutes' time. "There it is," he said, pointing upward.

Daniel, Ezra, and Henderson surrounded the tree, a medium-sized balsam fir. The etched out words read, *KIT CARSON 1844*.

"I can't figure out why Carson carved his initials so high up in the tree," Henderson said as he bit his lip. "What'd he do, stand on his horse?"

"You've got to remember, he carved it in the middle of the winter," Daniel explained. "He was probably standing on several feet of snow."

Henderson turned an embarrassing shade of red, wondering why he hadn't thought of that.

"Well, I guess this proves we're on the right trail, doesn't it?" Ezra stated with an emphatic note as he stared at the initials.

"I'll bet Fremont and Carson and all the men near froze to death when they were up here," Henderson said. "Was it February?"

"Early February at that," Ezra stated. "They had to stay up here on this ridge in order to avoid the deeper snow of the hollows. Their main Indian guide deserted them on one of those cold nights."

"You don't suppose one of those Indians following us was Fremont's guide, do you?" Henderson asked.

"I doubt it," Ezra said. "The guide was a Washo. The three Indians we've been seeing are from the Sacramento Valley side of the Sierras, not Washo."

Daniel gently kicked Sandy's ribs. "Come on boys. Let's find that spring. Then we'll invite those Indians into our camp and find out who they are and what they want." As he said those words he had an uneasy feeling. He began to wish he were wearing his temple garments.

CHAPTER NOTES

The following statement is attributed to John C. Fremont, a Missourian, after he rose to the position of U.S. Senator in 1850: "Spanish law has clearly and absolutely secured Indians fixed rights of property in the lands that they occupy…and some particular provision will be necessary to divest them of these rights."

It is a fact that the Indian population of Alta California was around 310,000 at the beginning of the Spanish incursion in 1769. By 1848, when Daniel Browett began leading the Battalion boys out of California, the Indian population stood at only 150,000. Two thirds of that number perished in the first ten years of the U.S. takeover. By 1852, a quarter of a million fortune hunters had arrived in California. By 1860, there were only 50,000 natives left alive.

43

July 1848

Pleasant Valley, California

NO DOUBT ABOUT IT, DANIEL AND THE other two scouts ought to have returned by now. That was the consensus among the Battalion boys at Pleasant Valley, who after more than a week were getting restless.

"They were gone only a week on their first trip to Iron Mountain," said John Cox to Robert Pixton.

Pixton replied, "You're right. They left May second and six days later they had made it back down, even as far as Mormon Island."

John slowly turned and looked in the direction of the Sierras. "It can't be more than a two- or three-day ride to the summit and less than that back here because it would be all downhill."

"Maybe they went *over* the summit," Pixton surmised. "Maybe they wanted to make certain the trail's a good one all the way to the big lake, and maybe all the way to the Humboldt."

John shook his head. "Daniel wouldn't do that. He said he'd be back in a week. I'd sure like it if he were back in camp when we get there."

The two men, with several other Battalion boys, were mining for gold in the creeks near Pleasant Valley. Surprisingly, gold seemed to be everywhere in this part of California. John had discovered that all a person had to do was look for gravel bars in the middle of the streams or heavy water runoff. Gold was also easily found on the downstream side of large boulders, in cracks above the waterline, along the edge of the stream, and in the streaks of gravel that settles above the streambeds.

"I suppose we'll end up leaving tomorrow, regardless," Pixton said. Last night, around the campfire, most of the men favored breaking camp at Pleasant Valley to follow Daniel's trail east, up the spine of Iron Mountain.

When Pixton and Cox got back to camp, they found the rest of the Battalion boys beginning to pack up.

"We've already decided to leave tomorrow," said Jonathan Holmes, the man who had been chosen as Daniel's first counselor. "I've assigned Henry Bigler and Addison Pratt and a few others to stay behind a day or two and round up animals that have strayed off, and to watch for Daniel in case he returns by another route."

"I've no cause to argue," John said.

Two days later, on the Fourth of July, John and the Battalion boys were camped in another pretty little meadow, a good ten miles from Pleasant Valley. With forty-five wagons and three hundred animals, the going had been slow. Because James Sly, who had been private in Company B, had found it, the men named the meadow Sly Park.

"I think we ought to limber up the cannon," John said to Jonathan Holmes as the men ate their dinner. The sky in the west had the makings of a glorious sunset. In Daniel's absence, Holmes had taken charge of all the occasional informal meetings held by the Battalion boys.

"Well, I guess it'd be a good way to celebrate America's independence," Holmes said. "I know right where the powder is."

When the powder had been placed in the four-pounder, John said, "This'll serve two other purposes when it goes off."

"What're you thinkin' of?" Pixton asked him.

"If Daniel is nearby, he'll hear it," John said. "And it'll tend to scare off all the pesky Indians we've been seeing." Ten days had gone by since Daniel had left with Ezra Allen and Henderson Cox. And the remaining Battalion boys had seen Indians every day of those ten, sometimes trading with them.

The cannon went off, making a loud boom. John thought that if Daniel were anywhere around, say within five to eight miles, he ought to hear the report of the cannon. The Indians scattered at the sound; none could be seen anywhere just now.

Holmes ordered the company to remain at Sly Park the next day so that men with broken wagons could fix them. This also allowed Henry Bigler and his group to catch up—provided he had left Pleasant Valley.

There was still no sign of Daniel the following day.

"I'm riding out to find Daniel," Holmes said that morning. "I need a few men to go with me."

John Cox volunteered and so did eight other men. John was glad there was a party of at least ten. Indians had made their appearance again.

"I've got my musket and my pistol loaded," John told Holmes as they men rode out.

"Good," Holmes replied. "Stay on the alert. I'm getting a bad feeling about the Indians here."

"Me, too," said John. He didn't say so, but he was getting a bad feeling not only about Indians, but also a bad feeling about Daniel and his two companions.

Holmes turned to face Pixton and the others who were staying behind. "Say your prayers for us, and for Brother Browett too. Pray individually, in your messes, and in a group prayer with the entire company."

"When can we expect you back?" Pixton asked.

"Today's the sixth," Holmes replied. "We'll be back no later than the twelfth. I promise."

"It's getting gloomy around here," Pixton said dejectedly.

"Be cheerful," said Holmes. "Be cheerful. Hope for the best."

Daniel's trail was hard to follow, especially for a man like John Cox who had no training in such matters. The other men were no better. John could see the trail here and there for the first day, but a combination of rain, wind, and melting snow had obliterated the trail of the three horses and two mules in Daniel's party by the end of the second day.

"Where they've gone from here is anyone's guess," Holmes said as he looked down upon a string of silver lakes from the summit.

"I can't see any tracks at all now," John moaned as he led his horse back and forth along the summit. A brisk wind was blowing. John figured the wind always blew at the tops of the mountains in America. He'd been on top of smaller mountains in the Malvern Hills area of England, and the wind blew there too. He'd been there once with Wilford Woodruff, the Apostle who baptized him. Wilford baptized several of John's friends there too, many of them in a pond on the John Benbow farm. Daniel Browett was one of them.

"If this is the way out of the Sierras, we're in for a lot of work," Holmes said with a sad shake of his head. "It's not a wagon road now, and it won't be much of one even after we get through here."

John agreed. "It's going to be a rough route, but probably no worse than going over the Truckee. Seems to me it's going to be a little shorter, and we don't have to cross the Truckee forty-seven times."

Holmes fired his pistol three times into the air. "This is Daniel's last chance. If he doesn't find us we have to assume that either he is scouting clear to the Humboldt, or something's happened to him."

"I can't believe you didn't find Daniel," Pixton said to John Cox on Wednesday when the search party returned.

"They've been up there all right," John said. "But we couldn't find them. We fired shots into the air several times, but all we did was scare up some birds."

"Well, I'm anxious to get going," Pixton said.

"It's not going to be a picnic up there," John said. "It's going to take a lot of labor—even blood, sweat, and tears—to get these wagons over the summit."

"I didn't expect it to be easy," Pixton said.

Holmes had already made an assessment. He made the decision to layover for one more day to allow for the final repairs of wagons and equipment to be made, for more packing and organization. A few were sick, including Addison Pratt who had served as the branch president in San Francisco after Sam Brannan ran off to the gold fields.

John began to assess the possibilities. Surely Daniel would not have gone too much farther than the summit of the Sierras. And surely he would not have just taken off in order to be with his two wives. Daniel had two wagons in the company, plus several head of horses and about ten head of cattle. John couldn't see Daniel on his horse riding hell-bent-for-leather toward the Salt Lake Valley with Henderson Cox and Ezra Allen. Daniel had been elected the leader of this company of men, one woman, wagons, and livestock. Of all persons on the earth, Daniel Browett wouldn't shirk such a responsibility. But what could have happened? Had something spooked the men's horses? Had they fallen off and banged their heads on the rocks? Or had they run into bad Indians?

44

"INDIANS OFF TO THE LEFT," one of the men in the road-clearing crew said as John Cox sunk his pick into a granite outcropping.

John, along with several other men, had been assigned to the crew by Jonathan Holmes. It had been six days since the wagons left Sly Park. Henry Bigler's group had caught up with them. John had just commented on how he enjoyed the fresh leeks for dinner they found at last evening's campground. It had been a long time since he had anything green to eat.

Last fall John enjoyed an abundance of California fruit—apples, pears, pomegranates, and all manner of fruit. With today being the eighteenth of July, the fruit harvest was more than two months away. Spring crops had been decimated at Sutter's Fort, including most of the wheat.

"Watch the horses," one of the men said. The crew had tied their horses to some trees. The Indians did not appear anxious to steal them, however. The Battalion boys had already worked the area in the morning. On their return trip, they decided to improve the road they had cleared.

"Are my eyes playing tricks on me, or do I see what I see?" said Azariah Smith, one of the crew. He had worked for Daniel at the gristmill site for a while, and then was hired away by James Marshall to work at the sawmill site at Coloma. He was there the day Marshall made the first discovery of gold.

"Them Indians are wearing white man's clothes," Henry Bigler said.

John hadn't paid too much attention to the Indians who had shown themselves this morning. There had been Indians off and on during the entire trip. He jerked his head up at Bigler's words and caught a band of Indians, a dozen or more, riding through the chaparral on horses.

"It ain't just any white man's clothes," moaned James Sly.

John's heart stopped beating. Sly was right. John recognized Daniel's tan hickory shirt. Another Indian was wearing Ezra Allen's red vest. Still another wore Henderson's blue and white plaid shirt.

"Dear Lord, dear God," said Samuel Rogers.

As if someone had rung a bell, all the men in the road-clearing crew stopped working. There was not a sound among them. In an eerie silence, the Indians disappeared into the trees.

John didn't say so, but one of the Indians was riding Sandy, Daniel's horse.

It was a minute or two until the men began speaking again.

"I think we'd better take a look around," Azariah said solemnly. The men slowly threw down their shovels and picks, walked to their tied-up horses, and mounted.

John mounted his horse and turned him down the mountain. "There's a spring just below us," he told the other men. "We passed the creek that flows out of it on the way up. Let's find the spring."

"Maybe they camped there," Bigler said.

"The Indians?" Azariah asked innocently.

"No, Daniel and his two companions," Bigler answered.

The sound of rushing water beckoned John in a matter of minutes. A stream was making its way downhill to the Cosumnes River. He turned his horse uphill, following the small stream. Tall trees cast long, gloomy shadows as the afternoon sun sunk lower in the west.

In a few minutes more, John found himself looking at a dead campfire at the base of a lively spring that gushed out of the mountain.

"Look over here, boys," said Henry Bigler.

Still mounted, John urged his horse a few steps away from the campfire. A lump came to his throat. A mound of dirt was as conspicuous as a white man's shirt on a wild Indian.

"Our brethren are in that grave," said James Sly.

A dark, gloomy feeling told John that James was right; Daniel lay under that shallow pile of dirt, and Ezra Allen and Henderson Cox, too. How they had met their fate he did not know. But he knew they were dead.

"What'll we do now?" Azariah said.

"I don't want to start digging," John said, still gloomy.

"Me neither," said James.

"Let's hoof it back to camp," John said. "We need everyone here. *Everyone.*"

On the way down the men began to talk about the three dead scouts. The puzzling thing was how they had died. The whole situation was complicated on that score, John thought to himself. There were a lot of questions to be answered. He wanted to follow the Indians, capture them, and somehow squeeze a confession out of them. But he didn't speak the language of a Maidu, a Miwok, or a Nisenan—whatever those Indians were. He didn't speak Spanish either, in case they spoke that language. He wasn't very good at sign language either. He didn't exactly know how to gain a murder confession out of an Indian in sign language, but he was angry enough to try.

"It happened right at their campfire," James Sly said.

"Do you think they invited the Indians into their camp?" Bigler asked the men.

"Maybe, maybe not," Azariah said. "Maybe the Indians attacked them in the middle of the night."

"The answer might be under that pile of dirt," Francis Hammond said.

"How do you figure?" Samuel Rogers asked.

"By what kind of wounds they have," Francis said. "We ought to be able to tell if they fought back, or if they were surprised."

The reality of Daniel's death was slowly settling over John. Hearing the men talk about it confirmed the fact that Daniel had been murdered, that he wasn't going to lead the Battalion boys to the Salt Lake Valley, and that someone would have to tell his two wives. He hoped that loathsome duty wouldn't fall to him.

"I don't even want to look in that grave," John said. "I want to remember Daniel how he was, not how he is now."

"Suit yourself," Bigler said. "I'm sure it won't be pretty."

All John wanted to think about was Daniel's smile with slightly crooked teeth, his blond hair blowing in the wind, the sprightly way he walked, and the fact that he was one of the best friends a man could ever have. John could remember when Daniel moved next door to Robert Harris in Deerhurst, England, and opened his own cooper shop there. John and Robert were boyhood friends and Daniel was quickly brought into their circle of friendship. Just as quickly Daniel courted Robert's sister, Elizabeth, and married her in a double wedding ceremony—along with Robert and Hannah Eagles. And just as quickly Daniel began supplying barrels to the John Benbow farm, and that led him to join the United Brethren congregation, under the leadership of Thomas Kington. The next year, all six hundred members of that congregation joined the Church—one at a time, converted by Elder Wilford Woodruff. John became a convert at the same time, as part of the United Brethren. And when many of the converts decided to emigrate to the United States, Daniel became president of a company of Saints headed for Nauvoo. John was part of that company too, and arrived in America on the *Echo*.

"Well, I'm not looking," John said as tears filled his eyes. Despite his testimony of the gospel, death was hard to understand in these circumstances. The last thing he wanted to do was to leave his old friend Daniel Browett in a shallow grave at the tops of the Sierra Mountains.

Leek Springs, where the Battalion boys had made camp, turned out to be only six miles from the spring where Daniel was buried in the shallow grave. Travel back to the spring the next morning was slow, however, with hard, heavy pulling. The oxen groaned as they pulled the wagons up the final miles of the spine of the mountain. Jonathan Holmes' wagon broke down halfway up, which delayed the men's arrival at the spring.

There had been a somber, sad, solemn mood among everyone all night and it pervaded into the morning hours, too. No one wanted to believe Daniel Browett was dead.

"He was like a father to me," Jonathan wept as he repaired his wagon.

When the entire company reached the spring and found the shallow grave, John Cox changed his mind.

"I want to know what happened," he said as some of the Battalion boys took shovels and picks out of the wagons and began the work to unearth the bodies.

"You don't have to look, we'll tell you what we learn," Robert Pixton said as he began digging.

It didn't take long. The grave was opened in just minutes, for it was a shallow grave. It was a shocking sight.

"Oh, dear God," said John as he peered into the grave.

The men were still uncovering the three bodies, but this is what John saw. Either an axe or a hatchet had been sunk into Daniel's face. He had been shot directly into one eye with an arrow, but the arrow had been removed. His body was naked, and so were the bodies of the other two men. Both Daniel and Ezra Allen's bodies lay on top of the body of Henderson Cox. Ugly gashes, some caused by arrows, others by knives, and others by hatchets, covered all three bodies. A withe was around Ezra's neck.

"This is the worst sight I've ever seen," said William Coray. He wheeled suddenly and pointed. "Keep Melissa back; I don't want her to see this." Melissa was the only woman in the company.

Arrows, some broken, some blood-stained, littered the ground. So did blood-stained rocks, some with locks of hair adhering to them; they had been used as weapons to kill the three Battalion boys.

Tears streaked down John's dusty face, and down the faces of all the men.

"Look what I found," said Azariah Smith, more than a dozen feet away from the grave. He reached into the chaparral and pulled out a pouch of gold. It was a double pouch, in fact, with a long buckskin string attached. It was blood-stained, too.

"It's Ezra's," James Sly said. "I'd recognize it anywhere. I saw him make it."

"When the Indians took Ezra's clothes off, they must have accidentally dumped the pouch in the bushes," Azariah said.

"It's still full of gold," Azariah Smith said as he handed the pouch over to Jonathan Holmes. Holmes had been chosen the new leader of the company during a solemn meeting the night previous.

"Conclusion number one," John stated to the men suddenly. "The attack on Daniel and his men was done in the dead of night." John felt himself losing the shock over the fact that Daniel was dead, and losing a bit of his sadness. But now a surge of anger swept over him. He wanted to organize a posse and chase the Indians, and kill them if they could be caught. He would shoot the Indian wearing Daniel's clothing first.

"That makes sense," Jonathan Holmes stated. "If it had been done in the daylight, even Indians wouldn't miss a pouch full of gold."

"Maybe Ezra was struck in the head, and the force of the blow cut the string," Pixton said. "He has that withe around his neck."

"Maybe so," said Samuel Thompson. He went to the grave and slowly rolled over the decomposed body of Ezra Allen. Ezra had been struck in the mouth with an axe; the lower jaw had been cut in two. His head had been beaten with rocks too. In places, through matted hair, his brains could be seen.

"Conclusion number two," John shot out. "That means Ezra's body was dragged here. He was killed a ways from here, so he must have put up a fight."

"I'd agree to that," said Thompson.

"Let me see that gold pouch," John said. Holmes handed it to him. "Looks like Ezra was defending himself. Look at all the blood and the tussocks."

"These three men put up a gallant fight," Holmes concluded. "But I'd say there were a dozen or more Indians. They didn't have a chance."

"It was Indians, I'm sure of it," John said. "It was those dirty Indians who were wearing our friends' clothes."

In about an hour, after the shock of this morbid scene had begun to drift away from everyone, Holmes thought it a good idea to begin the reburial process. "Let's dig a deep grave," he said as he began the work with his own shovel.

"How about going after the Indians who did this?" John asked his new leader.

Holmes appeared to think about the prospect for a few minutes, but afterward he said, "We best bury our men and get going again. Remember what the brethren said when Joseph Smith was assassinated? They told us not to take revenge, but that vengeance belongs to the Lord."

Visions of wild Indians burning in hell swept over John. He thought of the time when his good friend Robert Harris began to hunt down the apostates who caused the death of the Prophet Joseph Smith. Robert paid no attention to what the brethren had said. John felt like paying no attention now. He could take some of the strongest men, like Henry Bigler and James S. Brown, and track down the Indians within a day. He wondered how those wild

Indians would like to be hacked to pieces with an axe, the way they had done to Daniel, Ezra, and Henderson. He could see a shallow grave with the bodies of the wild Indians who had killed his friends.

Somehow Jonathan Holmes read John's mind. "Leave it alone, Brother Cox. Leave it be."

John shook himself, and shook away some of the feeling he had for those bad Indians.

"Help me dig a good grave for our friends," Jonathan said.

John found his pick. With all his strength he began to let out his frustration. The pick made a deadening sound as it buried itself in the mountain soil of the Sierras.

The stars were barely making their appearance in the broad California sky when John Cox rolled up in his wool blanket to make a try for sleep. Visibility was poor. The faint light in the west, the last of a setting sun, had faded to nothingness. Stars lit the sky, but there was no moon.

The company had just had a group prayer; John had said his personal prayers, too. Jonathan Holmes was trying to decide how many men to put on guard for the night, and who the men should be. Suddenly the cattle and the horses turned restless, almost to the point of a stampede.

"Indians!" someone screamed.

Melissa Coray screamed too, a blood-curdling scream.

John jumped to his feet. The cattle and the horses were running all around the top the mountain now, shaking the ground like an earthquake. John could feel it, the feeling of evil, and it had the company surrounded.

Jonathan Holmes' voice roared in the darkness. "Get your guns! Indians! Get your guns!"

John's only regret was that he wouldn't be able to see which Indian wore Daniel's clothing. His musket was already primed and loaded. He put it to his shoulder but quickly realized he would not be able to see an Indian if one stood only twenty feet from him, so completely had night descended upon the camp.

Robert Pixton had been asleep. "What spooked the livestock?" he said as he bailed out of his blanket.

"Indians," John said. "Them *murdering* Indians." Second by second the darkness intensified. Tall, dark trees seemed to snuff out what little light drifted downward from the big stars in the sky.

"Could have been a grizzly," said Samuel Thompson in a low but frightened voice.

"It was Indians," John said. "I can feel it. It was Indians. They're out there somewhere."

"Get the cannon out!" Jonathan yelled.

John didn't need any more invitation than that. He knew where Daniel's wagon was parked. It carried the two cannons purchased from Sutter. "Come on boys," he said as he ran. "Help me out."

From the dying embers of the evening campfire, someone lit a torch. By the light of the torch, the Battalion boys removed the six-pounder from Daniel's wagon. "Stuff it with extra gunpowder," someone said in the dark.

John found himself wishing there were a cannonball to slide into the barrel. And he wished the cannon were aimed at the filthy rotten Indians who had killed Daniel, Ezra, and Henderson.

The cannon belched a flame twenty feet long when it went off. It shook the mountain worse than the stampeding of three hundred livestock. If the cattle and horses weren't frightened before, they were now.

"Wow!" someone exclaimed. "Every Indian on the mountain ought to be running now." The smoke and smell of burned gunpowder drifted through the camp.

"And so's our livestock," said another. "How're we gonna find 'em in the morning?"

"We'll worry about that come morning," said a third. "We just need to make certain we're all alive when the sun comes up."

Sleep didn't come to John Cox. After things quieted down and most of the cattle had been retrieved, he lay on his blanket still blaming the Indians for the death of his friend. Then it came to him. The bad Indians of Iron Mountain had swung the hatchets, shot the arrows, thrust the knives, and beat on the three murdered men's heads with rocks, but the blame could go to other men and other circumstances, too. The Spaniards had killed Daniel, and so had the Mexicans. They had mistreated the Indians, abused them, killed them, tortured them, forced them to work in the missions, and brought diseases to them. The Mexicans and Spaniards had riled up the Indians, and so had the Americans. John Fremont killed Daniel. Fremont had killed enough Indians on his trips through California, Oregon, and Mexican territory to fill a graveyard in a place like St. Louis or Independence. Gold had killed Daniel, because the gold miners from all over California had abused and killed Indians, too. There was blame to go all around—the Spanish soldiers, the padres, the Mexican governors and Mexican soldiers, and even the opportune settlers like Captain Sutter. Even failed policies like secularization were part of it.

Laman and Lemuel could be blamed, too. They were responsible for the murderous disobedient race known as Lamanites, and Lamanites were Indians. Indians had strange customs, strange habits, and strange ways. John brought to his mind a scripture out of the Book of Mormon, in the twentieth verse of Enos:

And I bear record that the people of Nephi did seek diligently to restore the Lamanites unto the true faith in God. But our labors were vain; their hatred was fixed, and they were led by their evil nature that they became wild, and ferocious, and a blood-thirsty people, full of idolatry and filthiness; feeding upon beasts of prey; dwelling in tents, and wandering about in the wilderness with a short skin girdle about their loins and their heads shaven; and their skill was in the bow, and in the cimeter, and the ax. And many of them did eat nothing save it was raw meat; and they were continually seeking to destroy us.

There had been no Indians in England. During his days on this long trip in western America John had seen his share of skin girdle-wearing Indians, and now he hated them. To him, they were bloodthirsty. They were filthy. With their axes and arrows they had killed one of the best persons to ever walk the face of the earth, his friend Daniel Browett.

When morning came, John had slept only two hours. Someone yelled that a third of the livestock was missing. Holmes immediately sent three groups of ten men into the timber to search for the livestock, and to find out if there were any Indians left on the mountain. John stayed in camp with the other ten. All morning the ten men dug the grave deeper, built a wall of rocks about three feet high and eight feet square around it, laid the decomposing bodies of the three murdered men inside, and then filled the center up with dirt to the tops of the rocks.

"Wolves can't get into that grave," John said to his fellow workers when they were finished. The grave was on a side hill, not far from the spring. Indians ate wolves, and wolves ate Indians. John wished they'd eat each other to oblivion.

Holmes found a large rock rounded on one end that served as a headstone. "I hope not," he said. "This is a sad time. Daniel was like a father to me."

William and Melissa Coray came by to see the grave. Melissa said, "That was the worst night of my life. I've never been so frightened. It wasn't the darkness. It was the feeling of evil all around, of murderers out there, wanting to kill us, too."

The sound of an axe biting into a balsam fir interrupted the conversation.

"What're you doing?" Holmes asked the axe man, Wilford Hudson, the best wheelwright among the Battalion boys. Wilford had discovered gold on Mormon Island and was a close personal friend to Ezra Allen.

Without missing a stroke, Wilford made his answer. "We can't make much of an inscription on a rock, but we can make a good one on this tree."

"If you get tired, let me spell you off," John replied, wishing he'd thought of it first.

Wilford didn't quit. He dug into the fir a few inches with his axe, smoothed it off, and then took out his knife. Letter by letter, he began, carving both upper case and lower case:

To the memory of Daniel Browett, Ezra H. Allen, Henderson Cox
Who was supposed to have Been Murdered by Indians
On the Night of the 27th of June 1848

"Do you think we'll ever see this place again?" John asked Wilford when the graveside services were over.

John let his gaze trace the inscription on the tree over and over again. Joseph Smith had been murdered on the twenty-seventh of June 1844. Daniel Browett had been murdered on the twenty-seventh of June 1848, and so had Ezra and Henderson. Evil white men had murdered Joseph. Evil red men had killed Daniel.

"It's a long ways from the Salt Lake Valley," Wilford answered as he fondled Ezra's blood-stained gold pouch, letting it pass from one hand to the other. "I'd like to keep Ezra alive in my memory until I see him in paradise. But he's gone from this life. It's just his remains buried under this tree. I'll take his memory with me."

John figured that was a good way to look at it. A terrible tragedy took place here, but he aimed to hang onto his good memories of Daniel Browett.

Men, including the hired herdsmen, were still searching for oxen, cows, mules, and horses that had stampeded off during the night. John was making the sad conclusion that it might take two days to recover the livestock, so frightened they had been. The animals would have a tendency to go downhill, maybe all the way back to Pleasant Valley.

"Sister Allen won't know how to take the news," Wilford said. "But I'll see to it she gets Ezra's gold." Ezra's wife and children were still in Winter Quarters.

A melancholy sadness came over John again. Elizabeth and Harriet, he was certain, would never see the burial place of their husband. Worse, the Indians had made off with Daniel's pouch of gold and all his livestock except one cow. He had seen an Indian riding Sandy, and the Indians had probably eaten Daniel's mule the first night after the murder. At least he had one cow to give to Elizabeth and Harriet, if the cow could make it to the Salt Lake Valley. There were a lot of Indians between this summit of the Sierras and the Salt Lake Valley, and a desert to cross, too.

CHAPTER NOTES

Daniel Browett, Ezra H. Allen, and Henderson Cox remain interred at the same spot in the Sierra Mountains. California immigrants including the gold rush seekers used the trail blazed by the returning members of the Mormon Battalion; the route became far more popular than the Truckee route. The Battalion boys named the site of the murders "Tragedy Springs." The memorial and the inscription there became one of the most frequently mentioned landmarks in gold rush journals.

The author of this book has visited the spot twice.

A small roadside park along California Highway 88 has been established at Tragedy Springs, the cooperative effort of the Daughters of Utah Pioneers, the Sierra Chapter of the Sons of Utah Pioneers, several Explorer Boy Scout troops, and the U.S. Forest Service. Visitors can drive right to the park. The rock cairn containing the bodies remains in place today, within easy walking distance. A bronze marker was installed in September 1987 when the roadside park was established.

The fir tree bearing the inscription carved by the Battalion boys remained standing until the winter of 1928-29. A work crew headed by the curator at Sutter's Fort State Historic Park, H. C. Peterson, removed the stump with the inscription intact in August 1931. He placed it within the park. Later, the stump was transferred by the State Parks Department to the Marshall Gold Discovery Park at Coloma, where it remains prominently displayed.

The returning Battalion boys at this point became known as the Holmes-Thompson company. Over the next few days the company traveled southeast over a jumble of steep hillsides, granite domes, snow-covered peaks, and then descended into rocky canyons. By 21 July 1848 the company had reached a site they named Rock Creek in Rock Valley, now part of a private ranch property within the Eldorado National Forest. There, Samuel Rogers penned a letter to Captain Sutter, the federally appointed superintendent of Indian affairs for the region. Rogers wrote the account of the discovery of the bodies of Daniel Browett, Ezra Allen, and Henderson Cox. Rogers left the letter at Rock Creek, hoping it would somehow reach the hands of white men and subsequently reach Sutter. In his diary, Rogers said he did this so that the Indians could be properly punished. There is no indication in any surviving documents that Rogers' message ever reached John Sutter.

The two cannons Daniel purchased from Sutter arrived with the Holmes-Thompson company in the Salt Lake Valley. For years the cannons seemed to be missing. Thanks to efforts of the Mormon Battalion organization, the two cannons were recently identified. They had been stored by the Church for these many years without proper identification.

45

July 1848

Council Point, Iowa

WHEN RICHARD SLATER TOLD ROBERT Harris about gold being discovered in California, Robert felt so happy he could hardly contain himself.

"Daniel's gonna come back a rich man," Richard said as the two men visited outside Robert's little log home in a new Mormon settlement called Council Point. Winter Quarters had been abandoned. Kanesville, just north, formerly known as Council Bluffs, was the new headquarters of the Church in Iowa. Robert had helped build a tabernacle there, a huge log structure; it was assembled in three weeks.

Robert jumped in the air and clicked his heels. "Hear that Hannah? Whoopee!"

Hannah was more curious than excited. "It sounds too good to be true. How'd all this happen?"

Slater, one of Robert's former messmates in the Battalion, let a big smile come over his face. He told the story of the gold discovery—James Marshall and the sawmill contract, Daniel Browett and the gristmill contract, and how gold had become easy pickings in places like Mormon Island.

Slater opened a leather pouch. He let gold nuggets run through his fingers; he spread a few over his palm. "This is just a portion of what I mined in just a few days there, before I left."

"Why'd you ever come back?" Henry Eagles asked. Henry had built a cabin right next to Robert and Hannah.

"A lot of people have asked me that," Richard said. "I felt the tuggings of home, of my wife and family, and the Church."

"But you could have been rich if you would have stayed another month or two," Henry lamented.

"But I am," Richard confessed. "I'm reunited with my family."

"I guess I can relate to that," Henry said.

Richard went on to say that he had nearly five hundred dollars in gold, plus he had been paid by Samuel Brannan to deliver copies of the California Star to St. Louis.

"Do you think Daniel will have that much money?" Hannah asked.

Richard Slater laughed a big laugh. "More, much more," he said. "And a herd of horses and cattle, too. California is lousy with cattle. You see them everywhere. And wild horses, too."

This was nothing new to Robert; he had seen the wild cattle in California, and the wild horses.

Henry's eyes were big as saucers. "How many horses did you bring home?"

"There were ten of us," Slater explained. "We had quite a herd, but one night we lost eighteen of our horses to the Indians. It happened on the Platte, not too far out from here. The Pawnees got them."

"What if Indians get Daniel's horses and cattle?" Hannah asked.

"Not a chance," Slater predicted. "There'll be more than forty men in Daniel's group. They've all got their army muskets. Plus they've bought pistols, balls, and gunpowder. I don't reckon the Indians will bother Daniel."

Robert turned his muscular body and stared west. The Salt Lake Valley seemed more inviting now than ever, and closer. Hannah was pregnant again. He pictured his family of seven children safely ensconced on a huge ranch north of the Great Salt Lake somewhere. He'd seen plenty of good spots on his trip there last fall. He pictured a big herd of cattle and horses. And he pictured a pouch full of gold. Gold to buy food, gold to buy clothing, gold to buy farm implements.

Hurry home, Daniel. Hurry home.

46

August 1848

Carson River

"BROTHER HOLMES, I THINK I OUGHT to go with the packers to the Salt Lake Valley," John Cox said one night in early August. The Battalion boys were camped along the Carson River. Because Addison Pratt killed a rattlesnake here, the boys had named the place "Rattlesnake Camp." Pratt was not a Battalion veteran. He was a missionary who had returned from the Society Islands to San Francisco.

"You must have a good reason why," Jonathan Holmes replied.

"I do," John answered. "Someone's got to tell Daniel's wives about how the Indians got him. I reckon it's a hard thing, but I'd like to do it."

Jonathan nodded his head in approval. He was well aware that John Cox and Daniel Browett—and Elizabeth—had roots that traced together back in England. It would be an awkward thing for the fourteen Mormon Battalion veterans who had just caught the Holmes-Thompson company to have to break the bad news to Elizabeth and Harriet. None of them were there when the bodies were discovered. None of them knew Daniel and Elizabeth in England, or much at all in Nauvoo for that matter.

"Well, pack up your horse and mule then. We'll see to it that your wagon makes it to the Salt Lake Valley," Jonathan said. John had broken both axle-trees out of his wagon coming out of the Sierras, but the wagon was in fairly good shape now.

Holmes' decision pleased John. Another good friend to Daniel Browett, Jacob Kemp Butterfield, was among the packers. John reasoned that Butterfield could help break the news to Elizabeth and Harriet, and perhaps say something to bring them comfort and solace.

Indians had been a constant problem ever since the Battalion boys left Tragedy Springs where Daniel was buried. Yesterday Digger Indians shot arrows and threw rocks at them as they crossed the river. Indians stole several head of cattle last night.

Once the company descended into a valley, far below Tragedy Springs, curious Indians had followed the wagon train on a daily basis. After one of the Battalion boys, an expedition hunter, killed an antelope, the Indians began stealing horses and cattle at every opportunity.

"How will we handle Brother Browett's cow?" John asked. It was so lame it was not expected to make it alive to the valley.

"Take up a collection for Daniel's wives," Jonathan said.

Samuel Rogers was standing nearby, overhearing the conversation. "Let me be the first to donate," he said as he walked toward John. "Let's go to my saddlebags. I'll give a hundred and fifty dollars in gold."

This brought tears to the eyes of John Cox again.

"I don't envy either of you," said one of the packers, Thomas Dunn, to John Cox and Jacob Kemp Butterfield.

"Thanks for the concern," John said. "I'll be glad to be in the valley, but we don't look forward to breaking the bad news to Elizabeth and Harriet."

"It'll end up being one of the worst days in my life," said Butterfield.

Thomas, a former corporal in Company B, had not joined Daniel's group in Pleasant Valley last June. Instead, Dunn and thirteen other Battalion boys remained at the Mormon Island diggings for as long as they could, and then struck out for the Salt Lake Valley in a pack train of mules and horses. They overtook the Holmes-Thompson company just three days earlier.

Butterfield had been a private in Company A, one of the first to enlist during the process that had taken place in Council Bluffs. At six-foot-two-inches, he was the tallest man in the Battalion.

John remembered Thomas as the soldier who left Council Bluffs with all the other enlistees, but returned to Council Bluffs for a day to visit his sick wife and baby. Like all Company B veterans, Dunn had spent the winter of

1846-47 in San Diego while John, Daniel, and Robert were in Los Angeles.

The pack train had made the Humboldt. The Indians were bold here, too. Last night the Indians shot one of the horses with a poisoned arrow. This morning, however, three Northern Piutes carrying bows and arrows had ridden into camp. John showed them the injured horse. One of the Piutes, a more elderly man, wept at the sight of the wound. He jumped off his horse, put his hands beside the wound, and sucked out the poison. The horse was expected to live, but it was slowing them down considerably.

"I've had it in for Indians," John said slowly. "But after last night, I've decided all Indians aren't bad. However, on Judgment Day I'd hate to be in the shoes of the Indians who murdered my good friend Daniel Browett."

"How do you figure it happened?" Butterfield asked. "The murders, I mean."

John did a mental calculation. It was now the eighth of August. Daniel, Ezra, and Henderson died forty-two days ago. "Well, we've had a lot of time to think about that, and talk about it, too," John began.

"How was it that Daniel went out alone, with only two companions?" Butterfield asked.

"We tried to talk him out of it," John explained. "But the weight of leadership bore hard on him. He wanted to get us to the valley as quickly as possible. He was too anxious, I suppose."

"And the thoughts of getting back to Elizabeth and Harriet," Butterfield added.

"Yes, that was part of it, definitely," John said.

"So what happened, that night they were killed?" Dunn asked.

"Here's our theory, based on what we saw at the Tragedy Springs site, or at Daniel's campground," John began. "We all know how the Indians operate. We think the Indians acted friendly on purpose, trying to gain Daniel's trust. They probably followed at a distance for a day or two, then one night came closer and struck up a friendship. I'd guess there were only two or three Indians at this point. The act worked, so Daniel and the others probably fed them supper. Then they sat around the campfire sharing stories the best they could, despite the language barrier. We all speak a little Spanish now that we've been in California for all these months. And we all understand a little of the Indian sign language. I'll bet the Indians asked if they could camp with Daniel, and Daniel let them. But what Daniel didn't know, I'd be willing to bet, was that these two or three Indians had murder on their minds from the beginning, and had a dozen or more companions lurking in the trees, keeping out of sight. The Indians had their eyes on Daniel's horse, Sandy, and on his mules, and on the contents of their saddlebags, and the contents of their packs."

"So you think they jumped them during the night?" Dunn asked, his interest piqued.

"Could have been during the dead of night, or the next morning, who knows for certain?" John answered. "It looked to us like our three Battalion boys put up a fight. They killed Ezra a little distance away from the campfire area where they killed Daniel and Henderson. The Indians shot them with arrows, beat them with axes, and caved their heads in with rocks. All that indi-cates to me that the Indians must have been plenty mad at them for putting up such a battle."

"Gosh," Butterfield said. "I'm glad I didn't have to look at the bodies. Must have been dreadful."

"It was," John said. "It was worse than dreadful. The sight's been burned into my brain forever. But I still have the capacity to remember Daniel the way he was alive."

John was thinking of Daniel the missionary, the man who helped Wilford Woodruff convert all the United Brethren; Daniel the leader on the ship Echo, on the steamboat up the Mississippi, the wagon train across Iowa, sergeant in the Battalion, and the leader chosen to take the Battalion boys to the Salt Lake Valley.

"He was a nice man," John concluded, "a great man. I'll remember him that way, too."

47

Late September 1848

Salt Lake Valley

NOT A DAY WENT BY IN THE SALT Lake Valley that Elizabeth didn't dream of Daniel's return.

"I'd think them Battalion boys would be here by now," she said on a late September morning from her hut in the Salt Lake fort.

"If it gets any later Daniel won't have time to build us a house or pick out his farm ground," Harriet said. New arrivals to the valley were being assigned farm ground farther and farther out.

"I don't like the prospects of staying here all winter again," Elizabeth groaned. Nothing about her abode had changed. Her hut had the same hardened dirt floor, and same dirt roof, and the same door opening covered by a cloth greased with fat. Mice were coming in because of the approaching winter.

The leaves in the foothills to the east, and on the Wasatch Mountains, were already turning their fall colors. A dusting of snow covered the peaks. Formations of geese had been seen flying overhead the past few days, headed south.

"It'd be nice if Robert and Hannah would show up too," Elizabeth said. Brigham Young had arrived, leading a new company from Winter Quarters to the Salt Lake Valley. So had other companies, with more expected any time. The population of Salt Lake was swelling almost daily. The Church needed huts in the fort for the new arrivals, but Elizabeth and Harriet still needed theirs.

Later in the day, when Elizabeth and Harriet were milling around in the fort compound, a rider arrived from the north country. He reported that a pack train consisting of Mormon Battalion veterans was nearing Salt Lake and was expected to arrive within two hours. This news stirred up Elizabeth's heart, but also brought a lot of questions.

"Pack train?" she remarked to Harriet.

"Brigham's whole idea of having Daniel and half the Battalion stay in California was to work until spring and bring back horses, cattle, and provisions," Harriet said back to her.

Elizabeth dashed to her hut and so did Harriet. "What are you going to wear?" she asked Harriet.

"My cleanest dirty dress," she said, a reference to the fact it was hard to keep anything clean in a hut with a dirt floor.

Elizabeth stooped to open her trunk. On top was the baby memorabilia she had placed there: Moroni's clothing and toys. Her eyes watered. She rummaged through the trunk until she found what she was looking for.

"I've never seen you wear that green dress," Harriet commented. Elizabeth had pulled a silk and cashmere dress out of the trunk.

Elizabeth unfolded it, held it up, and draped it in front of her body. The dress was a light pastel green, wrinkled, but showed few wear marks. "It's my wedding dress," she said.

"It's beautiful, but why green?"

"I originally chose pink," Elizabeth said as she began brushing out the wrinkles. "Hannah and I were married in a double ceremony, remember? Hannah chose green because green is a sign of fertility."

"Oh, yes, I remember about the symbolism of colors," Harriet remarked. "If Hannah wore a green dress, it certainly worked for her."

Behind the dress, Elizabeth chuckled and crossed her fingers. As of June eleventh, she had been married for thirteen years. The green fertility dress had produced for her only one child, and that child was buried in Winter Quarters. Daniel would be here within two hours. She said a prayer in her heart. She prayed for another child. And then another.

"In November, Moroni would have been two years old," Elizabeth said as she fought back tears.

"He would have been a handful by now," Harriet said. "I can just see him out in the fort compound, toddling around, playing with the other children."

"What are you going to name your first child?" Elizabeth asked.

Harriet began to laugh. "Depends on whether it's a boy or a girl."

"If my first one is a boy, I'm naming him Daniel," Elizabeth said emphatically. "I hope my first one is a boy, and I hope your first one is a boy. It'd be nice to fill up the valley with a lot of people named Browett, wouldn't it?"

"Yes, it would," Harriet answered, appearing to be daydreaming now about her husband.

Elizabeth lapsed into dreaming too. She decided she didn't care who got the first night with Daniel. Half a husband was better than no husband at all.

The late afternoon weather under gray skies was chilly, with a threat of rain. Elizabeth fought off the urge to wear a coat or even a shawl. As the packers filed their way toward the fort, she stood there in her green dress looking for Daniel.

"What if he's not in the pack train?" Harriet asked with a concerned look. Word had already seeped through the gathering crowd that this was only the first group of several Battalion boys that was expected to arrive in the valley this fall. Some of the men arriving had been, in fact, part of a wagon train that was expected to arrive within another week or so.

"He might not be, but I've got my hopes up," Elizabeth replied. She said a prayer in her heart. *Please God, let him be in this pack train.*

The pack train was a long one, made up of horses and mules. Elizabeth counted twenty-four riders. In their dress, the men looked more like Indians or Mexicans than American soldiers. But each man carried a musket and had a pistol strapped around him.

Harriet began to weep. "I'm not seeing Daniel," she said.

Elizabeth tried to keep her hopes up, but she couldn't see Daniel either. She vaguely recognized a few of the returning men in the lead riders. Finally, toward the end of the train, she recognized John Cox. He was riding a black horse with one stocking foot and leading a brown mule with a rounded belly. John wore buckskin pantaloons, a bright red shirt, and a broad-brimmed funny-looking hat.

"There's Brother Cox," Elizabeth said to Harriet. Elizabeth had resigned herself to the fact that Daniel was not in this group. She felt disappointed, even slightly bitter. But there was nothing to do but pin her hopes on the future. "He'll know whether or not Daniel's in the wagon train that'll be here in a few days."

As they approached John, John slowly dismounted and took off his funny hat. His eyes met Elizabeth's and then he looked away. Elizabeth had caught John with misty eyes. A feeling came over her. In full sight of the more than one hundred people who had gathered around the packers to greet them, Elizabeth collapsed to her knees, soiling her green dress.

Harriet felt it too. Something was wrong. She stood there in stony silence, waiting for John Cox to say something.

The rest of the crowd was boisterous. A few wives were hugging and kissing their husbands. Men swept children into their arms, cried, and then bounced their smaller children into the air. Others were receiving reports that their families were either on their way to the valley or still on the Missouri.

Tears gushed down Elizabeth's hand-covered face. She began to sob in uncontrolled waves.

John finally turned to face the two women, gripping the reins so tightly that the veins of his hands stood out. "I'm sorry. I'm so sorry," he finally said.

Elizabeth rose to her feet and sought Harriet's embrace. The two women wept together.

An eerie silence fell over the crowd. The other returning packers began to whisper the tragic story of how Daniel Browett, Ezra Allen, and Henderson Cox met their fate. Men, women, and children turned to stare at the sobbing women.

After a few minutes, when Elizabeth and Harriet gained a little control, John said to them, in a choked voice, "Indians got him. He's buried in California, in the tops of the Sierra Mountains. On resurrection morning he'll have a beautiful view."

Elizabeth finally let John's sad gaze meet her teary green eyes. "I never thought it would come to this."

"It's a terrible sacrifice you've made, both you and Harriet," John replied.

Elizabeth closed her eyes. "I hope the Savior takes good care of him."

"He will," Harriet added. "I know He will."

EPILOGUE

As I stated in the beginning, this series of historical novels is based on a true story. The majority of the characters are real. Here is a brief, and true, summary of each character as I have been able to glean the information from family history records. Robert Harris is my great-great-great grandfather; Daniel Browett was his brother-in-law and therefore a great-great-great uncle to me.

Robert and Hannah Harris

Robert arrived at Winter Quarters practically penniless. Due to poor circumstances, Robert and Hannah were not able to make it to the Salt Lake Valley until 1850. They traveled in the Aaron Johnson Company, which was plagued with cholera. Four persons in the company died but Robert, Hannah, and their children all arrived safely.

I do not know exactly how Robert and Hannah learned of Daniel's death. It would be logical to assume, however, that they learned from Battalion veterans who returned there late that summer from California. I assume they learned of the gold discovery from Richard Slater, who had been hired by Samuel Brannan to take copies of the *California Star* to Missouri. Several of them still had to journey to the Mormon settlements on the Missouri to find their families. Perhaps John Cox broke the news to Robert and Hannah. While living at Council Point, Iowa, Hannah had another child, a boy. Robert and Hannah named him Daniel Browett Harris. Daniel was born 29 October

1848 and later served as a bishop in Layton, Utah.

Several English converts, many of them Robert's friends, had settled in the area now known as Kaysville, Utah. Robert and Hannah lived somewhere in Salt Lake until February, 1851, when they moved into a small log home with Edward Phillips—a twelve by fourteen structure with a dirt roof. According to the personal history of Joseph Harris (Robert and Hannah's oldest son), they lived with the Phillips family until they could build their own home. Robert's first home in Kaysville was a "wattle" house, made of poles, willows, and mud.

"Kays Ward," the first ward in Kaysville, was organized in 1851 at the home of Edward Phillips.

Robert and Hannah's farm was located west of present-day Kaysville, near the Great Salt Lake. They eventually replaced the wattle house with a nice log home. Because Robert built a home with a large room, Church meetings were held there in later years.

Hannah continued to be fruitful. But just as she had lost a son while living at Winter Quarters (Robert Harris III), she also lost her next child, a daughter, who was born shortly after her arrival in the Salt Lake Valley. The girl, Maria, died the day she was born.

Robert and Hannah had a total of fifteen children, with only two of them passing away as babies. From the other thirteen, they had a total of 132 grandchildren. I estimate that by now Robert and Hannah have around 200,000 descendents!

By contrast, Daniel and Elizabeth Browett had no living descendents. Their only child, Moroni, died at Winter Quarters.

While Robert lived in Kaysville he worked on the Salt Lake Temple. In 1857, during the Utah War, Robert served as a captain in the Legion. He was sent east to Echo Canyon to help build walls and dig trenches to make it more difficult for the U.S. Army to invade Utah. During the latter part of the war, Robert moved his family to somewhere in the Payson or Spanish Fork area until things cooled down.

Another notable event occurred while Robert lived in the Kaysville area. He was sent on a mission. He served in the Cotton Mission, south of St. George, Utah, on land that is in the current state of Nevada, near Overton. Brigham Young, upon finding Robert there, sent him home. Brigham said, "You go home; you have done enough for the Church."

In 1869, however, Robert left Kaysville to help settle the Portage, Utah, area. He established a farm just west of the I-15 exit. The farm is still owned by a family member, David Robert Harris. Robert lived on this farm until 1875 when he moved back to Kaysville. He had suffered a farm injury (he fell off a corn wagon) and never totally recovered. He bought a farm with a brick home on the main road between Kaysville and Holmes Creek. On 29 February 1876, Robert died at age 68, "very suddenly." Wilford Woodruff spoke at his funeral in Kaysville.

Hannah lived for another twelve years. She died 29 September 1888 in Portage, where she was living with some of her children

Robert and Hannah are buried in the Kaysville cemetery. Elizabeth Browett is buried with them, and Elizabeth's name appears on the same headstone. Several of Robert's friends and acquaintances are buried in Kaysville, including: John Gailey, John Hyrum Green, Joseph "Cap" Hill, William Kay, Edward Phillips, James Robins, and Levi Roberts.

Robert was born 16 December 1807 in Hucclescote, England, the son of a butcher and cattle buyer, Robert Harris, Sr., and Sarah Oakey. Some records show he was born on that date but others say he was born on 26 December (his grave marker reads this way.) He had two sisters, Elizabeth and Dianah. Elizabeth married Daniel Browett. Dianah married Thomas Bloxham. Robert also had two brothers—William and John, neither of whom emigrated to America. Just as portrayed in the first volume of the novel, William died before Robert left for Nauvoo. John managed a pub in Apperley and never joined the Church—and neither did William to my knowledge.

Hannah Maria Eagles Harris was born 10 June 1817 in Hucclecote, Gloucestershire, England, to Thomas Eagles and Ann Sparks Eagles. Her parents were Methodist; Robert's parents were Anglican. For this reason, Robert and Hannah were married twice, first in a Methodist chapel 18 March 1835, and second in the St. Mary de Lode Church (Anglican) on 28 September of the same year.

Robert at first resisted joining the Church. When Wilford Woodruff began his missionary work among members of the United Brethren, Daniel, Elizabeth, and Dianah were among the first converts. Robert, who participated in pugilism (bare-fisted boxing), tried to throw Woodruff out of his home when Hannah invited a group of investigators into her parlor to hear the gospel. When the Spirit protected Woodruff, it provided the spiritual awakening Robert needed and he was soon baptized.

By the time Robert and Hannah emigrated to America, they had three children—Joseph, Elizabeth, and William. A fourth—Thomas—was born on the ship *Echo*. The Church organized a presidency of six men on each Mormon immigrant vessel. Robert served in the presidency on the *Echo*; Daniel Browett was the president or company leader. The *Echo* left Liverpool 16 February 1841 with a company of 109 Saints. The ship arrived in New Orleans on 16 April. Everyone transferred to a steamboat. The steamboat carrying Robert and Hannah, and Daniel and Elizabeth, arrived in Nauvoo 1 May 1841.

Robert served in the Nauvoo Legion and helped build the Nauvoo Temple. He and his wife lived on property they owned near the temple. Robert and Hannah were endowed in the temple 6 February 1846. That spring, in April or May, they left Nauvoo forever and made their way, with the other Saints, to Council Bluffs. And of course Robert enlisted in the Mormon Battalion in mid-July.

Daniel and Elizabeth Browett

Daniel Browett's remains are still buried in the grave at Tragedy Springs, along with the remains of Ezra Allen and Henderson Cox.

Just as portrayed in this novel, Elizabeth and Harriet had made it to the Salt Lake Valley in late 1847 and were waiting there for Daniel to return in September 1848. The two women were informed of Daniel's death by returning Battalion veterans.

The veterans presented Elizabeth money in the form of donated gold, collected on the way back to the Salt Lake Valley. We do not know how much Elizabeth received, but one man, Samuel Rogers, donated $150.

Like Robert and Hannah, Elizabeth settled in Kaysville where she became a schoolteacher. Children called her "Aunt Browett." She later married another Battalion veteran, William Johnstun, who had been a private in Company C. She was a plural wife to him. In California, William had worked for James Marshall at Coloma and was there when gold was discovered. Johnstun was in Pleasant Valley when Daniel was chosen president of the company to lead the Battalion boys to the Salt Lake Valley. She remained married to him for only two years and then they separated. William ultimately settled in Arizona and died in New Mexico.

Elizabeth lived until 4 March 1899 and died in Kaysville at the age of 85. She is buried in the Kaysville cemetery next to Robert and Hannah. All their names are on the same tombstone.

Not much is known about Harriet Barnes Clifford Browett, Daniel's second wife, after Daniel died. Late in her life, Elizabeth gave a deposition in an attempt to gain a pension from the government for being the wife of a soldier. The pension was denied because Daniel had entered into polygamy. At any rate, Elizabeth said this about Harriet: "Harriet died the next year after we came to Salt Lake City...She died somewhere back on the plains. She came here with us in 1847, I believe, and she went back to the states again and was returning the next year when she was taken sick with the cholera and died."

Elizabeth Harris Browett was born 16 June 1813 in Sandhurst, Gloucestershire, England, the daughter of Robert Harris, Sr., and Sarah Oakey. She had an older sister, Dianah, and three older brothers, William, John, and Robert.

Daniel Browett was born 18 December 1809 in Tewkesbury, Gloucestershire, England, the oldest son of Thomas Browett, Jr., and Martha Pulham Browett. Daniel's parents were Quaker. Daniel and Elizabeth were married 2 June 1834. They witnessed the marriage of Robert and Hannah a year later.

Daniel and Elizabeth joined a small, independent organization in England called the United Brethren. They even became lay preachers under the direction of Thomas Kington, the leader of the United Brethren. Funding came chiefly from a wealthy farmer, John Benbow. By 1840 the United Brethren had 42 places licensed for worship and one chapel (most meetings were held in members' homes). Membership had grown to about 600.

When Elder Wilford Woodruff arrived in England that year, he was directed by the Spirit to Benbow's home. Ultimately, Woodruff baptized all 600 members except one. Daniel and Elizabeth were among the first baptized. By May, Daniel had been ordained an elder and frequently helped Woodruff in his missionary labors. Woodruff spent several nights in the Browett home.

When Mormon converts began to emigrate to the United States, Daniel was chosen by the Apostles to be the leader of a company of Saints that would board the ship *Echo*. Daniel had six assistants, or counselors. He chose Robert as one of his counselors. The ship arrived in New Orleans 16 April 1841. Daniel then arranged steamboat passage for the 109 members of the company, all Mormons. They arrived in Nauvoo on 1 May 1841.

Like Robert, Daniel helped build the Nauvoo Temple and served in the Nauvoo Legion. Daniel owned a forty-acre farm just east of Nauvoo.

Daniel was asked by Church leaders to enter into the practice of plural marriage. Harriet Clifford Barnes, a widow, became his second wife. Daniel and his two wives were endowed in the Nauvoo Temple 6 February 1846. They left Nauvoo that spring and made their way to Council Bluffs. Daniel joined the Mormon Battalion there and served as a sergeant in Company E.

Ezra Allen

Ezra was born 28 July 1814 in Madrid, New York. He married Sarah Fiske on 25 December 1837. They were converted to the Church while still living in New York. They moved to a settlement 20 miles north of Nauvoo in 1843, and later moved into Nauvoo. Ezra supported his family by working on the Nauvoo Temple. In Nauvoo, he suffered from the ague. Ezra and Sarah lost an infant son there.

Ezra served as a fifer in Company C, which entitled him to three dollars more a month than a regular private. He left a wife, a son, and a daughter.

Ezra's wife, Sarah, kept a diary. This is what she wrote about Ezra's death:

"In the spring of 1848 I began to look forward to the return of my husband. I looked forward to the time when his strong arms would lift these burdens of care from my shoulders. I gathered grapes from the lowlands near the river [at Winter Quarters] and made wine and prepared such dainties as I could that would please him. At length the news came that a company of brethren was expected to cross the river at the ferry in a few days. I felt anxious to go to the ferry to meet him, but circumstances would not permit so I remained at home waiting and watching, listening to the sound of every footstep that approached my door.

"After several days word was brought to me that he had been killed by Indians in California or the Sierra Nevada Mountains. I learned that a purse containing about $120 in gold dust had been found belonging to my husband and it was being brought to me. Thus were my hopes and expectations blasted in a moment... There were marks of blood upon it and it seemed to me as the price of his life."

In 1851 Sarah exchanged her gold dust for cash and goods to migrate west to the Salt Lake Valley. She reserved enough gold to make a ring, which she wore all the rest of her life. She married Joel Ricks in 1852 and they resided in the Utah communities of Centerville, Farmington, and Logan.

After Sarah's death, her daughter, Amorett, received the gold ring. The buckskin bag went to Ezra's son, Alexander. Afterward, it passed into the hands of the oldest grandson, Guy Poulsen, who on his death turned it over to Preston Nibley.

Henderson Cox

Henderson was the 15th child of Jehu and Sarah Cox. He was born 6 November 1829 near the Wabash River, Warren, Indiana. Later his parents settled in the Ozark Mountains in Missouri. There, they joined the Church in 1835. Henderson did not join the church until 1843 when his parents lived in Nauvoo. He was brought by his parents to Council Bluffs where the Mormon Battalion was being formed in 1846. He joined Company A at the age of 17 and marched off, never to see his parents again.

Henderson's parents were on their way to the Salt Lake Valley when Henderson died. On 27 June 1848, the day of his death, they were in their 49th day with the wagon train on the prairie. They did not learn of their son's tragic death until they arrived in the valley.

Like most of the Battalion veterans, Henderson worked the gold mines in California prior to his return trip. Like Daniel Browett, Henderson carried his gold in his packs. The Indians took it when they took his horse and personal belongings.

Daniel and Robert's messmates in the Battalion:

John Cox

John, who was a messmate to both Daniel and Robert in Company E, was also a boyhood friend to Robert in England. John was born 8 August 1810 in Deerhurst, Gloucestershire. He married Eliza Roberts, a sister to Levi Roberts, on 1 March 1836. And like Levi and others, John and his wife joined the United Brethren congregation and were converted to the Church by Wilford Woodruff in 1840. The Coxes emigrated to Nauvoo on the ship *Echo* in 1841. After his discharge from the Battalion, John stayed in California and worked. Like so many others, he mined for gold in early 1848, and was returning in the same company when Daniel Browett was killed. His wife, Eliza, was still in Iowa when she heard that three Battalion members had been killed by Indians. She went into hysteria because she thought that the Cox who had been killed was her husband, but it was Henderson Cox, the 18-year-old former soldier. John returned to Eliza and brought her out to the Salt Lake Valley where they eventually settled in Weber County. John served as a bodyguard to Brigham Young in the 1860s. Later, John helped settle Oxford, Idaho. He died in 1880 and is buried with his wife in Oxford. They had twelve children.

Robert Pixton

Pixton was a messmate of both Daniel and Robert in Company E and served as the cook. When Pixton decided to stay in California and work until spring, he sent a mule with Robert Harris to be given to his wife in Winter Quarters. Robert delivered the mule.

Pixton was born 27 February 1819 in Manchester, Lancastershire, England. He married Elizabeth Cooper on 5 May 1839. Robert emigrated to America the next year. While on board the ship, he converted to the Church and came to Nauvoo. His wife and daughter emigrated in 1843. Like so many others, the Pixtons lost a child at Winter Quarters while Robert served in the Battalion. Sister Pixton worked in St. Louis to earn enough money for the trip to the Salt Lake Valley. She left in May and arrived in the valley on 22 September 1848. A week later the Thompson-Holmes company arrived from California and Pixton was reunited with his wife and children. They lived in the fort in Salt Lake until they got their city lot, given to them by Willard Richards in gratitude for Sister Pixton helping him out during a severe spell of sickness in the Richards family. The lot is part of the land where the Kearns building now stands. Pixton served a mission to England in 1862. When he returned he continued to farm and run a merchandise store. Later the Pixtons were called on to help colonize Dixie. Pixton died in 1881 and is buried in the Salt Lake City cemetery. Sister Pixton then went to England to do genealogy work and returned to do temple work in St. George and Salt Lake. The Pixtons had ten children.

Levi Roberts

Levi also served as a private in Company E and was a messmate to Robert

Harris and Daniel Browett. Levi was born 10 May 1810 in Apperley, Gloucestershire, and was a boyhood friend to Robert Harris in England. He married Harriet Ann Effort 18 August 1835. Like Robert and Daniel, Levi and his wife became converts of Wilford Woodruff. The Roberts had been members of the United Brethren. Levi and Harriet emigrated to Nauvoo on the same ship, the *Echo*. While living in Nauvoo, Levi served as one of the bodyguards to the Prophet Joseph Smith. After his release from the Battalion, Levi debated whether or not to stay and work in California. At the last minute he changed his mind and returned with Robert Harris, and like Robert, emigrated to the Salt Lake Valley in 1850. Levi and his family settled in Kaysville. In 1865 he build his second home there, a nice log cabin. The home is now on display at the Pioneers' Trails Village near *This Is The Place* Monument. Later in life Levi took a second wife, Sarah Davis. Altogether, Levi had ten children. He and Harriet are buried in the Kaysville cemetery.

Richard Slater

Slater was born 26 September in Lancastershire, England, and married Ann Corbridge in 1834. They were baptized in 1840 and emigrated to Nauvoo and rented property on Hyde Street. He served as a private in Company E of the Battalion and was a messmate to Robert Harris and Daniel Browett. After discharge he worked in California until the spring of 1848. He worked at Sutter's Fort, running the bowling alley and selling food and assorted drinks. He was hired by Samuel Brannan, along with nine others, to carry copies of Brannan's newspapers back east. They crossed the Truckee Pass in the Sierras during a treacherous time of the year, April. Some of the men stayed in the Salt Lake Valley, but Richard continued east. He met Brigham Young on the plains; Brigham was on his way from Winter Quarters to the Salt Lake Valley again. The newspapers promoted California and told of the discovery of gold. Richard took seeds and fruit tree starts from California to Iowa. The Slaters stayed in Iowa until 1852 when they migrated to Utah and settled in North Ogden before pioneering Slaterville. The Slaters had twelve children.

Other characters in this historical novel series:

John Benbow

Benbow made it to the Salt Lake Valley in 1848 and served as a captain of fifty in the Wilford Woodruff company during the trip. While living in Winter Quarters, Benbow's wife, Jane, died on 27 November 1846. Just before John and Jane Benbow left Nauvoo, John took a plural wife. He married a sister to Elder John Taylor, Agnes. She was 58 at the time and John 46. They never lived together and they later separated.

After Benbow arrived in the valley he stayed with his nephew and foster son, Thomas Benbow, who had made it a year earlier. Thomas had built a little log home on the bank of Little Cottonwood Creek on what is now Vine Street and 5800 South. John selected a spot farther north and built a log home there, near present 5300 South. He remained single until 3 September 1851 when he married Rosetta Wright King Peacock. Benbow built a second home in 1862 near 700 East and 5300 South. Rosetta had a son by her first marriage and a daughter by her second husband. John and Rosetta had a daughter together and named her Isabella.

Right after his arrival in the valley, Benbow was appointed by Brigham Young to be the superintendent of fencing for the Saints in his area. Benbow continued to be unselfish in his devotion to helping people. He assisted in building three meeting houses in Utah, for example, and he sent his team and hired man across the plains six times to assist Mormon immigrants. Benbow died 12 May 1874.

Benbow is remembered as the financial force behind the organization of the United Brethren in England. Thomas Kington, the man who organized the group, worked for Benbow. When Elder Wilford Woodruff arrived at the Benbow farm in the spring of 1840, Benbow became the first person baptized of the United Brethren group. Woodruff later baptized all the other members except one. Benbow financed the printing of the Book of Mormon in England.

Thomas Bloxham

Thomas married Dianah Harris in England, so he was Robert Harris' brother-in-law. Just as indicated in this volume, Dianah died at Winter Quarters, leaving five children. Up to this point, Thomas had never joined the

Church. But he was baptized shortly afterward. He then married Elizabeth Sheen Morris, a widow of John Morris. She was also native to England and 15 years older than Thomas. Thomas brought his children and new wife to the Salt Lake Valley in 1848, settling in Kaysville near Robert Harris and other old friends. In late 1850 Thomas accepted a call to help settle Iron County. He later returned to Kaysville and lived there until 1870. His sons acquired farm ground in Idaho so Thomas, with his sons, moved to Bannock County, Idaho, along the Marsh Valley. They helped establish the community of Cambridge. Thomas died there at age 75 on 28 April 1883. He is buried in the Cambridge cemetery.

Martha Browett

Martha Pulham, Daniel Browett's mother, was born 4 June 1779, in Southam, Gloucestershire. She married Thomas Browett in 1812 and he made his living as an ironmonger (hardware) in Tewkesbury. Thomas died in 1824 when Daniel was only 13. There were four other living children at the time: Thomas Jr., Martha Rebecca, John, and William.

Martha joined the Church about the same time as Daniel and Elizabeth and emigrated to America on the ship *Echo* along with her daughter, Rebecca. Her three other sons remained in England. Martha never remarried. She was endowed in the Nauvoo Temple at the same time as Daniel and Elizabeth. She apparently came to the Salt Lake Valley with the Robert Harris family. A "Sister Browett" is listed on the roster of the Aaron Johnson Company. I have not been able to find a death date for her.

Rebecca Browett

Rebecca is portrayed in this historical series as flighty and hard to please. That's just my guess based on her relationship with her husband, Orson Hyde. Rebecca (her full name was Martha Rebecca Browett) became the second wife, plural, to Orson during the Nauvoo period. She and her mother crossed Iowa with Orson. She also traveled to the Salt Lake Valley with Orson. However, Rebecca and Orson later separated and divorced. She had no children. Rebecca later married Thomas McKenzie but that marriage ended in divorce, also. Rebecca took back her maiden name and was known as Martha Browett in Salt Lake City. She was an expert seamstress and she made her living by sewing for many of the wealthy families there. Years of constant eyestrain brought about almost complete blindness during the last thirty years of her life. She passed away 30 October 1904 at the age of 86. She is buried in the Gilette family plot in the Salt Lake City cemetery. A small leather steamer trunk, brought by her on the ship *Echo* from England, is on exhibit in the Pioneer Memorial Building.

Rebecca was born 22 June 1819, the only daughter of Thomas Browett and Martha Puller. She had four brothers. Of them, only Daniel emigrated to the United States with Rebecca and her mother.

Jacob Kemp Butterfield

Jacob is my great-great-great grandfather on my mother's side. He was born 17 February 1814 in Farmington, Maine. He was baptized by his uncle, Josiah Butterfield, on 29 May 1834 at Saco, Maine.

Jacob lived in Kirtland and later moved to Dearborn, Indiana, where he met and married Louisa Walker, and they moved to Nauvoo in 1840 where they had three daughters, but two died in infancy. Jacob and his brother, Abel, served a special short-time mission in 1843, to "preach the gospel and disabuse the public mind" with regard to the arrest of the Prophet Joseph Smith. Jacob's uncle, Josiah Butterfield, served as a member of the First Council of the Seventy in the early days of the Church. Because the Walker family grew tired of mob persecutions in Nauvoo, they left Nauvoo and took Louisa with them. So Jacob was left alone.

After crossing Iowa, Jacob volunteered for the Mormon Battalion, and was the tallest man in the Battalion at six-feet, two-inches. He was one of the first to volunteer so he served in Company A as a private. After discharge he stayed in California and worked at Sutter's Fort tanning cowhides and making wagon tongues. He made his way to the Salt Lake Valley in 1848 and in 1850 married Sarah Jennings Hayes in a ceremony performed by Heber C. Kimball. They had only two children, a set of twins, who both died. However, Jacob married a daughter of Sarah by a previous marriage, also named Sarah. Jacob and Sarah had thirteen children, and I descended through one of them. Jacob also married Ellen Barrass in 1858. She bore him four children. Jacob died 22

November 1889 and is buried in Taylorsville, Utah.

John Hyrum Green

Robert Harris' oldest son, Joseph, married two of Green's daughters—Charlotte and Mary Elizabeth. Therefore John Hyrum Green is my great-great-great grandfather because I descended from Joseph and Charlotte.

Green was born 25 March 1801 in Acton Beauchamp, Worcestershire, and married Susannah Phillips on 3 February 1835. Susannah was a sister to Edward Phillips, a close friend to Robert Harris. The Greens, who by now had five children, were converted to the Church by Wilford Woodruff. They had been members of the United Brethren congregation. They emigrated to America in September 1841 on the *Harmony* with Thomas Kington as the company leader. Kington was the man who organized the United Brethren. While in Nauvoo, the Greens lived not too far away from Robert and Hannah Harris. John's Nauvoo property was set on fire by mobbers shortly before the Greens crossed the plains to Council Bluffs. While living in Winter Quarters, a daughter, Mary Elizabeth, was born. The Greens emigrated to Utah in 1849, wintered in the Big Cottonwood Canyon, and then permanently settled in Kaysville. John Hyrum Green died there on 16 April 1886. He had Susannah had fifteen children. He had two other wives in Utah, but neither bore him children.

Thomas Kington

Kington, the founder of the United Brethren congregation in England, eventually emigrated to Utah and settled in Wellsville. He served as a patriarch there and that's where he died 1 July 1874 at the age of 80.

Thomas was born 18 May 1794 in Bodenham, Herefordshire. In later life he was a Methodist preacher of John Wesley's stamp, zeal, and inspiration. To him, the dead influence of a formal religion was not enough to save a soul. Methodism had settled down into a rut of self-satisfied formality. With a revivalist's zeal he annoyed the more formal and better paid preachers of the denomination. As a result, he was expelled around 1830. He went to work as a farm manager for John Benbow, but did not give up his desire to preach. He formed a new society called the United Brethren, organized to prepared to hear the "further light and truth" of some future gospel knowledge. By 1840, when Wilford Woodruff came into the area, Kington had attracted around 600 members.

Kington was out preaching and working his circuit when Wilford Woodruff came to the Benbow farm. Benbow was immediately baptized and Kington followed a few days later. Eventually all former United Brethren members were baptized into the Church except one man, Phillip Helot. In May of 1840 Thomas held a feast and prayer meeting in his home for a hundred members of the Church who had been baptized by Woodruff. An outraged vicar of the Church of England led a mob against the prayer meeting and nearly destroyed Kington's home. Kington was ordained a high priest during a general conference held in Manchester 6 July 1840.

Kington led a company of Saints to America on the ship *Harmony* in 1841, reaching Quebec 25 June. Kington and his wife, Hannah Pitt—a sister to William Pitt—found several friends in Nauvoo including Daniel Browett and Willard Richards. Tragedy struck, however, and both his mother and his wife, Hannah, died from the effects of the grueling trip. Thomas then married a widow, Margaret Peizel Myers, on 5 January 1842. Their first child died at age one. He purchased a ten-acre farm in Nauvoo.

Thomas did not leave Nauvoo in early 1846. He arrived in Council Bluffs in June or July and it is assumed he traveled there with Daniel Browett and other former members of the United Brethren. Thomas remained in Iowa until 1850 when he traveled to Utah with Robert Harris in the Aaron Johnson Company. Thomas and his family arrived in the valley 12 September. He remained in Salt Lake for a time, moved to Davis County (probably Kaysville), and then eventually settled in the Ogden area. In 1853 Wilford Woodruff visited Kington there and chose a place to establish a fort to help protect the Saints. The site became known as Kington Fort. Kington was called to serve as Bishop there. The bond of friendship between Kington and Woodruff continued throughout their lifetimes. Kington, who with Margaret Pisel fathered eight children, died in Wellsville 1 July 1874.

Edward Phillips

Edward and his family emigrated to Utah in 1849 and settled in

Kaysville. When Robert Harris arrived the next year, Edward invited Robert and his family to stay in a small log home with them. Edward supplemented his living as a farmer both in Nauvoo and in Utah by being a blacksmith.

Edward was also English, born at Oxenhall Parish, Gloucestershire, on 2 April 1813. His father, a farmer, died at an early age so Edward learned blacksmithing to help raise the family.

Edward's mother and grandparents were Methodist. When Thomas Kington and John Benbow organized the United Brethren, she joined, and so did her children, including Edward. Edward, even though only in his early twenties, became a lay preacher in that organization. When Wilford Woodruff preached in the area in 1840, Edward and his family were baptized into the Church. Edward was 27. In a historical sketch of his life, Edward is quoted as saying this about the United Brethren: "It seemed to me that we had come to a precipice and could go no further until Brother Woodruff placed a bridge over the precipice and we went on with glad hearts rejoicing." After his baptism Woodruff ordained Edward a priest and placed him over two branches, Ashfield and Corcutt.

Edward was courting Hannah Simmons at the time but they did not get married until both of them were living near Nauvoo. Edward set sail on the *Caroline* 8 August 1841. Hannah Simmons came later. They lived at McQueen's Mill. During the time of the murder of Joseph and Hyrum Smith, Edward and Hannah went back to their farm to try to sell it and see the graves of their two children. According to the historical sketch of Edward's life,

Edward and Hannah "found some of the mob who participated in the murder…They narrowly escaped death as these fiends placed a pistol in the hands of an eight-year-old boy and told him to say, 'Damn you sir, I could kill you'." Edward and Hannah escaped.

The historical sketch says they left Nauvoo in May, so they likely traveled in the same company as Robert Harris and Daniel Browett. Edward did not serve in the Mormon Battalion. He and his family made it to the Salt Lake Valley in 1849. Edward, along with men like John Hyrum Green, Hector Haight, and William Kay, became the first settlers of Kaysville. Phillips Creek is named after him. Because of his success in raising wheat, Brigham Young asked him to give a report in the tabernacle. Both he and John Hyrum Green served as counselors to William Kay in the first bishopric in Kaysville. John Hyrum had married Edward's sister, Susannah. In later life, Edward took two plural wives. He had four children by Martha Annley Taylor.

Edward and Hannah had a total of 15 children. Edward passed away 1 December 1896 and is buried in Kaysville alongside his wife. A rock cottage built by Edward in 1862 still stands in Kaysville at 358 W. Center.

BIBLIOGRAPHY

While it is not normal to publish a bibliography for a novel, I do it here to demonstrate the depth of the research it has taken to write the fourth and fifth books in this series.

Bagley, Will. *A Road From El Dorado, The 1848 Trail Journal of Ephraim Green*, The Prairie Dog Press, Salt Lake City, Utah, 1991.

Bagley, Will. *Scoundrel's Tale, The Samuel Brannan Papers*, Utah State University Press, Logan, Utah, 1999.

Bennett, Richard E. *We'll Find the Place, The Mormon Exodus*, 1846-1848, Deseret Book Company, Salt Lake City, Utah, 1997.

Bigler, David L., and Bagley, Will. *Army of Israel, Mormon Battalion Narratives*, Utah State University Press, Logan, Utah, 2000.

Bishop, M. Guy. *Henry William Bigler, Soldier, Gold Miner, Missionary, Chronicler*, Utah State University Press, Logan, Utah, 1998.

Brock, Richard K. *Emigrant Trails West: A Guide to the California Trail*, Trails West, Inc., Reno, Nevada, 2000.

Bryant, Edwin, *What I Saw in California*, University of Nebraska Press, Lincoln, Nebraska, 1985 (original printing in 1848).

Chalfant, William Y. *Dangerous Passage, The Santa Fe Trail and the Mexican War*, University of Oklahoma Press, Norman, Oklahoma, 1994.

Crockett, David R. *Saints Find the Place, Winter Quarters to the Salt Lake Valley*, LDS-Gems Press, Lehi, Utah, 1997.

Curran, Harold. *Fearful Crossing: The central Overland Trail Through Nevada*, Nevada Publications, Las Vegas, Nevada, 1982.

Dary, David. *The Santa Fe Trail, Its History, Legends, and Lore*, Alfred A. Knopf, a division of Random House, Inc., New York, N.Y. 2000.

Dawson, Joseph C. *Doniphan's Epic March, The 1st Missouri Volunteers in the Mexican War*, University Press of Kansas, 1999.

DeVoto, Bernard. *The Year of Decision, 1846*, Truman Valley Books, St. Martin's Griffin, New York, N.Y. 2000.

Dillon, Richard. *Captain John Sutter, Sacramento Valley's Sainted Sinner*, Western Tanager Press, Santa Cruz, California, 1967.

Egan, Ferol. Fremont, *Explorer for a Restless Nation*, University of Nevada Press, Reno, Nevada, 1985.

Ellison, R. S. *Fort Bridger, A Brief History*, Wyoming State Archives, Museums and Historical Department, 1981.

Fey, Marshall; King, R. Joe; Lepisto, Jack. *Emigrant Shadows: A History and Guide to the California Trail*, Western Trails Research Assn., Virginia City, Nevada, 2002.

Freedman, Russell. *In the Days of the Vaqueros, America's First True Cowboys*, Clarion Books, New York, N. Y., 2001.

Gardner, Mark L. *Wagons for the Santa Fe Trade*, University of New Mexico Press, Albuquerque, New Mexico, 2000.

Gay, Theressa. *James W. Marshall, The Discoverer of California Gold; A Biography*, The Talisman Press, Georgetown, California. 1967.

Hancock, Levi Ward. *The Levi Ward Hancock Journal, 1803-1846* (unpublished), LDS Church Archives.

Harlow, Neal. *California Conquered, War and Peace on the Pacific 1846-1850,* University of California Press, Berkeley and Los Angeles, California, 1982.

Holmes, Gail George. *Old Council Bluffs; Mormon Developments, 1846-1853, in the Missouri and Platte River Valleys of SW Iowa and E Nebraska,* Omaha LDS Institute of Religion, Omaha, Nebraska, 2000.

Hunt, Thomas H. *Ghost Trails to California,* Nevada Publications, Las Vegas, Nevada, 1974.

Hyslop, Stephen G. *Bound for Santa Fe, The Road to New Mexico and the American Conquest,* University of Oklahoma Press, 2002.

Larsen, Karen M. and Paul D. *Remembering Winter Quarters/Council Bluffs,* Action Group, Omaha, Nebraska, 1998.

Maynes, Shirley N. *Five Hundred Wagons Stood Still, Mormon Battalion Wives,* Corporate Edge Printing, 1999.

McLynn, Frank. *Wagons West, The Epic Story of America's Overland Trails,* Grove Press, New York, N. Y., 2002.

Nevins, Allan. Fremont, *Pathmarker of the West,* University of Nebraska Press, Lincoln, Nebraska, 1939.

Noble, David Grant. *Santa Fe; History of an Ancient City,* School of American Research Press, Santa Fe, New Mexico, 1989.

Norris, David L., *William H. Emory, Soldier-Scientist,* The University of

Arizona Press, Tucson, Arizona, 1998.

Owens, Kenneth N. *Gold Rush Saints, California Mormons and the Great Rush for Riches,* The Arthur H. Clark Co., Spokane, Washington, 2004.

Peterson, Charles S. *Mormon Battalion Trail Guide,* Utah State Historical Society, Logan, Utah, 1972.

Ricketts, Norma Baldwin. *Mormons and the Discovery of Gold,* Odyssey Press, Mesa, Arizona 1998.

Ricketts, Norma Baldwin. *The Mormon Battalion, U.S. Army of the West,* Utah State University Press, Logan, Utah, 1996.

Roberts, David. *A Newer World; Kit Carson, John C. Fremont, and the Claiming of the American West,* Simon & Schuster, New York, New York, 2000.

Scott, Richard. *Eyewitness to the Old West,* Roberts Rinehart Publishers, New York, N. Y., 2004.

Standage Family, *Henry Standage's Journal; An Account of His Experiences in the Mormon Battalion* (unpublished), 1972.

Talbot, Dan. *A Historical Guide to the Mormon Battalion and Butterfield Trail,* Westernlore Press, Tucson, Arizona, 1992.

Bowen, Ezra. *The Old West, The Forty-Niners,* Time-Life Books, New York, N. Y., 1974.

Bowen, Ezra. *The Old West, The Mexican War,* Time-Life Books, New York, N. Y., 1974.

Bowen, Ezra. *The Old West, The Pioneers,* Time-Life Books, New York, N. Y., 1974.

Tyler, Daniel, *A Concise History of the Mormon Battalion in the Mexican War,* Publishers Press, Salt Lake City, Utah, 7th printing, 2000.

Vestal, Stanley. Kit Carson, *The Happy Warrior of the Old West,* Houghton Mifflin Co., New York, N.Y., 1928.

Vestal, Stanley. *The Old Santa Fe Trail,* University of Nebraska Press, Lincoln, Nebraska, 1996.

Weber, David J. *The Mexican Frontier, 1821-1846, The American Southwest Under Mexico,* University of New Mexico Press, Albuquerque, New Mexico, 1982.

Weems, John Edward. *To Conquer A Peace, The War Between the United States and Mexico,* Doubleday and Company, Inc., Garden City, New York, 1974.

Woolsey, Ronald C. Migrants West, *Toward the Southern California Frontier,* Grizzly Bear Publishing, Claremont, California, 1966.

Young, Stanley. *The Missions of California,* Chronicle Books, San Francisco, California, 1998.